THE
SILVER TREASURY

BEING THE HOLIDAY EDITION OF

POETRY FOR HOME AND SCHOOL

SELECTED AND ARRANGED BY

ANNA C. BRACKETT AND IDA M. ELIOT

ILLUSTRATED

NEW YORK & LONDON
G. P. PUTNAM'S SONS
The Knickerbocker Press
1889

Press of
G P. Putnam's Sons
New York

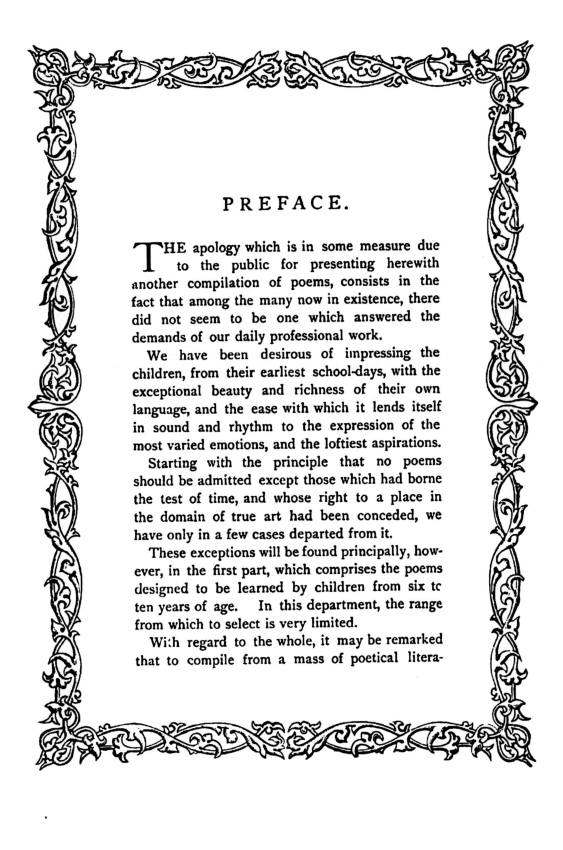

PREFACE.

THE apology which is in some measure due to the public for presenting herewith another compilation of poems, consists in the fact that among the many now in existence, there did not seem to be one which answered the demands of our daily professional work.

We have been desirous of impressing the children, from their earliest school-days, with the exceptional beauty and richness of their own language, and the ease with which it lends itself in sound and rhythm to the expression of the most varied emotions, and the loftiest aspirations.

Starting with the principle that no poems should be admitted except those which had borne the test of time, and whose right to a place in the domain of true art had been conceded, we have only in a few cases departed from it.

These exceptions will be found principally, however, in the first part, which comprises the poems designed to be learned by children from six to ten years of age. In this department, the range from which to select is very limited.

With regard to the whole, it may be remarked that to compile from a mass of poetical literature which extends in an unbroken line for more than four hundred years, is no easy task, nor do we suppose that any critic will be entirely satisfied. We hope, however, that the members of our own profession may find the volume to supply a want which has been for many years recognized.

The arrangement may possibly call for a word of explanation. It is based upon the practical wants of the school-room. The poems may be learned in the order in which they stand, without the monotony arising from arranging all the poems of one author together. The double index will make it easy to refer to any author or any selection, when desired.

Our acknowledgments are due and are hereby gratefully tendered to all those authors and publishers who have at once and freely, given us the right to use poems. Though, as has been said, the volume is especially designed for the use of schools, it is hoped and believed that it will be found of practical value in the family and home.

A. C. B.

9 West 39th St., New York City.
March, 1876.

INDEX OF AUTHORS.

v

LIST OF ILLUSTRATIONS.

POETRY.

* I *

LULLABY OF AN INFANT CHIEF.

O, hush thee, my babie, thy sire was a knight,
Thy mother a lady both lovely and bright;
The woods and the glens from the tower which we see,
They all are belonging, dear babie, to thee.

O, fear not the bugle, though loudly it blows,
It calls but the warders that guard thy repose;
Their bows would be bended, their blades would be red
Ere the step of a foeman draws near to thy bed.

O, hush thee, my babie, the time soon will come,
When thy sleep shall be broken by trumpet and drum;
Then hush thee, my darling, take rest while you may,
For strife comes with manhood, and waking with day.
Sir Walter Scott.

* 2 *

THE OLD MAN IN THE WOOD.

There was an old man who lived in a wood,
  As you shall plainly see;
He thought he could do more work in one day
  Than his wife could do in three.

" With all my heart," the old dame said;
　" And if you will allow,
You shall stay at home to-day,
　And I'll go follow the plow.

" But you must milk the tiny cow,
　Lest she should go quite dry;
And you must feed the little pigs
　That are within the sty;

" And you must watch the speckled hen,
　Lest she should go astray;
Not forgetting the spool of yarn
　That I spin every day."

The old woman took the stick in her hand,
　And went to follow the plow;
The old man put the pail on his head,
　And went to milk the cow.

But Tiny she winced, and Tiny she flinched,
　And Tiny she tossed her nose;
And Tiny gave him a kick on the shin,
　Till the blood ran down to his toes.

And a " Ho, Tiny!" and a "So, Tiny!
　Pretty little cow, stand still!
If ever I milk you again," he said,
　" It shall be against my will."

And then he went to feed the pigs
　That were within the sty;
He knocked his nose against the shed,
　And caused the blood to fly.

And then he watched the speckled hen,
　Lest she should go astray;
But he quite forgot the spool of yarn
　That his wife spun every day.

And when the old woman came home at night,
  He said he could plainly see
That his wife could do more work in a day
  Than he could do in three !

And when he saw how well she plowed,
  And made the furrows even,
Said his wife could do more work in a day
  Than he could do in seven !

• 3 •

What does little birdie say
In her nest at peep of day?
Let me fly, says little birdie,
Mother, let me fly away.
Birdie, rest a little longer,
Till the little wings are stronger,
So she rests a little longer,
Then she flies away !

What does little baby say
In her bed at peep of day?
Baby says, like little birdie,
Let me rise and fly away.
Baby, sleep a little longer,
Till the little limbs are stronger,
If she sleeps a little longer,
Baby too shall fly away.

Alfred Tennyson.

• 4 •

OVER IN THE MEADOW

Over in the meadow,
  In the sand, in the sun,
Lived an old mother-toad
  And her little toadie one.

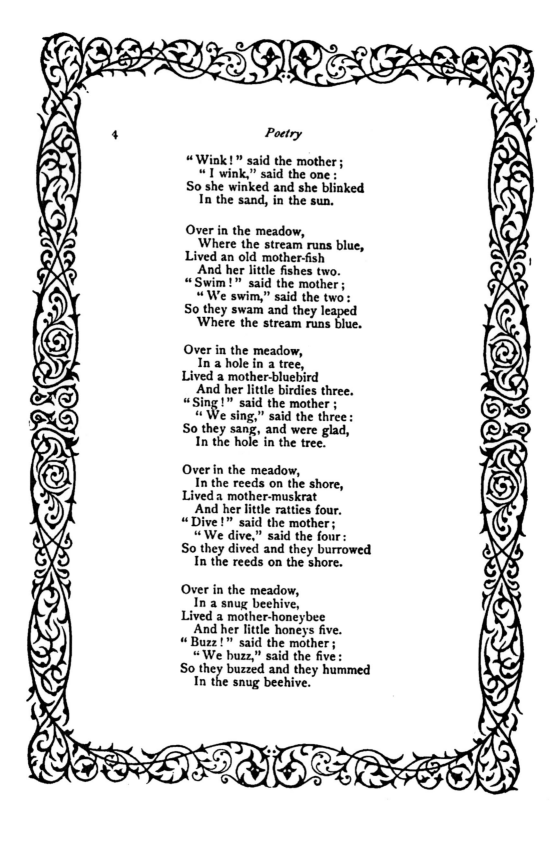

"Wink!" said the mother;
"I wink," said the one:
So she winked and she blinked
In the sand, in the sun.

Over in the meadow,
Where the stream runs blue,
Lived an old mother-fish
And her little fishes two.
"Swim!" said the mother;
"We swim," said the two:
So they swam and they leaped
Where the stream runs blue.

Over in the meadow,
In a hole in a tree,
Lived a mother-bluebird
And her little birdies three.
"Sing!" said the mother;
"We sing," said the three:
So they sang, and were glad,
In the hole in the tree.

Over in the meadow,
In the reeds on the shore,
Lived a mother-muskrat
And her little ratties four.
"Dive!" said the mother;
"We dive," said the four:
So they dived and they burrowed
In the reeds on the shore.

Over in the meadow,
In a snug beehive,
Lived a mother-honeybee
And her little honeys five.
"Buzz!" said the mother;
"We buzz," said the five:
So they buzzed and they hummed
In the snug beehive.

Over in the meadow,
  In a nest built of sticks,
Lived a black mother-crow
  And her little crows six.
"Caw !" said the mother;
  " We caw," said the six:
So they cawed and they called
  In their nest built of sticks.

Over in the meadow,
  Where the grass is so even,
Lived a gay mother-cricket
  And her little crickets seven.
"Chirp!" said the mother;
  "We chirp," said the seven :
So they chirped cheery notes
  In the grass soft and even.

Over in the meadow,
  By the old mossy gate,
Lived a brown mother-lizard
  And her little lizards eight.
"Bask!" said the mother;
  "We bask," said the eight:
So they basked in the sun
  On the old mossy gate.

Over in the meadow,
  Where the clear pools shine,
Lived a green mother-frog
  And her little froggies nine.
"Croak!" said the mother;
  '' We croak," said the nine :
So they croaked, and they plashed,
  Where the clear pools shine.

Over in the meadow,
  In a sly little den,
Lived a gray mother-spider
  And her little spiders ten.

"Spin!" said the mother;
 "We spin," said the ten:
So they spun lace webs
 In their sly little den.

Over in the meadow,
 In the soft summer even,
Lived a mother-fire-fly
 And her little flies eleven.
"Shine!" said the mother;
 "We shine," said the eleven:
So they shone like stars
 In the soft summer even.

Over in the meadow,
 Where the men dig and delve,
Lived a wise mother-ant
 And her little anties twelve.
"Toil!" said the mother;
 "We toil," said the twelve:
So they toiled, and were wise.
 Where the men dig and delve.
                    Olive A. Wadsworth.

• 5 •

WISHING.

Ring-ting! I wish I were a Primrose,
A bright yellow Primrose, blowing in the spring!
 The stooping boughs above me,
 The wandering bee to love me,
The fern and moss to creep across,
 And the Elm-tree for our king!

Nay-stay! I wish I were an Elm-tree,
A great lofty Elm-tree, with green leaves gay!
 The winds would set them dancing,
 The sun and moonshine glance in,
The birds would house among the boughs,
 And sweetly sing.

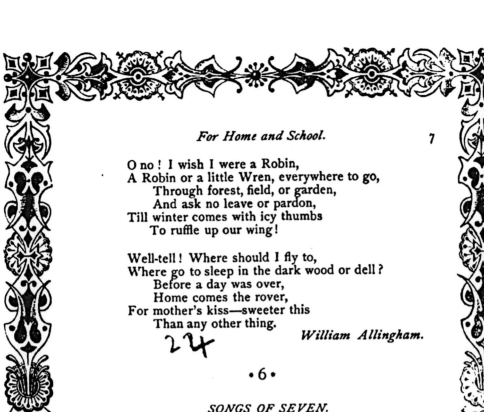

O no! I wish I were a Robin,
A Robin or a little Wren, everywhere to go,
   Through forest, field, or garden,
   And ask no leave or pardon,
Till winter comes with icy thumbs
   To ruffle up our wing!

Well-tell! Where should I fly to,
Where go to sleep in the dark wood or dell?
   Before a day was over,
   Home comes the rover,
For mother's kiss—sweeter this
   Than any other thing.
                     William Allingham.

24

• 6 •

SONGS OF SEVEN.

SEVEN TIMES ONE. EXULTATION.

There's no dew left on the daisies and clover,
   There's no rain left in heaven;
I've said my " seven times " over and over,
   Seven times one are seven.

I am old, so old, I can write a letter;
   My birthday lessons are done;
The lambs play always, they know no better;
   They are only one times one.

O moon! in the night I have seen you sailing
   And shining so round and low;
You were bright! ah bright! but your light is failing—
   You are nothing now but a bow.

You moon, have you done something wrong in heaven,
   That God has hidden your face?
I hope if you have you will soon be forgiven,
   And shine again in your place.

O velvet bee, you're a dusty fellow,
　You've powdered your legs with gold!
O brave marsh-mary buds, rich and yellow,
　Give me your money to hold!

O columbine, open your folded wrapper,
　Where two twin turtle doves dwell!
O cuckoo-pint, toll me the purple clapper!
　That hangs in your clear green bell.

And show me your nest with the young ones in it;
　I will not steal them away;
I am old! you may trust me, linnet, linnet—
　I am seven times one to-day.

Jean Ingelow.

• 7 •

BEAUTIFUL GRANDMAMMA.

Grandmamma sits in her quaint arm-chair;
Never was lady more sweet and fair;
Her gray locks ripple like silver shells,
And her own brow its story tells
Of a gentle life and peaceful even,
A trust in God, and a hope in heaven.

Little girl Mary sits rocking away
In her own low seat, like some winsome fay;
Two doll babies her kisses share,
And another one lies by the side of her chair;
May is as fair as the morning dew,
Cheeks of roses, and ribbons of blue.

"Say, Grandmamma," says the pretty elf,
"Tell me a story about yourself.
When you were little, what did you play?
Were you good or naughty the whole long day?
Was it hundreds and hundreds of years ago?
And what makes your soft hair as white as snow?"

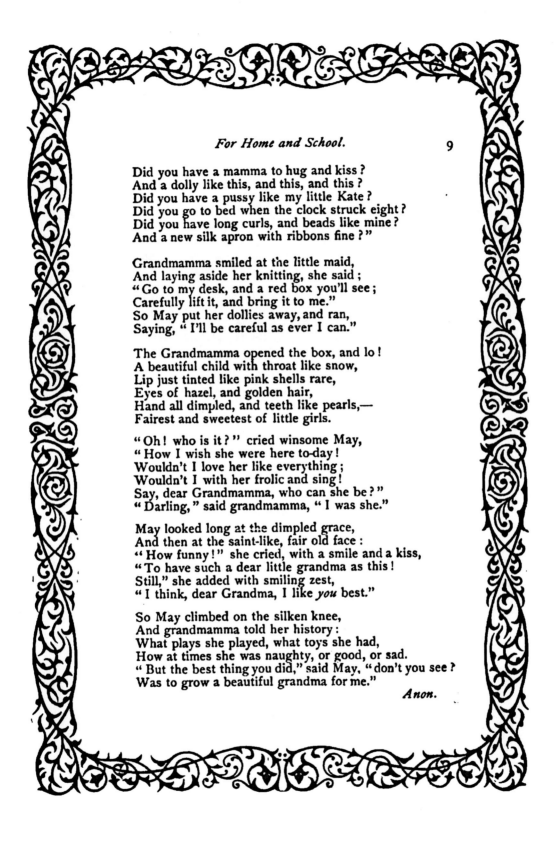

Did you have a mamma to hug and kiss?
And a dolly like this, and this, and this?
Did you have a pussy like my little Kate?
Did you go to bed when the clock struck eight?
Did you have long curls, and beads like mine?
And a new silk apron with ribbons fine?"

Grandmamma smiled at the little maid,
And laying aside her knitting, she said;
"Go to my desk, and a red box you'll see;
Carefully lift it, and bring it to me."
So May put her dollies away, and ran,
Saying, "I'll be careful as ever I can."

The Grandmamma opened the box, and lo!
A beautiful child with throat like snow,
Lip just tinted like pink shells rare,
Eyes of hazel, and golden hair,
Hand all dimpled, and teeth like pearls,—
Fairest and sweetest of little girls.

"Oh! who is it?" cried winsome May,
"How I wish she were here to-day!
Wouldn't I love her like everything;
Wouldn't I with her frolic and sing!
Say, dear Grandmamma, who can she be?"
"Darling," said grandmamma, "I was she."

May looked long at the dimpled grace,
And then at the saint-like, fair old face:
"How funny!" she cried, with a smile and a kiss,
"To have such a dear little grandma as this!
Still," she added with smiling zest,
"I think, dear Grandma, I like *you* best."

So May climbed on the silken knee,
And grandmamma told her history:
What plays she played, what toys she had,
How at times she was naughty, or good, or sad.
"But the best thing you did," said May, "don't you see?
Was to grow a beautiful grandma for me."

Anon.

· 8 ·

VAGRANT PANSIES.

They are all in the lily-bed, cuddled close together—
Purples, Yellow Cap and little Baby Blue :
How they ever got there, you must ask the April weather,
The morning and the evening winds, the sunshine and the dew.

Why they should go visiting the tall and haughty lilies
Is very odd, and none of them will condescend to say :
They might have made a call upon the jolly daffodillies ;
They might have come to my house any pleasant day.

They don't have a good time, I think, their little faces
Look so very solemn underneath each velvet hood.
I wonder, don't they feel among the garden's airs and graces
That shy cousin Violet is happier in the wood ?

Ah, my pretty pansies, it's no use to go a-seeking ;
There isn't any good time waiting anywhere :
I fancy even Violet is troubled—mildly speaking—
When somebody plucks her, finding her so fair.

There's nothing left for you, my pets, but just to do your
 duty—
Bloom, and make the world sweet—that's the best for you ;
There isn't much that's lovelier than your bashful beauty,
My purples, my Yellow Cap, my little Baby Blue.
     Nelly M. Hutchinson.

· 9 ·

NURSERY SONG.

As I walked over the hill one day,
I listened and heard a mother sheep say,
" In all the green world there is nothing so sweet
As my little lammie with his nimble feet,
  With his eyes so bright,

And his wool so white—
Oh, he is my darling, my heart's delight."
And the mother-sheep and the little one,
Side by side lay down in the sun,
And they went to sleep on the hillside warm,
While my little lammie lies here on my arm.

I went to the kitchen, and what did I see
But the old gray cat with her kittens three!
I heard her whispering soft; said she,
" My kittens with tails so cunningly curled
Are the prettiest things that can be in the world.
        The bird on the tree,
        And the old ewe, she
        May love their babies exceedingly,
        But I love my kittens there
        Under the rocking-chair;
I love my kittens with all my might,
I love them at morning, noon, and night;
Now I'll take up my kitties, the kitties I love,
And we'll lie down together beneath the warm stove."
Let the kittens sleep under the stove so warm,
While my little kitten lies here on my arm.

I went to the yard, and saw the old hen
Go clucking about with her chickens ten.
She clucked, and she scratched, and she bustled away,
And what do you think I heard the hen say?
I heard her say, " The sun never did shine
On anything like to these chickens of mine!
You may hunt the full moon and the stars if you please,
But you never will find such ten chickens as these.
My dear downy darlings, my sweet little things,
Come, nestle now cosily under my wings."
        So the hen said
        And the chickens all sped,
As fast as they could to their nice feather bed;
And there let them sleep in their feathers so warm,
While my little chick lies here on my arm.
                                        Mrs. Carter.

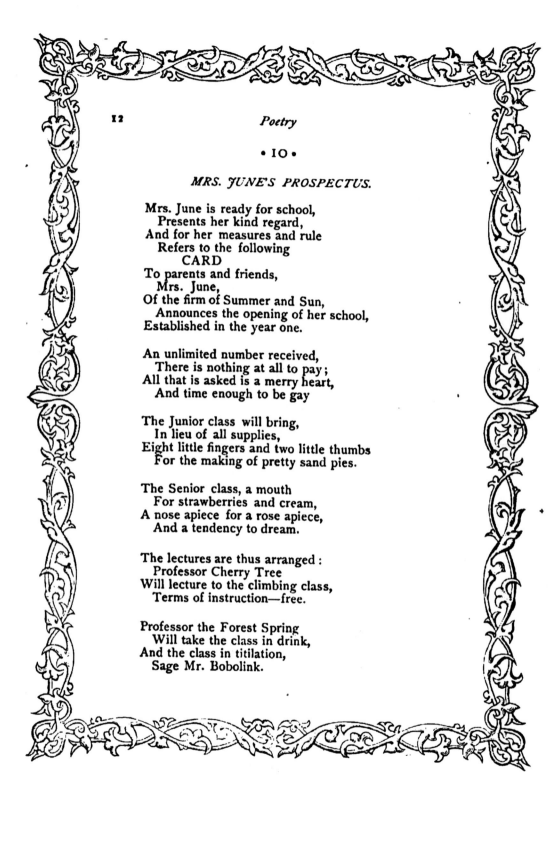

• IO •

MRS. JUNE'S PROSPECTUS.

Mrs. June is ready for school,
  Presents her kind regard,
And for her measures and rule
  Refers to the following
      CARD
To parents and friends,
  Mrs. June,
Of the firm of Summer and Sun,
  Announces the opening of her school,
Established in the year one.

An unlimited number received,
  There is nothing at all to pay;
All that is asked is a merry heart,
  And time enough to be gay

The Junior class will bring,
  In lieu of all supplies,
Eight little fingers and two little thumbs
  For the making of pretty sand pies.

The Senior class, a mouth
  For strawberries and cream,
A nose apiece for a rose apiece,
  And a tendency to dream.

The lectures are thus arranged :
  Professor Cherry Tree
Will lecture to the climbing class,
  Terms of instruction—free.

Professor the Forest Spring
  Will take the class in drink,
And the class in titilation,
  Sage Mr. Bobolink.

Young Mr. Ox Eye Daisy
  Will demonstrate each day
On botany, on native plants,
  And the properties of hay.

Miss Nature, the class in fun
  (A charming class to teach);
And the swinging class and the bird's-nest class
  Miss Hickory and Miss Beech.

And the sleepy class at night,
  And the dinner class at noon,
And the fat, and laugh and roses class,
  They fall to Mrs. June.

And she hopes her little friends
  Will be punctual as the sun,
For the term, alas! is very short,
  And she wants them every one.

Susan Coolidge.

• II •

PUSSY'S CLASS.

"Now, children," said Puss, as she shook her head,
"It is time your morning lesson was said."
So her kittens drew near with footsteps slow,
And sat down before her all in a row.

"Attention, class!" said the cat mamma,
"And tell me quick where your noses are!"
At this all the kittens sniffed the air,
As if it were filled with a perfume rare.

"Now, what do you say when you want a drink?"
The kittens waited a moment to think,
And then the answer came clear and loud—
You ought to have heard how those kittens *meow'd!*

"Very well. 'Tis the same with a sharper tone,
When you want a fish or a bit of bone.
Now what do you say when children are good?"
And the kittens purred as soft as they could.

"And what do you do when children are bad?
When they tease and pull?" Each kitty looked sad.
"Pooh!" said their mother, "That isn't enough;
You must use your claws when children are rough."

"And where are your claws? No, no, my dear,"
As she took up a paw, "See, they're hidden here."
Then all the kittens crowded about,
To see their sharp little claws brought out.

They felt quite sure they should never need
To use such a weapon—oh no, indeed!
But their wise mamma gave a pussy's "*pshaw!*"
And boxed their ears with her softest paw.

"Now *sptsss* as hard as you can," she said;
But every kitten hung down its head.
"*Sptsss!* I say," cried the mother cat;
But they said, "Oh mamma, we can't do that."

"Then go and play," said the fond mamma;
"What sweet little idiots kittens are!
Ah well! I was once the same, I suppose,"
And she looked very wise and rubbed her nose.

M. M. D

• 1 2 •

HUNTING EGGS.

"Who wants to hunt eggs?" shouted Charlie the bold;
   "Who wants to climb on the hay?"
"Oh, I!" clamored Fannie and Will;
   "And I, too," pleaded three-year-old May.

So they rushed to the barn, helter-skelter, and soon
    Were driving about with a zest,
In the corners and rafters, the mangers and hay,
    To see who could find the first nest.

"And who gets the most eggs shall beg Grandma to bake
    A cake we can share all around;"
So Fannie suggested; and the boys cried "Hurrah!
    We'll have every egg can be found!"

Nimble Charlie went clambering about like a cat,
    And soon counted, one, two, three, four!
And then, with the pearly white eggs in his hat,
    Slid carefully down to the floor.

"There's a nest!" Fannie cried, from far up on the mow,
    "Right here in the hay! one, two, three!"
And in her white apron she gathered them up,
    As happy and glad as could be.

"Old Speckle's on mine!" shouted Will, but just then,
    With a cackle, away the hen flew.
"Dear me!" said poor Will, "I was sure I would beat,
    And here I have got only two!"

"Where's May?" they all questioned; Oh, where has she
       gone?"
    "Here! here I is. I's foun' a nes'!"
And her curly brown head from the manger popped out,
    Just under the nose of Black Bess.

"Oh, sit still now, May, or horsie may bite!"
    But she counted, "one, two, three, four, five!"
And they rushed to her rescue with laugh and with shout;
    "She's got the most, sure as you live!"

But there she was sitting in sweetest content;
    And down in her snug little lap
Five soft little kitties lay rolled into balls,
    Contentedly taking a nap.

                    Zion's Herald.

• 13 •

THE CHICKEN'S MISTAKE.

A little chick one day
    Asked leave to go on the water,
Where she saw a duck with her brood at play,
    Swimming and splashing about her.

Indeed she began to peep and cry
    When her mother wouldn't let her;
"If the ducks can swim there, why can't I ?
    Are they any bigger or better ? "

Then the old hen answered : " Listen to me,
    And hush your foolish talking ;
Just look at your feet and you will see
    They were only made for walking."

But chicky wistfully eyed the brook,
    And didn't half believe her,
For she seemed to say, by a knowing look,
    Such stories couldn't deceive her.

And as her mother was scratching the ground,
    She muttered, lower and lower,
"I know I can go there and not be drowned,
    And so, I think, I'll show her."

Then she made a plunge where the stream was deep,
    And saw, too late, her blunder,
For she had hardly time to peep ;
    When her foolish head went under.

And now I hope her fate will show
    The child my story reading,
That those who are older sometimes know
    What you will do well in heeding;

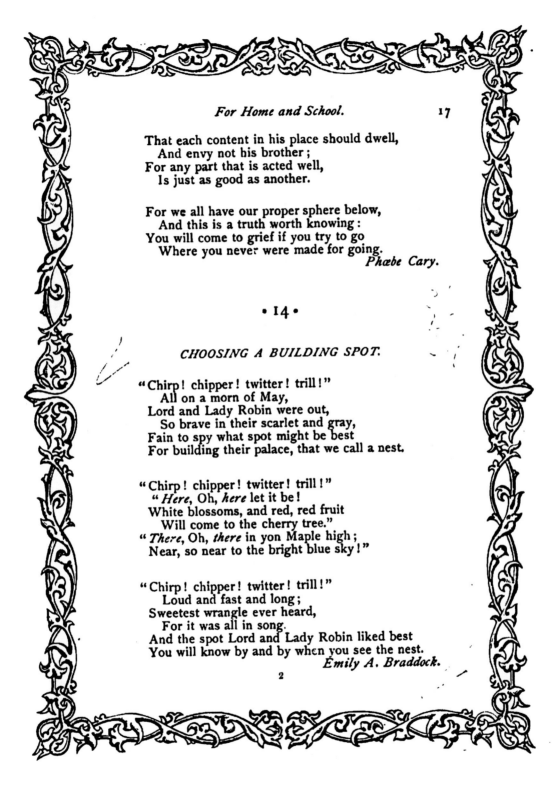

That each content in his place should dwell,
  And envy not his brother;
For any part that is acted well,
  Is just as good as another.

For we all have our proper sphere below,
  And this is a truth worth knowing:
You will come to grief if you try to go
  Where you never were made for going.
               Phœbe Cary.

• 14 •

CHOOSING A BUILDING SPOT.

"Chirp! chipper! twitter! trill!"
  All on a morn of May,
Lord and Lady Robin were out,
  So brave in their scarlet and gray,
Fain to spy what spot might be best
For building their palace, that we call a nest.

"Chirp! chipper! twitter! trill!"
  "*Here*, Oh, *here* let it be!
White blossoms, and red, red fruit
  Will come to the cherry tree."
"*There*, Oh, *there* in yon Maple high;
  Near, so near to the bright blue sky!"

"Chirp! chipper! twitter! trill!"
  Loud and fast and long;
Sweetest wrangle ever heard,
  For it was all in song.
And the spot Lord and Lady Robin liked best
You will know by and by when you see the nest.
            Emily A. Braddock.

· 15 ·

THE MOUNTAIN AND THE SQUIRREL.

The Mountain and the Squirrel
Had a quarrel
And the former called the latter " Little Prig."
Bun replied :
" You are doubtless very big ;
But all sorts of things and weather
Must be taken in together
To make up a year,
And a sphere ;
And I think it no disgrace
To occupy my place.
If I'm not so large as you
You're not so small as I,
And not half so spry ;
I'll not deny you make
A very pretty squirrel track,
Talents differ ; all is well and wisely put ;
If I cannot carry forests on my back,
Neither can you crack a nut."

Ralph Waldo Emerson.

· 16 ·

AUTUMN SONG OF A LITTLE GIRL.

The Autumn has filled me with wonder to-day,
The wind seems so sad while the trees look so gay ;
The sky is so blue while the fields are so brown ;
While bright leaves and brown leaves drift all through the
      town ;—
I wish I could tell why the world changes so ;—
But I am a little girl,—I cannot know !

The sun rises late. and then down goes so soon
I think it is evening before it is noon!
Of the birds and the flowers hardly one can be found
Though the little brown sparrows stay all the year round;—
I wish I could tell you where all the birds go;
But I am a little girl,—I cannot know!

Oh, Autumn! why banish such bright things as they?
Pray turn the world gently,—don't scare them away!
And now they are gone, will you bring them again?
If they come in the Spring,—I may not be here then;—
Why go they so swiftly,—then come back so slow?
Oh, I'm but a little girl,—I cannot know!

H. C. B.

· 17 ·

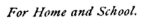

ADVICE.

There was once a pretty chicken;
But his friends were very few,
For he thought that there was nothing
In the world but what he knew.
So he always in the farm-yard
Had a very forward way,
Telling all the hens and turkeys
What they ought to do and say.
"Mrs. Goose," he said, "I wonder
That your goslings you should let
Go out paddling in the water;
It will kill them to get wet."

"And I wish, my old Aunt Dorking,"
He began to her one day,
"That you wouldn't sit all summer
In your nest upon the hay;
Won't you come out to the meadow
Where the grass with seeds is filled?"
"If I should," said Mrs. Dorking,

"Then my eggs would get all chilled."
"No they won't," replied the chicken;
"And no matter if they do.
Eggs are really good for nothing;
What's an egg to me or you?"

"What's an egg?" said Mrs. Dorking,
"Can it be you do not know
You yourself were in an eggshell
Just one little month ago?
And if kind wings had not warmed you,
You would not be out to-day,
Telling hens, and geese, and turkeys
What they ought to do and say!
To be very wise, and show it,
Is a pleasant thing, no doubt;
But when young folks talk to old folks,
They should know what they're about."

Anonymous.

• 18 •

SUPPOSE.

Suppose, my little lady,
  Your doll should break her head;
Could you make it whole by crying
  Till your eyes and nose were red?
And wouldn't it be pleasanter
  To treat it as a joke,
And say you're glad 'twas dolly's,
  And not your head that broke?

Suppose you're dressed for walking,
  And the rain comes pouring down;
Will it clear off any sooner
  Because you scold and frown?
And wouldn't it be nicer
  For you to smile than pout,
And so make sunshine in the house
  When there is none without?

Suppose your task, my little man,
  Is very hard to get;
Will it make it any easier
  For you to sit and fret?
And wouldn't it be wiser,
  Than waiting like a dunce,
To go to work in earnest
  And learn the thing at once?

Suppose that some boys have a horse,
  And some a coach and pair;
Will it tire you less while walking
  To say "It isn't fair?"
And wouldn't it be nobler
  To keep your temper sweet,
And in your heart be thankful
  You can walk upon your feet?

Suppose the world don't please you,
  Nor the way some people do;
Do you thing the whole creation
  Will be altered just for you?
And isn't it, my boy or girl,
  The wisest, bravest plan,
Whatever comes, or doesn't come,
  To do the best you can?

Phœbe Cary.

• 19 •

THE CROW'S CHILDREN.

A huntsman, bearing his gun a-field,
  Went whistling merrily,
When he heard the blackest of black crows
  Call out from a withered tree :—

"You are going to kill the thievish birds,
  And I would, if I were you;
But you must not touch my family,
  Whatever else you do."

"I'm only going to kill the birds
　That are eating up my crop;
And if your young ones do such things,
　Be sure they'll have to stop."

"O," said the crow, "my children
　Are the best ones ever born:
There isn't one among them all
　Would steal a grain of corn."

"But how shall I know which ones they are?
　Do they resemble you?"
"O no," said the crow; "they're the prettiest birds,
　And the whitest, ever flew."

So off went the sportsman whistling,
　And off, too, went his gun;
And its startling echoes never ceased
　Again till the day was done.

And the old crow sat untroubled,
　Cawing away in her nook;
For she said, "He'll never kill my birds,
　Since I told him how they look.

"Now there's the hawk, my neighbor,
　She'll see what'll come to pass soon
And that saucy, whistling blackbird
　May have to change his tune."

When, lo! she saw the hunter
　Taking his homeward track,
With a string of crows as long as his gun,
　Hanging down his back.

"Alack, alack!" said the mother,
　"What in the world have you done?
You promised to spare my pretty birds,
　And you've killed them, every one."

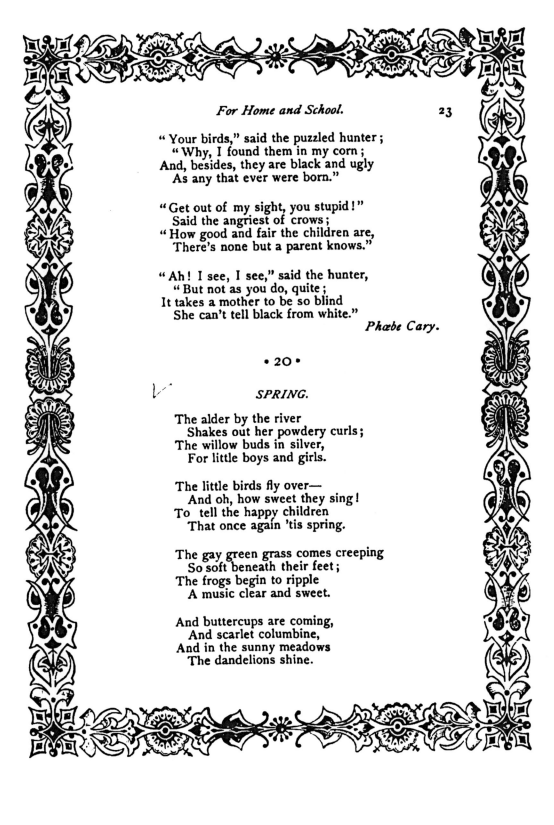

"Your birds," said the puzzled hunter;
    "Why, I found them in my corn;
And, besides, they are black and ugly
    As any that ever were born."

"Get out of my sight, you stupid!"
    Said the angriest of crows;
"How good and fair the children are,
    There's none but a parent knows."

"Ah! I see, I see," said the hunter,
    "But not as you do, quite;
It takes a mother to be so blind
    She can't tell black from white."

Phœbe Cary.

• 20 •

SPRING.

The alder by the river
    Shakes out her powdery curls;
The willow buds in silver,
    For little boys and girls.

The little birds fly over—
    And oh, how sweet they sing!
To tell the happy children
    That once again 'tis spring.

The gay green grass comes creeping
    So soft beneath their feet;
The frogs begin to ripple
    A music clear and sweet.

And buttercups are coming,
    And scarlet columbine,
And in the sunny meadows
    The dandelions shine.

And just as many daisies
  As their soft hands can hold,
The little ones may gather,
  All fair in white and gold.

Here blows the warm, red clover,
  There peeps the violet blue;
O, happy little children,
  God made them all for you.

Celia Thaxter.

• 21 •

FLOWER-GIRLS.

O, my little sea-side girl,
  What is in your garden growing?
"Rock-weeds and tangle-grass,
  With the slow tide coming, going;
Samphire and marsh-rosemary,
  All along the west shore creeping;
Sand-wort, beach-peas, pimpernel,
  Out of nooks and corners peeping."

O, my little prairie girl,
  What's in bloom among your grasses?
"Spring-beauties, painted-cups,
  Flushing when the south wind passes;
Beds of rose-pink centaury;
  Compass-flowers to northward turning;
Larkspur, orange-gold puccoon;
  Leagues of lilies flame-red burning."

O, my little mountain girl,
  Have you anything to gather?
"White everlasting-bloom,
  Not afraid of wind or weather;
Sweet brier, leaning on the crag
  That the lady-fern hides under;
Hare bells, violets white and blue;
  Who has sweeter flowers, I wonder?"

" O, my little maidens three,
    I will lay your pretty posies—
Sea scented, cloud-bedewed,
    Prairie grasses, mountain-roses—
On a bed of shells and moss.
    Come and bend your bright heads nearer !
Though so fair your blossoms are,
    You three human flowers are dearer."

                      Lucy Larcom.

• 22 •

IN THE TREE TOP.

" Rock-a-by, baby, up in the tree-top !"
    Mother his blanket is spinning ;
And a light little rustle that never will stop,
    Breezes and boughs are beginning.
Rock-a-by, baby, swinging so high !
        Rock-a-by !

" When the wind blows, then the cradle will rock."
    Hush ! now it stirs in the bushes ;
Now with a whisper, a flutter of talk,
    Baby and hammock it pushes.
Rock-a-by, baby ! shut pretty eye !
        Rock-a-by !

" Rock with the boughs, rock-a-by, baby, dear ! "
    Leaf tongues are singing and saying ;
Mother she listens, and sister is near,
    Under the tree softly playing.
Rock-a-by, baby ! mother's close by !
        Rock-a-by !

Weave him a beautiful dream, little breeze !
    Little leaves, nestle around him !
He will remember the song of the trees,
    When age with silver has crowned him.
Rock-a-by, baby ! wake by-and-by !
        Rock-a-by !

                      Lucy Larcom.

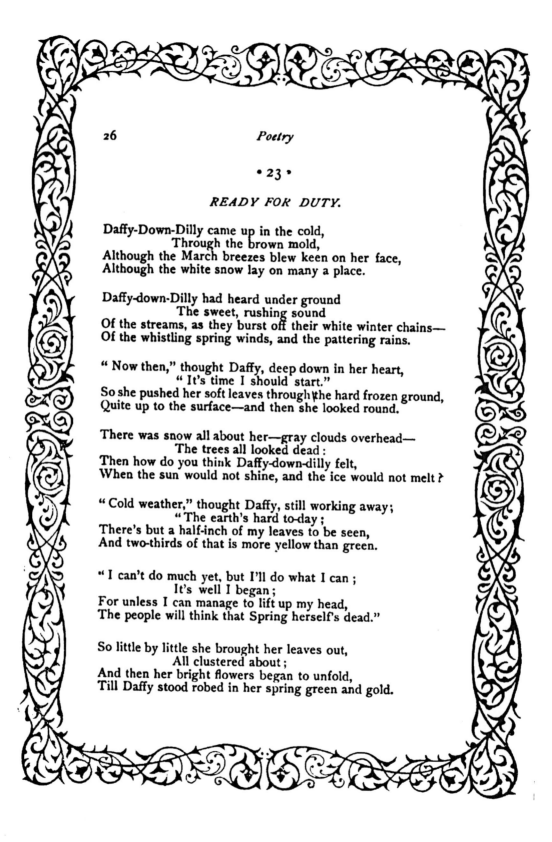

• 23 •

READY FOR DUTY.

Daffy-Down-Dilly came up in the cold,
　　　Through the brown mold,
Although the March breezes blew keen on her face,
Although the white snow lay on many a place.

Daffy-down-Dilly had heard under ground
　　　The sweet, rushing sound
Of the streams, as they burst off their white winter chains—
Of the whistling spring winds, and the pattering rains.

" Now then," thought Daffy, deep down in her heart,
　　　" It's time I should start."
So she pushed her soft leaves through the hard frozen ground,
Quite up to the surface—and then she looked round.

There was snow all about her—gray clouds overhead—
　　　The trees all looked dead :
Then how do you think Daffy-down-dilly felt,
When the sun would not shine, and the ice would not melt ?

" Cold weather," thought Daffy, still working away;
　　　" The earth's hard to-day ;
There's but a half-inch of my leaves to be seen,
And two-thirds of that is more yellow than green.

" I can't do much yet, but I'll do what I can ;
　　　It's well I began ;
For unless I can manage to lift up my head,
The people will think that Spring herself's dead."

So little by little she brought her leaves out,
　　　All clustered about ;
And then her bright flowers began to unfold,
Till Daffy stood robed in her spring green and gold.

Ever faithfully Yours
Bayard Taylor

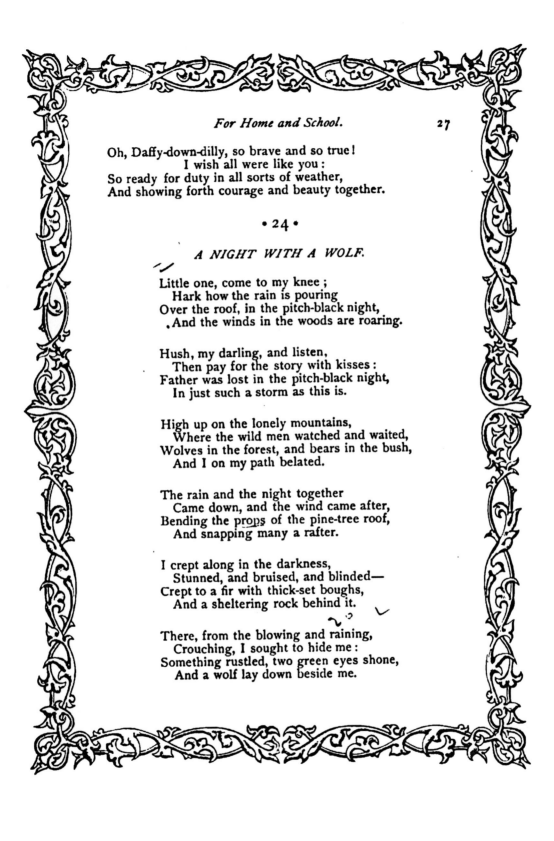

Oh, Daffy-down-dilly, so brave and so true!
I wish all were like you:
So ready for duty in all sorts of weather,
And showing forth courage and beauty together.

• 24 •

A NIGHT WITH A WOLF.

Little one, come to my knee;
  Hark how the rain is pouring
Over the roof, in the pitch-black night,
  And the winds in the woods are roaring.

Hush, my darling, and listen,
  Then pay for the story with kisses:
Father was lost in the pitch-black night,
  In just such a storm as this is.

High up on the lonely mountains,
  Where the wild men watched and waited,
Wolves in the forest, and bears in the bush,
  And I on my path belated.

The rain and the night together
  Came down, and the wind came after,
Bending the props of the pine-tree roof,
  And snapping many a rafter.

I crept along in the darkness,
  Stunned, and bruised, and blinded—
Crept to a fir with thick-set boughs,
  And a sheltering rock behind it.

There, from the blowing and raining,
  Crouching, I sought to hide me:
Something rustled, two green eyes shone,
  And a wolf lay down beside me.

Little one, be not frightened :
　I and the wolf together,
Side by side, through the long, long night,
　Hid from the awful weather.

His wet fur pressed against me ;
　Each of us warmed the other ;
Each of us felt, in the stormy dark,
　That beast and man were brother.

And when the falling forest
　No longer crashed in warning,
Each of us went from our hiding-place
　Forth in the wild, wet morning.

Darling, kiss me in payment :
　Hark, how the wind is roaring ;
Father's house is a better place
　When the stormy rain is pouring.
　　　　　　　　　　　　Bayard Taylor.

• 25 •

GOLDEN-TRESSED ADELAIDE.

Sing, I pray, a little song,
　Mother dear !
Neither sad nor very long :
It is for a little maid,
Golden-tressed Adelaide !
Therefore let it suit a merry, merry ear,
　Mother dear ?

Let it be a merry strain,
　Mother dear !
Shunning e'en the thought of pain.

For our gentle child will weep,
If the theme be dark and deep;
And we will not draw a single, single tear,
    Mother dear!

Childhood should be all divine,
    Mother dear!
And like an endless summer shine;
Gay as Edward's shouts and cries,
Bright as Agnes' azure eyes:
Therefore bid thy song be merry;—dost thou hear,
    Mother dear?
                Barry Cornwall.

• 26 •

MY HEART'S IN THE HIGHLANDS.

My heart's in the Highlands, my heart is not here;
My heart's in the Highlands a-chasing the deer;
Chasing the wild deer, and following the roe,
My heart's in the Highlands wherever I go.
Farewell to the Highlands, farewell to the North,
The birthplace of valor, the country of worth;
Wherever I wander, wherever I rove,
The hills of the Highlands forever I love.
Farewell to the mountains high covered with snow;
Farewell to the straths and green valley below;
Farewell to the forests and wild-hanging woods;
Farewell to the torrents and loud-pouring floods.
My heart's in the Highlands, my heart is not here,
My heart's in the Highlands a-chasing the deer;
Chasing the wild deer, and following the roe,
My heart's in the Highlands wherever I go.
                Robert Burns.

• 27 •

THE WIND AND THE MOON.

Said the Wind to the Moon, " I will blow you out.
   You stare
   In the air
   Like a ghost in a chair,
Always looking what I am about.
I hate to be watched ; I will blow you out."

The wind blew hard, and out went the Moon.
   So, deep
   On a heap
   Of cloudless sleep,
Down lay the Wind, and slumbered soon—
Muttering low—" I've done for that Moon."

He turned in his bed ; she was there again !
   On high
   In the sky
   With her ghost eye,
The Moon shone white and alive and plain ;
Said the Wind—" I will blow you out again."

The Wind blew hard, and the Moon grew dim.
   " With my sledge
   And my wedge
   I have knocked off her edge.
If only I blow right fierce and grim
The creature will soon be dimmer than dim."

He blew, and he blew, and she thinned to a thread.
   " One puff
   More's enough
   To blow her to snuff !
One good puff more where the last was bred,
And glimmer, glum will go the thread."

He blew a great blast and the thread was gone;
  In the air
  Nowhere
  Was a moonbeam bare;
Far off and harmless the sky-stars shone;
Sure and certain the Moon was gone!

The Wind took to his revels once more
  On down,
  In town,
  Like a merry-mad clown,
He leaped and halloed with whistle and roar.
"What's that?" The glimmering thread one more

He flew in a rage—he danced and blew;
  But in vain
  Was the pain
  Of his bursting brain;
For still broader the moon-scrap grew,
The broader he swelled his big cheeks, and blew.

Slowly she grew—till she filled the night
  And shone
  On her throne
  In the sky alone,
A matchless, wonderful, silvery light,
Radiant and lovely, the queen of the night.

Said the Wind: "What a marvel of power am I!
  With my breath,
  Good faith,
  I blew her to death—
First blew her away right out of the sky—
Then blew her in; what strength am I!"

But the Moon knew nothing about the affair;
  For high
  In the sky
  With her one white eye,
Motionless miles above the air,
She had never heard the great Wind blare.

       George MacDonald.

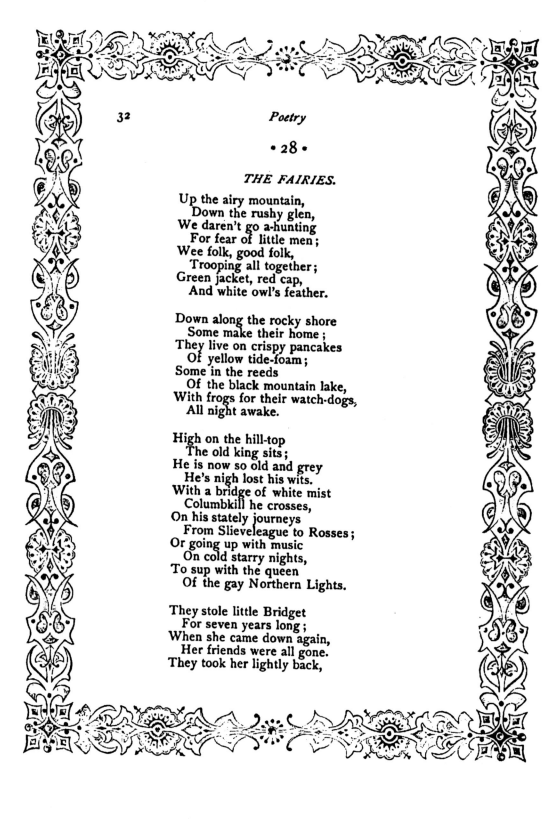

• 28 •

THE FAIRIES.

Up the airy mountain,
　Down the rushy glen,
We daren't go a-hunting
　For fear of little men;
Wee folk, good folk,
　Trooping all together;
Green jacket, red cap,
　And white owl's feather.

Down along the rocky shore
　Some make their home;
They live on crispy pancakes
　Of yellow tide-foam;
Some in the reeds
　Of the black mountain lake,
With frogs for their watch-dogs,
　All night awake.

High on the hill-top
　The old king sits;
He is now so old and grey
　He's nigh lost his wits.
With a bridge of white mist
　Columbkill he crosses,
On his stately journeys
　From Slieveleague to Rosses;
Or going up with music
　On cold starry nights,
To sup with the queen
　Of the gay Northern Lights.

They stole little Bridget
　For seven years long;
When she came down again,
　Her friends were all gone.
They took her lightly back,

Between the night and morrow,
They thought that she was fast asleep,
　But she was dead with sorrow.
They have kept her ever since
　Deep within the lakes,
On a bed of flag leaves,
　Watching till she wakes.

By the craggy hill-side,
　Through the mosses bare,
They have planted thorn trees
　For pleasure here and there.
Is any man so daring
　As to dig one up in spite,
He shall find the thornies set
　In his bed at night.

Up the airy mountain,
　Down the rushy glen,
We daren't go a-hunting,
　For fear of little men;
Wee folk, good folk,
　Trooping all together;
Green jacket, red cap,
　And white owl's feather.

William Allingham.

• 29 •

LITTLE WHITE LILY.

Little white Lily
Sat by a stone,
Drooping and waiting
Till the sun shone.
Little white Lily
Sunshine has fed;
Little white Lily
Is lifting her head.

Little white Lily
Said, " It is good ;
Little white Lily's
Clothing and food."
Little white Lily,
Dressed like a bride!
Shining with whiteness,
And crowned beside !

Little white Lily
Droopeth with pain,
Waiting and waiting
For the wet rain.
Little white Lily
Holdeth her cup ;
Rain is fast falling
And filling it up.

Little white Lily
Says, " Good again,
When I am thirsty
To have fresh rain ;
Now I am stronger,
Now I am cool ;
Heat cannot burn me,
My veins are so full."

Little white Lily
Smells very sweet !
On her head, sunshine,
Rain at her feet.
" Thanks to the sunshine
Thanks to the rain ! "
Little white Lily
Is happy again !

Geo. MacDonald.

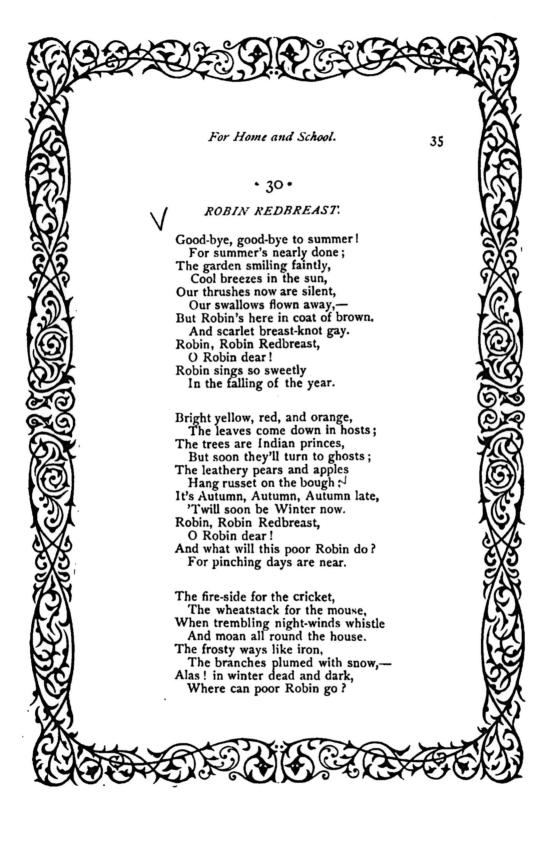

• 30 •

ROBIN REDBREAST.

Good-bye, good-bye to summer!
  For summer's nearly done;
The garden smiling faintly,
  Cool breezes in the sun,
Our thrushes now are silent,
  Our swallows flown away,—
But Robin's here in coat of brown.
  And scarlet breast-knot gay.
Robin, Robin Redbreast,
  O Robin dear!
Robin sings so sweetly
  In the falling of the year.

Bright yellow, red, and orange,
  The leaves come down in hosts;
The trees are Indian princes,
  But soon they'll turn to ghosts;
The leathery pears and apples
  Hang russet on the bough;
It's Autumn, Autumn, Autumn late,
  'Twill soon be Winter now.
Robin, Robin Redbreast,
  O Robin dear!
And what will this poor Robin do?
  For pinching days are near.

The fire-side for the cricket,
  The wheatstack for the mouse,
When trembling night-winds whistle
  And moan all round the house.
The frosty ways like iron,
  The branches plumed with snow,—
Alas! in winter dead and dark,
  Where can poor Robin go?

Robin, Robin Redbreast,
  O Robin dear!
And a crumb of bread for Robin,
  His little heart to cheer.

W. Allingham.

31 •

TO THE LADY-BIRD.

Lady-bird! lady-bird! fly away home;—
  The field-mouse has gone to her nest,
The daisies have shut up their sleepy red eyes,
  And the bees and the birds are at rest.

Lady-bird! lady-bird! fly away home,—
  The glow-worm is lighting her lamp,
The dew's falling fast, and your fine speckled wings
  Will flag with the close-clinging damp.

Lady-bird! lady-bird! fly away home,—
  Good luck if you reach it at last!
The owl's come abroad, and the bat's on the roam,
  Sharp set from their Ramazan fast.

Lady-bird! lady-bird! fly away home,—
  The fairy bells tinkle afar!
Make haste, or they'll catch you, and harness you fast
  With a cobweb to Oberon's car.

Lady-bird! lady-bird! fly away home,—
  To your house in the old willow-tree,
Where your children, so dear, have invited the ant
  And a few cosy neighbors to tea.

Lady-bird! lady-bird! fly away home,—
  And if not gobbled up by the way,
Nor yoked by the fairies to Oberon's car,
  You're in luck—and that's all I've to say.

Mrs. Southey.

• 32 •

CHRISTMAS TIMES.

'Twas the night before Christmas, and all through the house
Not a creature was stirring, not even a mouse,
The stockings were hung by the chimney with care,
In the hope that St. Nicholas soon would be there.
The children were nestled all snug in their beds,
While visions of sugar-plums danced in their heads,
And mamma in her kerchief, and I in my cap,
Had just settled our brains for a long winter's nap;
When out on the lawn there arose such a clatter,
I sprang from the bed to see what was the matter.
Away to the window I flew like a flash,
Tore open the shutters and threw up the sash;—
The moon on the breast of the new-fallen snow
Gave the lustre of mid-day to objects below,—
When what to my wondering eyes should appear
But a miniature sleigh, and eight tiny reindeer,
With a little old driver so lively and quick
I knew in a moment it must be St. Nick.
More rapid than eagles his coursers they came,
And he whistled, and shouted, and called them by name :—
"Now, Dasher! now, Dancer! now, Prancer! now, Vixen!
On, Comet! on, Cupid! on, Dunder and Blixen!
To the top of the porch, to the top of the wall,
Now, dash away! dash away! dash away all!"
As dry leaves before the wild hurricane fly,
When they meet with an obstacle mount to the sky,
So up to the house top the coursers they flew
With the sleigh full of toys, and St. Nicholas too.
And then in a twinkling, I heard on the roof
The prancing and pawing of each tiny hoof.
As I drew in my head, and was turning around,

Down the chimney St. Nicholas came with a bound.
He was dressed all in fur, from his head to his foot,
And his clothes were all tarnished with ashes and soot;
A bundle of toys he had flung on his back,
And he looked like a pedler just opening his pack.
His eyes—how they twinkled! his dimples how merry!
His cheeks were like roses, his nose like a cherry;
His droll little mouth was drawn up like a bow,
And the beard of his chin was as white as the snow;
The stump of a pipe he held tight in his teeth,
And the smoke it encircled his head like a wreath.
He was chubby and plump, a right jolly old elf,
And I laughed when I saw him, in spite of myself.
A wink of his eye, and a twist of his head,
Soon gave me to know I had nothing to dread.
He spoke not a word, but went straight to his work,
And filled all his stockings,—then turned with a jerk,
And laying his finger aside of his nose,
And giving a nod, up the chimney he rose.
He sprang to his sleigh, to his team gave a whistle,
And away they all flew, like the down of a thistle;
But I heard him exclaim, ere he drove out of sight,
" Merry Christmas to all, and to all a good night ! "

Clement C. Moore.

· 33 ·

A BALLAD.

TRANSLATED FROM HERDER.

Among green, pleasant meadows,
　All in a grove so wild,
Was set a marble image
　Of the Virgin and the child.

Here oft, on summer evenings,
　A lovely boy would rove,
To play beside the image
　That sanctified the grove.

Oft sat his mother by him,
  Among the shadows dim,
And told how the Lord Jesus
  Was once a child like him.

" And now from highest heaven
  He doth look down each day,
And sees whate'er thou doest;
  And hears what thou dost say ! "

Thus spoke his tender mother;
  And on an evening bright,
When the red, round sun descended
  'Mid clouds of crimson light,

Again the boy was playing,
  And earnestly said he,
"O beautiful child Jesus,
  Come down and play with me !

" I will find thee flowers the fairest
  And weave for thee a crown ;
I will get thee ripe, red strawberries,
  If thou wilt but come down !

" O holy, holy Mother,
  Put him down from off thy knee
For in these silent meadows
  There are none to play with me ! "

Thus spoke the boy so lovely,
  The while his mother heard,
And on his prayer she pondered,
  But spoke to him no word.

That self-same night she dreamed
  A lovely dream of joy;
She thought she saw young Jesus
  There playing with her boy.

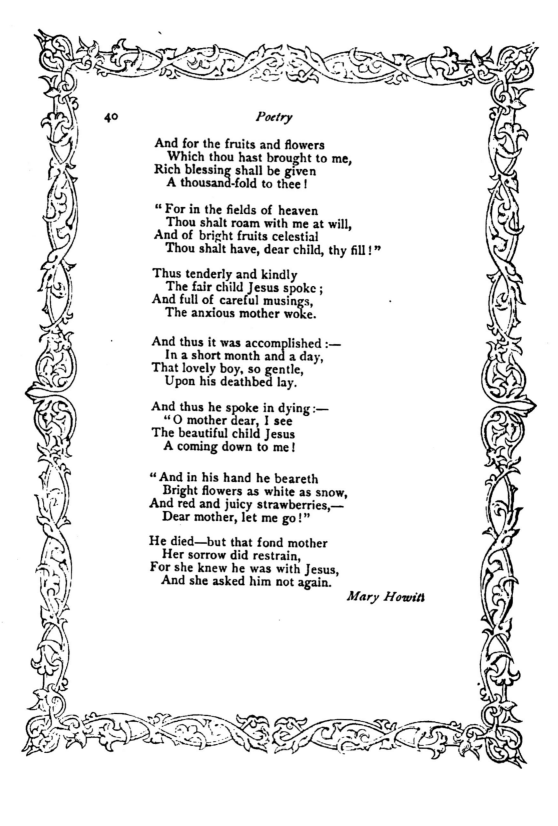

And for the fruits and flowers
  Which thou hast brought to me,
Rich blessing shall be given
  A thousand-fold to thee !

" For in the fields of heaven
  Thou shalt roam with me at will,
And of bright fruits celestial
  Thou shalt have, dear child, thy fill ! "

Thus tenderly and kindly
  The fair child Jesus spoke ;
And full of careful musings,
  The anxious mother woke.

And thus it was accomplished :—
  In a short month and a day,
That lovely boy, so gentle,
  Upon his deathbed lay.

And thus he spoke in dying :—
  " O mother dear, I see
The beautiful child Jesus
  A coming down to me !

" And in his hand he beareth
  Bright flowers as white as snow,
And red and juicy strawberries,—
  Dear mother, let me go ! "

He died—but that fond mother
  Her sorrow did restrain,
For she knew he was with Jesus,
  And she asked him not again.

                      Mary Howitt

• 34 •

MABEL ON MIDSUMMER DAY.

" Arise, my maiden, Mabel,"
  The mother said; " Arise,
For the golden sun of midsummer
  Is shining in the skies.

" Arise, my little maiden,
  For thou must speed away,
To wait upon thy grandmother
  This livelong summer day.

" And thou must carry with thee
  This wheaten cake so fine,
This new-made pat of butter,
  This little flask of wine.

" And tell the dear old body,
  This day I cannot come,
For the good man went out yester-morn,
  And he is not come home.

" And more than this, poor Amy
  Upon my knee doth lie;
I fear me with this fever-pain
  The little child will die !

" And thou canst help thy grandmother;
  The table thou canst spread
Canst feed the little dog and bird;
  And thou canst make her bed.

" And thou canst fetch the water
  From the lady-well hard by ;
And thou canst gather from the wood
  The fagots brown and dry .

·" Canst go down to the lonesome glen,
  To milk the mother-ewe ;
This is the work, my Mabel,
  That thou wilt have to do.

" But listen now, my Mabel,
  This is midsummer day,
When all the fairy people
  From elf-land come away.

" And when thou'rt in the lonesome glen,
  Keep by the running burn,
And do not pluck the strawberry flower,
  Nor break the lady-fern.

" But think not of the fairy folk,
  Lest mischief should befall ;
Think only of poor Amy,
  And how thou lov'st us all.

" Yet keep good heart, my Mabel,
  If thou the fairies see,
And give them kindly answer
  If they should speak to thee.

" And when into the fir-wood
  Thou go'st for fagots brown,
Do not, like idle children,
  Go wandering up and down.

" But fill thy little apron,
  My child, with earnest speed ;
And that thou break no living bough
  Within the wood, take heed.

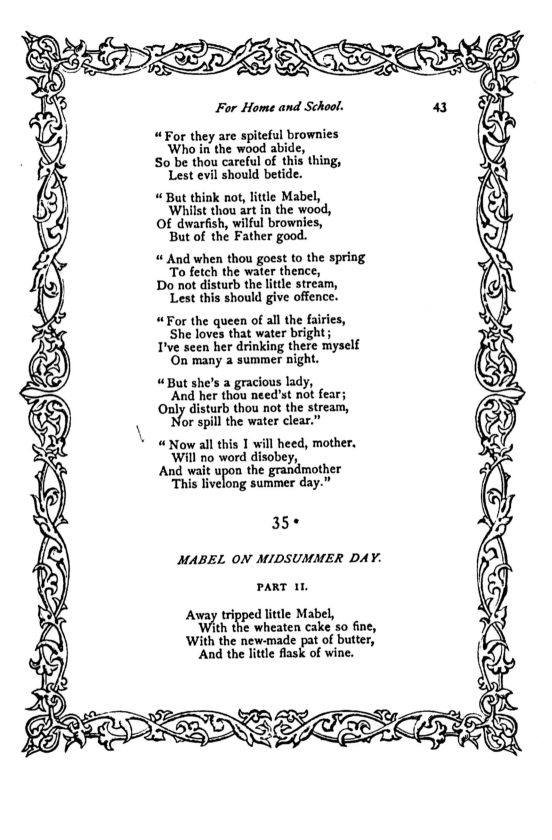

"For they are spiteful brownies
  Who in the wood abide,
So be thou careful of this thing,
  Lest evil should betide.

"But think not, little Mabel,
  Whilst thou art in the wood,
Of dwarfish, wilful brownies,
  But of the Father good.

"And when thou goest to the spring
  To fetch the water thence,
Do not disturb the little stream,
  Lest this should give offence.

"For the queen of all the fairies,
  She loves that water bright;
I've seen her drinking there myself
  On many a summer night.

"But she's a gracious lady,
  And her thou need'st not fear;
Only disturb thou not the stream,
  Nor spill the water clear."

"Now all this I will heed, mother.
  Will no word disobey,
And wait upon the grandmother
  This livelong summer day."

35 •

MABEL ON MIDSUMMER DAY.

PART II.

Away tripped little Mabel,
  With the wheaten cake so fine,
With the new-made pat of butter,
  And the little flask of wine.

And long before the sun was hot,
    And summer mist had cleared,
Beside the good old grandmother
    The willing child appeared.

And all her mother's message
    She told with right good-will,
How that her father was away,
    And the little child was ill.

And then she swept the hearth up clear,
    And then the table spread ;
And next she fed the dog and bird ;
    And then she made the bed.

"And go now," said the grandmother,
    "Ten paces down the dell,
And bring in water for the day,—
    Thou knowest the Lady-well."

The first time that good Mabel went,
    Nothing at all saw she,
Except a bird, a sky-blue bird,
    That sat upon a tree.

The next time that good Mabel went,
    There sat a lady bright
Beside the well,—a lady small,
    All clothed in green and white.

A courtsey low made Mabel,
    And then she stooped to fill
Her pitcher at the sparkling spring,
    But no drop did she spill.

"Thou art a handy maiden,"
    The fairy lady said ;
"Thou hast not spilt a drop, nor yet
    The fairy spring troubled !

" And for this thing which thou hast done,
　Yet mayest not understand,
I give to thee a better gift
　Than houses or than land.

" Thou shalt do well whate'er thou dost,
　As thou hast done this day ;
Shalt have the will and power to please,
　And shalt be loved alway."

Thus having said she passed from sight,
　And nought could Mabel see,
But the little bird, the sky-blue bird,
　Upon the leafy tree.

" And now go," said the grandmother,
　" And fetch in fagots dry ;
All in the neighboring fir-wood
　Beneath the trees they lie."

Away went kind, good Mabel,
　Into the fir-wood near,
Where all the ground was dry and brown
　And the grass grew thin and sere.

She did not wander up and down,
　Nor yet a live branch pull,
But steadily of the fallen boughs
　She picked her apron full.

And when the wild-wood brownies
　Came sliding to her mind,
She drove them thence, as she was told,
　With home-thoughts sweet and kind.

But all that while, the brownies
　Within the fir-wood still,
They watched her how she picked the wood,
　And strove to do no ill.

"And, oh, but she is small and neat,"
 Said one ; "'twere shame to spite
A creature so demure and meek,
 A creature harmless quite!"

"Look only," said another,
 "At her little gown of blue;
At her kerchief pinned about her head,
 And at her little shoe!"

"Oh, but she is a comely child,"
 Said a third; "and we will lay
A good-luck penny in her path,
 A boon for her this day.—
Seeing she broke no living wood;
 No live thing did affray!"

With that the smallest penny,
 Of the finest silver ore,
Upon the dry and slippery path,
 Lay Mabel's feet before.

With joy she picked the penny up,
 The fairy penny good;
And with her fagots dry and brown
 Went wandering from the wood.

"Now she has that," said the Brownies,
 "Let flax be ever so dear,
'Twill buy her clothes of the very best,
 For many and many a year!"

"And go now," said the grandmother,
 "Since falling is the dew,
Go down unto the lonesome glen,
 And milk the mother-ewe!"

All down into the lonesome glen,
　　Through copses thick and wild,
Through moist rank grass, by trickling streams,
　　Went on the willing child.

And when she came to the lonesome glen,
　　She kept beside the burn,
And neither plucked the strawberry-flower
　　Nor broke the lady-fern.

And while she milked the mother-ewe
　　Within this lonesome glen,
She wished that little Amy
　　Were strong and well again.

And soon as she had thought this thought,
　　She heard a coming sound,
As if a thousand fairy-folk
　　Were gathering all around.

And then she heard a little voice,
　　Shrill as the midge's wing,
That spake aloud,—" A human child
　　Is here ; yet mark this thing,—

" The lady-fern is all unbroke,
　　The strawberry-flower unta'en ?
What shall be done for her who still
　　From mischief can refrain ? "

" Give her a fairy cake ! " said one ;
　　" Grant her a wish ! " said three ;
" The latest wish that she hath wished,"
　　Said all, " whate'er it be ! "

Kind Mabel heard the words they spake,
　　And from the lonesome glen
Unto the good old grandmother
　　Went gladly back again.

Thus happened it to Mabel
On that midsummer day,
And these three fairy-blessings
She took with her away.

'Tis good to make all duty sweet,
To be alert and kind;
'Tis good like little Mabel,
To have a willing mind.

Mary Howitt.

· 36 ·

PIBROCH OF DONUIL DHU.

Pibroch of Donuil Dhu,
Pibroch of Donuil,
Wake thy wild voice anew,
Summon Clan-Conuil!
Come away, come away—
Hark to the summons!
Come in your war array,
Gentles and commons.

Come from deep glen, and
From mountain so rocky;
The war-pipe and pennon
Are at Inverlochy.
Come every hill-plaid, and
True heart that wears one!
Come every steel blade, and
Strong hand that bears one.

Leave untended the herd,
The flock without shelter;
Leave the corpse uninterred,
The bride at the altar;

Leave the deer, leave the steer,
   Leave nets and barges;
Come with your fighting gear,
   Broadswords and targes.

Come as the winds come, when
   Forests are rended;
Come as the waves come, when
   Navies are stranded.
Faster come, faster come,
   Faster and faster—
Chief, vassal, page and groom,
   Tenant and master!

Fast they come, fast they come—
   See how they gather!
Wide waves the eagle-plume,
   Blended with heather.
Cast your plaids, draw your blades,
   Forward each man set!
Pibroch of Donuil Dhu,
   Knell for the onset!
              Sir Walter Scott.

• 37 •

LADY MOON.

Lady Moon, Lady Moon, where are you roving?
   Over the sea.
Lady Moon, Lady Moon, whom are you loving?
   All who love me.
Are you not tired with rolling, and never
   Resting to sleep?
Why look so pale, and so sad, as forever
   Wishing to weep?
Ask me not this, little child, if you love me;
   You are too bold;
4

I must obey my dear Father above me,
    And do as I'm told.
Lady Moon, Lady Moon, where are you roving?
    Over the sea.
Lady Moon, Lady Moon whom are you loving?
    All who love me.

Lord Houghton.

• 38 •

WILLIE WINKIE.

Wee Willie Winkie rins through the town,
Up stairs and down stairs, in his nicht-gown,
Tirlin' at the windows, cryin' at the lock,
"Are the weans in their beds? for it's now ten o'clock."

Hey, Willie Winkie! are ye comin' ben?
The cat's singin' gay thrums to the sleepin' hen,
The doug's speldered on the floor, and disna gie a cheep,
But here's a waukrife laddie that winna fa' asleep.

Onything but sleep, ye rogue! glow'rin' like the moon,
Rattlin' in an airn jug wi' an airn spoon,
Rumblin', tumblin' roun' about, crawin' like a cock,
Skirlin' like a kenna-what—waukin' sleepin' folk!

Hey, Willie Winkie! the wean's in a creel!
Waumblin' aff a body's knee, like a vera eel,
Ruggin' at the cat's lug, and ravellin' a' her thrums
Hey, Willie Winkie! See, there he comes!

Wearie is the mither that has a storie wean,
A wee, stumpie stoussie, that canna rin his lane,
That has a battle aye wi' sleep, before he'll close an ee;
But a kiss frae aff his rosy lips gies strength anew to me.

William Miller.

• 39 •

ANSWER TO A CHILD'S QUESTION.

Do you ask what the birds say? The sparrow, the dove,
The linnet, and thrush say "I love, and I love!"
In the winter they're silent, the wind is so strong;
What it says I don't know, but it sings a loud song.
But green leaves, and blossoms, and sunny warm weather,
And singing and loving—all come back together.
But the lark is so brimful of gladness and love,
The green fields below him, the blue sky above,
That he sings and he sings, and forever sings he,
"I love my Love, and my Love loves me."

S. T. Coleridge.

• 40 •

THE CORAL GROVE.

Deep in the wave is a coral grove,
Where the purple mullet and gold-fish rove;
Where the sea-flower spreads its leaves of blue,
That never are wet with the falling dew;
But in bright and changeful beauty shine,
Far down in the green and glassy brine.
The floor is of sand, like the mountain drift,
And the pearl-shells spangle the flinty-snow;
From coral rocks the sea-plants lift
Their boughs, where the tides and billows flow;
The water is calm and still below,
For the winds and waves are absent there,
And the sands are bright as the stars that glow
In the motionless fields of upper air;
There, with its waving blade of green,
The sea-flag streams through the silent water,
And the crimson leaf of the dulse is seen

To blush like a banner bathed in slaughter;
There, with a light and easy motion,
The fan-coral sweeps through the clear deep sea;
And the yellow and scarlet tufts of ocean
Are bending like corn on the upland lea:
And life in rare and beautiful forms
Is sporting amid those bowers of stone,
And is safe, when the wrathful spirit of storms
Has made the top of the waves his own.
And when the ship from his fury flies,
When the myriad voices of ocean roar,
When the wind-god frowns in the murky skies,
And demons are waiting the wreck on shore;
Then, far below, in the peaceful sea,
The purple mullet and gold-fish rove
Where the waters murmur tranquilly
Through the bending twigs of the coral grove.

Jas. G. Percival.

· 41 ·

THE MAHOGANY-TREE.

Christmas is here;
Winds whistle shrill,
Icy and chill,
Little care we;
Little we fear
Weather without,
Sheltered about
The Mahogany-Tree.

Once on the boughs
Birds of rare plume
Sang in its bloom;
Night-birds are we;
Here we carouse,
Singing, like them,
Perched round the stem
Of the jolly old tree.

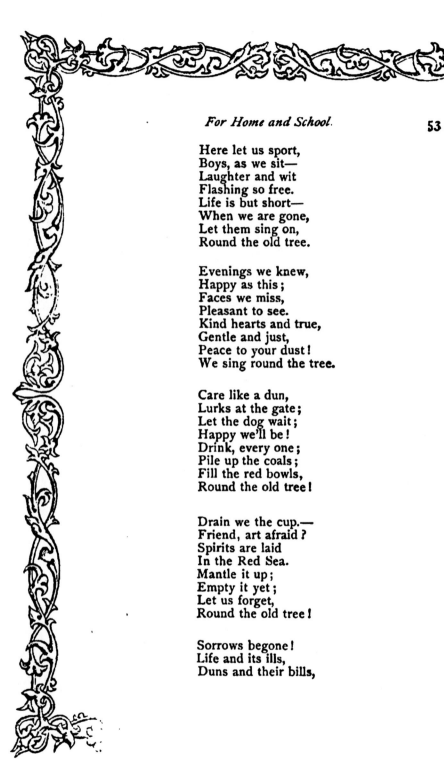

Here let us sport,
Boys, as we sit—
Laughter and wit
Flashing so free.
Life is but short—
When we are gone,
Let them sing on,
Round the old tree.

Evenings we knew,
Happy as this;
Faces we miss,
Pleasant to see.
Kind hearts and true,
Gentle and just,
Peace to your dust!
We sing round the tree.

Care like a dun,
Lurks at the gate;
Let the dog wait;
Happy we'll be!
Drink, every one;
Pile up the coals;
Fill the red bowls,
Round the old tree!

Drain we the cup.—
Friend, art afraid?
Spirits are laid
In the Red Sea.
Mantle it up;
Empty it yet;
Let us forget,
Round the old tree!

Sorrows begone!
Life and its ills,
Duns and their bills,

Bid we to flee.
Come with the dawn,
Blue-devil sprite;
Leave us to-night,
Round the old tree!
William Makepeace Thackeray.

• 42 •

JOHN BARLEYCORN.

There were three kings into the East,
  Three kings both great and high,
And they hae sworn a solemn oath
  John Barleycorn should die.

They took a plough and ploughed him down,
  Put clods upon his head,
And they hae sworn a solemn oath,
  John Barleycorn was dead.

But the cheerful spring came kindly on,
  And showers began to fall;
John Barleycorn got up again,
  And sore surprised them all.

The sultry suns of summer came,
  And he grew thick and strong,
His head well armed wi' pointed spears,
  That no one should him wrong.

The sober autumn entered mild,
  When he grew wan and pale;
His bending joints and drooping head
  Showed he began to fail.

His color sickened more and more,
  He faded into age;
And then his enemies began
  To show their deadly rage.

They've ta'en a weapon, long and sharp,
  And cut him by the knee;
Then tied him fast upon a cart,
  Like a rogue for forgerie.

They laid him down upon his back,
  And cudgelled him full sore;
They hung him up before the storm,
  And turned him o'er and o'er.

They filled up a darksome pit
  With water to the brim,
They heaved in John Barleycorn,
  There let him sink or swim.

They laid him out upon the floor,
  To work him farther woe,
And still, as signs of life appear'd,
  They tossed him to and fro.

They wasted o'er a scorching flame
  The marrow of his bones,
But a miller used him worst of all
  For he crushed him between two stones.

And they hae ta'en his very heart's blood,
  And drunk it round and round;
And still the more and more they drank,
  Their joy did more abound.

John Barleycorn was a hero bold,
  Of noble enterprise,
For if you do but taste his blood,
  'Twill make your courage rise;

'Twill make a man forget his woe;
  'Twill heighten all his joy;
'Twill make the widow's heart to sing,
  Though the tear were in her eye.

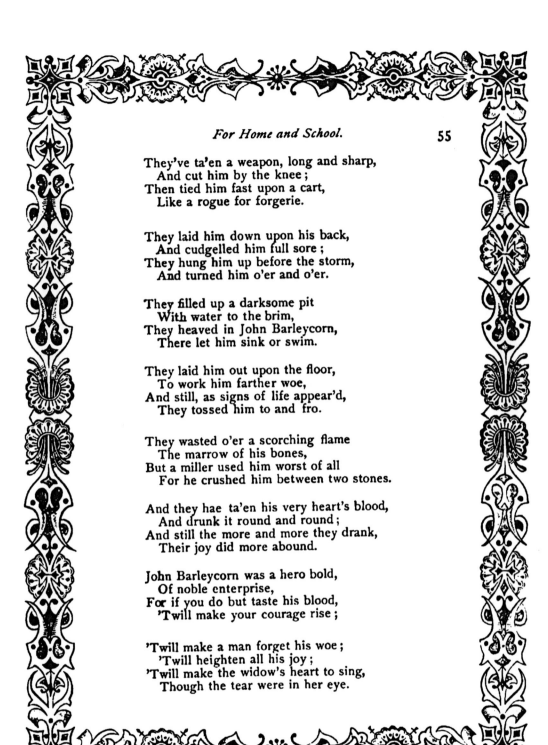

Then let us toast John Barleycorn
Each man a glass in hand;
And may his great posterity
Ne'er fail in old Scotland!

Robert Burns.

• 43 •

MARCH.

The cock is crowing,
The stream is flowing,
The small birds twitter,
The lake doth glitter,
The green field sleeps in the sun;
The oldest and youngest
Are at work with the strongest;
The cattle are grazing,
Their heads never raising;
There are forty feeding like one!

Like an army defeated
The snow hath retreated,
And now doth fare ill
On the top of the bare hill;
The Plough-boy is whooping anon, anon.
There's joy in the mountains;
There's life in the fountains;
Small clouds are sailing,
Blue sky prevailing;
The rain is over and gone!

William Wordsworth.

• 44 •

CHORAL SONG OF ILLYRIAN PEASANTS.

Up! up! ye dames, ye lasses gay!
To the meadows trip away.
'Tis you must tend the flocks this morn,

And scare the small birds from the corn.
　　Not a soul at home may stay:
　　　For the shepherds must go
　　　With lance and bow
To hunt the wolf in the woods to-day.

Leave the hearth and leave the house
　　To the cricket and the mouse:
　　Find grannam out a sunny seat,
With babe and lambkin at her feet.
　　Not a soul at home may stay:
　　　For the shepherds must go
　　　With lance and bow
To hunt the wolf in the woods to-day.
　　　　　　　　　S. T. Coleridge.

• 45 •

THE USE OF FLOWERS.

God might have bade the earth bring forth
　　Enough for great and small,
The oak-tree and the cedar-tree,
　　Without a flower at all.

We might have had enough, enough
　　For every want of ours,
For luxury, medicine and toil,
　　And yet have had no flowers.

The ore within the mountain mine
　　Requireth none to grow;
Nor doth it need the lotus-flower
　　To make the river flow.

The clouds might give abundant rain,
　　The nightly dews might fall,
And the herb that keepeth life in man
　　Might yet have drunk them all.

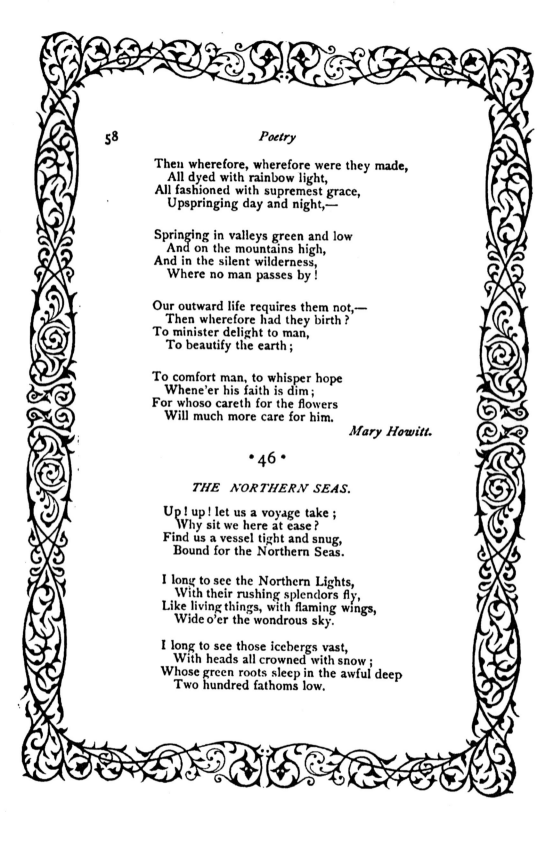

Then wherefore, wherefore were they made,
  All dyed with rainbow light,
All fashioned with supremest grace,
  Upspringing day and night,—

Springing in valleys green and low
  And on the mountains high,
And in the silent wilderness,
  Where no man passes by !

Our outward life requires them not,—
  Then wherefore had they birth ?
To minister delight to man,
  To beautify the earth ;

To comfort man, to whisper hope
  Whene'er his faith is dim ;
For whoso careth for the flowers
  Will much more care for him.

Mary Howitt.

• 46 •

THE NORTHERN SEAS.

Up ! up ! let us a voyage take ;
  Why sit we here at ease ?
Find us a vessel tight and snug,
  Bound for the Northern Seas.

I long to see the Northern Lights,
  With their rushing splendors fly,
Like living things, with flaming wings,
  Wide o'er the wondrous sky.

I long to see those icebergs vast,
  With heads all crowned with snow ;
Whose green roots sleep in the awful deep
  Two hundred fathoms low.

I long to hear the thundering crash
 Of their terrific fall ;
And the echoes from a thousand cliffs,
 Like lonely voices call.

There shall we see the fierce white bear,
 The sleepy seals aground ;
And the spouting whales that to and fro
 Sail with a dreary sound.

There may we tread on depths of ice,
 That the hairy mammoth hide ;
Perfect as when in times of old,
 The mighty creature died.

And while the unsetting sun shines on
 Through the still heaven's deep blue,
We'll traverse the azure waves, the herds
 Of the dread sea-horse to view.

We'll pass the shores of solemn pine,
 Where wolves and black bears prowl,
And away to the rocky isles of mist,
 To rouse the Northern fowl.

Up there shall start ten thousand wings,
 With a rushing, whistling din ;
Up shall the auk and fulmar start,—
 All but the fat penguin.

And there in the wastes of the silent sky,
 With the silent earth below,
We shall see far off to his lonely rock
 The lonely eagle go.

Then softly, softly will we tread
 By inland streams, to see
Where the pelican of the silent North
 Sits there all silently.

William Howitt.

• 47 •

THE WIND IN A FROLIC.

The wind one morning sprang up from sleep,
Saying, " Now for a frolic ! Now for a leap !
Now for a madcap galloping chase !
I'll make a commotion in every place !"
So it swept with a bustle right through a great town,
Creaking the signs and scattering down
Shutters, and whisking with merciless squalls,
Old women's bonnets and gingerbread stalls.
There never was heard a much lustier shout,
As the apples and oranges tumbled about ;
And the urchins that stand with their thievish eyes
Forever on watch, ran off each with a prize.
  Then away to the fields it went blustering and humming,
And the cattle all wondered whatever was coming.
It plucked by their tails the grave, matronly cows,
And tossed the colts' manes all about their brows,
Till, offended at such a familiar salute,
They all turned their backs and stood silently mute.
So on it went, capering and playing its pranks ;
Whistling with reeds on the broad river banks ;
Puffing the birds, as they sat on the spray,
Or the traveller grave on the king's highway.
It was not too nice to bustle the bags
Of the beggar, and flutter his dirty rags.
'Twas so bold that it feared not to play its joke
With the doctor's wig, and the gentleman's cloak.
Through the forest it roared, and cried gayly, " Now
You sturdy old oaks, I'll make you bow !"
And it made them bow without more ado,
Or it cracked their great branches through and through.
  Then it rushed like a monster o'er cottage and farm
Striking their inmates with sudden alarm ;
And they ran out like bees in a midsummer swarm.
There were dames with their kerchiefs tied over their caps,
To see if their poultry were free from mishaps ;

The turkeys they gobbled, the geese screamed aloud,
And the hens crept to roost in a terrified crowd;
There was rearing of ladders, and logs laying on,
Where the thatch from the roof threatened soon to be gone.
But the wind had passed on, and had met in a lane
With a schoolboy, who panted and struggled in vain,
For it tossed him, and twirled him, then passed, and he
    stood
With his hat in a pool, and his shoe in the mud.

William Howitt.

• 48 •

WE ARE SEVEN.

—A simple child,
  That lightly draws its breath,
And feels its life in every limb,
  What should it know of death?

I met a little cottage girl;
  She was eight years old she said;
Her hair was thick with many a curl,
  That clustered round her head.

She had a rustic woodland air,
  And she was wildly clad;
Her eyes were fair and very fair,
  Her beauty made me glad.

"Sisters and brothers, little maid,
  How many may you be?"
"How many? Seven in all," she said,
  And wondering looked at me.

"And where are they, I pray you tell?"
  She answered, "Seven are we;
And two of us at Conway dwell,
  And two are gone to sea.

"Two of us in the churchyard lie,
  My sister and my brother;
And in the churchyard cottage I
  Dwell near them, with my mother."

"You say that two at Conway dwell,
  And two are gone to sea,
Yet you are seven;—I pray you tell,
  Sweet maid, how this may be."

Then did the little maid reply,—
  "Seven boys and girls are we;
Two of us in the churchyard lie,
  Beneath the churchyard tree."

"You run about, my little maid,
  Your limbs they are alive;
If two are in the churchyard laid,
  Then ye are only five."

"Their graves are green, they may be seen,"
  The little maid replied;
"Twelve steps or more from my mother's door,
  And they are side by side.

"My stockings there I often knit,
  My kerchief there I hem;
And there upon the ground I sit,
  I sit and sing to them.

"And often, after sunset, sir,
  When it is light and fair,
I take my little porringer,
  And eat my supper there.

"The first that died was little Jane;
  In bed she moaning lay
Till God released her from her pain,
  And then she went away.

"So in the churchyard she was laid ;
  And when the grass was dry,
Together round the grave we played,
  My brother John and I.

"And when the ground was white with snow,
  And I could run and slide,
My brother John was forced to go,
  And he lies by her side."

"How many are you, then," said I,
  "If there are two in heaven !"
The little maiden did reply,
  "O master, we are seven."

"But they are dead, those two are dead !
  Their spirits are in heaven."
'Twas throwing words away ; for still
The little maid would have her will,
  And said, "Nay, we are seven."

Wm. Wordsworth.

• 49 •

THE FAIRIES OF THE CALDON-LOW.

"And where have you been, my Mary,
  And where have you been from me ?"
"I've been at the top of the Caldon-Low,
  The midsummer night to see !"

"And what did you see, my Mary,
  All up on the Caldon-Low ?"
"I saw the blithe sunshine come down,
  And I saw the merry winds blow."

"And what did you hear, my Mary,
  All up on the Caldon-Hill?"
"I heard the drops of water made
  And the green corn-ears to fill."

"Oh, tell me all, my Mary,—
  All, all that ever you know;
For you must have seen the fairies,
  Last night, on Caldon-Low."

"Then take me on your knee, mother,
  And listen, mother of mine;—
A hundred fairies danced last night,
  And the harpers they were nine.

"And merry was the glee of the harp-strings,
  And their dancing feet so small!
But, O, the sound of the talking
  Was merrier far than all!"

"And what were the words, my Mary,
  That you did hear them say?"
"I'll tell you all, my mother,—
  But let me have my way!

"And some they played with the water,
  And rolled it down the hill:—
'And this, they said,' shall speedily turn
  The poor old miller's mill;

"'For there has been no water
  Ever since the first of May;
And a busy man shall the miller be
  By the dawning of the day!

"'O, the miller, how he will laugh
  When he sees the mill-dam rise!
The jolly old miller, how he will laugh,
  Till the tears fill both his eyes!'

" And some, they seized the little winds
   That sounded over the hill,
And each put a horn into his mouth,
   And blew so sharp and shrill :—

" ' And there,' said they, ' the merry winds go,
   Away from every horn ;
And those shall clear the mildew dank
   From the blind old widow's corn !

" ' O, the poor, blind old widow,—
   Though she has been blind so long,
She'll be merry enough when the mildew's gone.
   And the corn stands stiff and strong !'

" And some they brought the brown lint seed,
   And flung it down from the low :—
' And this,' said they,—' by the sunrise,
   In the weaver's croft shall grow !

" ' O, the poor, lame weaver,
   How he will laugh outright
When he sees his dwindling flax-field
   All full of flowers by night !'

" And then upspoke a brownie,
   With a long beard on his chin :—
' I have spun up all the tow,' said he,
   ' And I want some more to spin.

" ' I've spun a piece of hempen cloth,
   And I want to spin another,—
A little sheet for Mary's bed,
   And an apron for her mother !'

" And with that I could not help but laugh,
   And I laughed out loud and free ;
And then on the top of the Caldon-Low
   There was no one left but me.

"And all in the top of the Caldon-Low
  The mists were cold and gray,
And nothing I saw but the mossy stones
  That round about me lay.

"But as I came down from the hill-top,
  I heard a jar below;
How busy the jolly miller was
  And how merry the wheel did go!

"And I peeped into the widow's field,
  And sure enough were seen
The yellow ears of the mildewed corn
  All standing stiff and green.

"And down by the weaver's croft I stole,
  To see if the flax were high;
But I saw the weaver at his gate,
  With the good news in his eye!

"Now this is all I heard, mother,
  And all that I did see;
So, prythee, make my bed, mother,
  For I'm tired as I can be!"

                                        Mary Howitt.

• 50 •

SIR PATRICK SPENCE.

The king sits in Dunfermline town,
  Drinking the blude-red wine;
"O, where shall I get a skeely skipper
  To sail this ship of mine?"

O, up and spake an eldern knight,—
  Sat at the king's right knee,—
"Sir Patrick Spence is the best sailor
  That sails upon the sea."

"The king sits in Dunfermline town,
 Drinking the blude-red wine."
—*p. 66.*

The king has written a braid letter,
  And sealed it with his hand;
And sent it to Sir Patrick Spence,
  Was walking on the strand.

"To Noroway, to Noroway,
  To Noroway o'er the faem,
The king's daughter of Noroway,
  'Tis thou maun bring her hame."

The first line that Sir Patrick read,
  Sae loud, loud, laughed he;
The next line that Sir Patrick read,
  The tear blinded his e'e.

"O, wha is this hae done this deed,
  This ill deed done to me;
To send me out, this time o' the year,
  To sail upon the sea?

"Be it wind, be it weet, be it hail, be it sleet,
  Our ship must sail the faem;
The king's daughter of Noroway,
  'Tis we maun fetch her hame.

"Make ready, make ready, my merry men all!
  Our gude ship sails the morn,"
"Now, ever alake, my master dear,
  I fear a deadly storm.

"Late, late yestreen, I saw the new moon
  Wi' the old moon in her arm;
And I fear, I fear, my master dear
  That we will come to harm."

They hadna sailed a league, a league,
  A league but barely three,
When the lift grew dark, and the wind blew loud,
  And gurly grew the sea.

The anchors brak, and the top-masts lap,
  It was sik a deadly storm;
And the waves came o'er the broken ship,
  Till all her sides were torn.

" O, where will I get a gude sailor
  To take my helm in hand,
Till I get up to the tall top-mast;
  To see if I can spy land ? "

" O, here am I, a sailor gude,
  To take the helm in hand,
Till you get up to the tall top-mast;
  But I fear you'll ne'er spy land."

He hadna gone a step, a step,
  A step but barely ane,
When a bout flew out of our goodly ship,
  And the salt sea it came in.

" Gae, fetch a web o' the silken claith,
  Another o' the twine,
And wap them into our ship's side,
  And let nae the sea come in."

They fetched a web o' the silken claith,
  Another o' the twine,
And they wapped them round that gude ship's side
  And still the sea came in.

O, laith, laith, were our gude Scots lords
  To weet their cork-heeled shoon!
But lang or a' the play was played,
  They wat their hats aboon.

And mony was the feather-bed
  They floated on the faem;
And mony was the gude lord's son,
  That never mair came hame.

The ladies wrang their fingers white,
  The maidens tore their hair,
A' for the sake of their true loves,
  For them they'll see nae mair.

O, lang, lang, may the ladies sit,
  Wi' their fans into their hand,
Before they see Sir Patrick Spence
  Come sailing to their land.

And lang, lang, may the maidens sit,
  Wi' their gold kaims in their hair,
A' waiting for their ain dear loves!
  For them they'll see nae mair.

O, forty miles off Aberdeen
  'Tis fifty fathoms deep,
And there lies gude Sir Patrick Spence,
  Wi' the Scots lords at his feet.

• 51 •

LANDING OF THE PILGRIM FATHERS.

The breaking waves dashed high
  On a stern and rock-bound coast,
And the woods against a stormy sky
  Their giant branches tossed;

And the heavy night hung dark
  The hills and waters o'er,
When a band of exiles moored their bark
  On the wild New England shore.

Not as the conqueror comes,
  They, the true-hearted, came;
Not with the roll of the stirring drums,
  And the trumpet that sings of fame;

Not as the flying come,
  In silence and in fear,—
They shook the depths of the desert gloom
  With their hymns of lofty cheer.

Amidst the storm they sang,
  And the stars heard and the sea!
And the sounding aisles of the dim wood rang
  To the anthems of the free!

The ocean-eagle soared
  From his nest by the white wave's foam,
And the rocking pines of the forest roared,—
  This was their welcome home!

There were men with hoary hair
  Amidst that pilgrim-band;—
Why had they come to wither there,
  Away from their childhood's land?

There was woman's fearless eye
  Lit by her deep love's truth;
There was manhood's brow, serenely high,
  And the fiery heart of youth.

What sought they thus afar?
  Bright jewels of the mine?
The wealth of seas, the spoils ot war?
  They sought a faith's pure shrine!

Ay, call it holy ground,
  The soil where first they trod!
The've left unstained what there they found,—
  Freedom to worship God!

                                Mrs. Hemans.

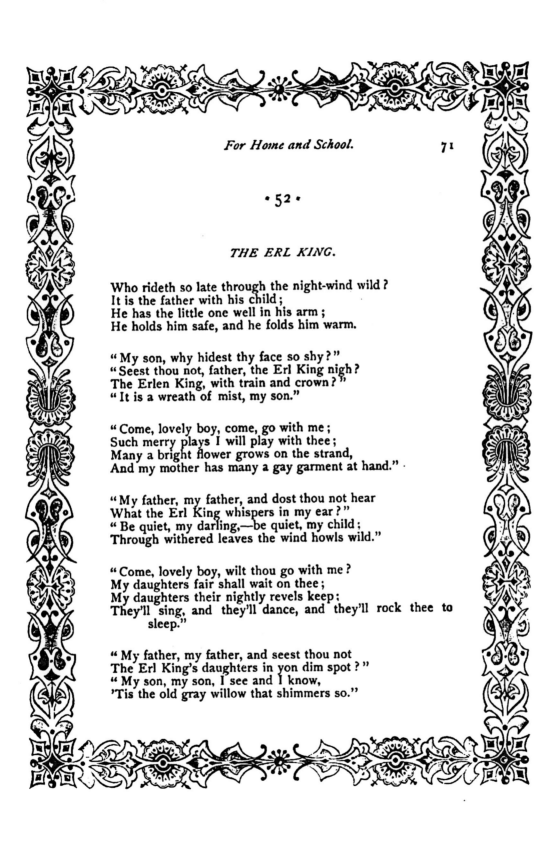

• 52 •

THE ERL KING.

Who rideth so late through the night-wind wild?
It is the father with his child;
He has the little one well in his arm;
He holds him safe, and he folds him warm.

"My son, why hidest thy face so shy?"
"Seest thou not, father, the Erl King nigh?
The Erlen King, with train and crown?"
"It is a wreath of mist, my son."

"Come, lovely boy, come, go with me;
Such merry plays I will play with thee;
Many a bright flower grows on the strand,
And my mother has many a gay garment at hand."

"My father, my father, and dost thou not hear
What the Erl King whispers in my ear?"
"Be quiet, my darling,—be quiet, my child;
Through withered leaves the wind howls wild."

"Come, lovely boy, wilt thou go with me?
My daughters fair shall wait on thee;
My daughters their nightly revels keep;
They'll sing, and they'll dance, and they'll rock thee to
  sleep."

"My father, my father, and seest thou not
The Erl King's daughters in yon dim spot?"
"My son, my son, I see and I know,
'Tis the old gray willow that shimmers so."

"I love thee ; thy beauty has ravished my sense ;
And, willing or not, I will carry thee hence."
"O, father, the Erl King now puts forth his arm !
O, father, the Erl King has done me harm !"

The father shudders ; he hurries on ;
And faster he holds his moaning son ;
He reaches his home with fear and dread,
And lo ! in his arms the child is dead !

From the German of Goethe.

• 53 •

THE DIRGE IN CYMBELINE.

To fair Fidele's grassy tomb
    Soft maids and village hinds shall bring
Each opening sweet, of earliest bloom,
    And rifle all the breathing spring.

No wailing ghost shall dare appear
    To vex with shrieks this quiet grove ;
But shepherd lads assemble here,
    And youthful virgins own their love.

No withered witch shall here be seen,
    No goblins lead their nightly crew ;
The female fays shall haunt the green,
    And dress thy grave with pearly dew.

The redbreast oft at evening's hours
    Shall kindly lend his little aid,
With hoary moss, and gathered flowers,
    To deck the ground where thou art laid.

When howling winds, and beating rain,
    In tempests shake thy sylvan cell ;
Or 'midst the chase on every plain,
    The tender thought on thee shall dwell ;

Each lonely scene shall thee restore,
 For thee the tear be duly shed;
Beloved, till life can charm no more;
 And mourned, till Pity's self be dead.
       Wm. Collins.

• 54 •

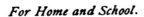

THE MOSS ROSE.

The Angel of the flowers one day
Beneath a rose-tree sleeping lay,—
That spirit to whose charge is given
To bathe young buds in dew from heaven.
Awakening from his slight repose,
The Angel whispered to the Rose,—
" O fondest object of my care,
Still fairest found where all is fair,
For the sweet shade thou'st given me,
Ask what thou wilt, 'tis granted thee."
Then said the Rose with deepened glow,—
" On me another grace bestow ; "—
The Angel paused in silent thought,—
What grace was there the flower had not?
'Twas but a moment,—o'er the Rose
A veil of moss the Angel throws,
And robed in Nature's simplest weed,
Could there a flower that Rose exceed?

• 55 •

THE FAITHFUL BIRD.

The greenhouse is my summer seat,
My shrubs, displaced from that retreat,
 Enjoy'd the open air;
Two goldfinches whose sprightly song
Had been their mutual solace long,
 Lived happy prisoners there.

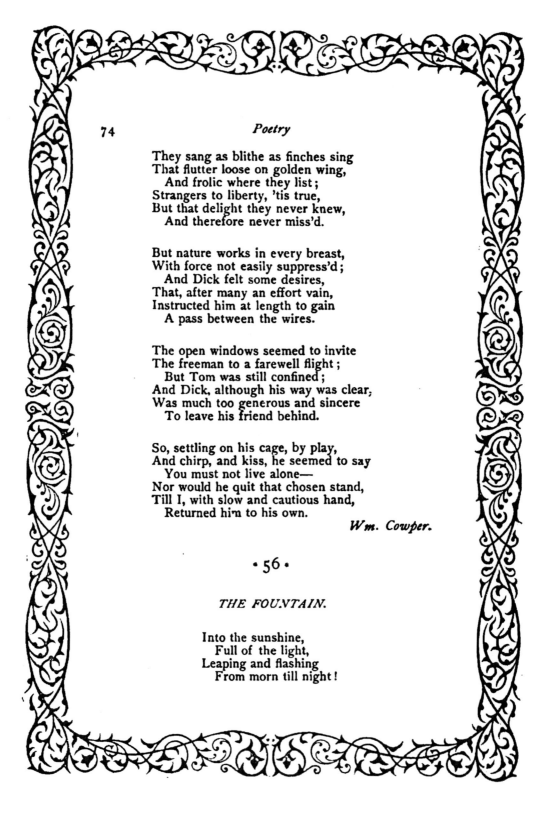

They sang as blithe as finches sing
That flutter loose on golden wing,
    And frolic where they list;
Strangers to liberty, 'tis true,
But that delight they never knew,
    And therefore never miss'd.

But nature works in every breast,
With force not easily suppress'd;
    And Dick felt some desires,
That, after many an effort vain,
Instructed him at length to gain
    A pass between the wires.

The open windows seemed to invite
The freeman to a farewell flight;
    But Tom was still confined;
And Dick, although his way was clear,
Was much too generous and sincere
    To leave his friend behind.

So, settling on his cage, by play,
And chirp, and kiss, he seemed to say
    You must not live alone—
Nor would he quit that chosen stand,
Till I, with slow and cautious hand,
    Returned him to his own.

                              Wm. Cowper.

• 56 •

THE FOUNTAIN.

Into the sunshine,
    Full of the light,
Leaping and flashing
    From morn till night!

"And Dick, although his way was clear,
Was much too generous and sincere
To leave his friend behind."—*p. 74.*

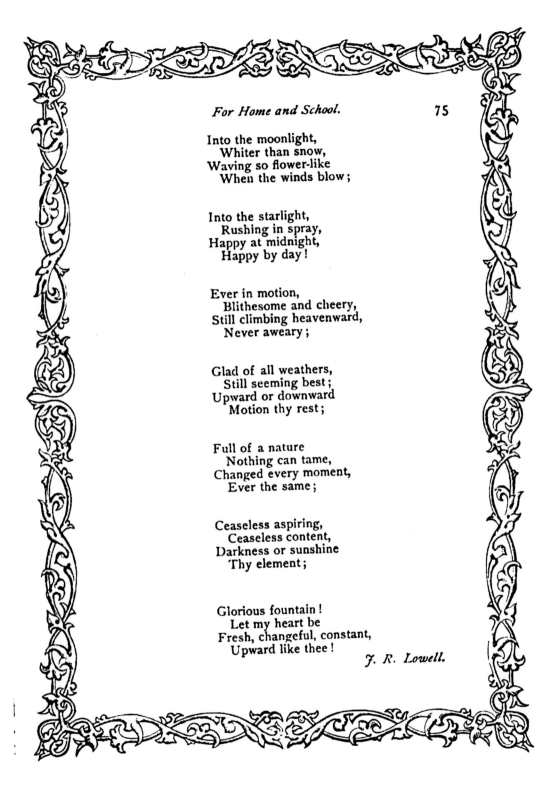

Into the moonlight,
　Whiter than snow,
Waving so flower-like
　When the winds blow;

Into the starlight,
　Rushing in spray,
Happy at midnight,
　Happy by day!

Ever in motion,
　Blithesome and cheery,
Still climbing heavenward,
　Never aweary;

Glad of all weathers,
　Still seeming best;
Upward or downward
　Motion thy rest;

Full of a nature
　Nothing can tame,
Changed every moment,
　Ever the same;

Ceaseless aspiring,
　Ceaseless content,
Darkness or sunshine
　Thy element;

Glorious fountain!
　Let my heart be
Fresh, changeful, constant,
　Upward like thee!

J. R. Lowell.

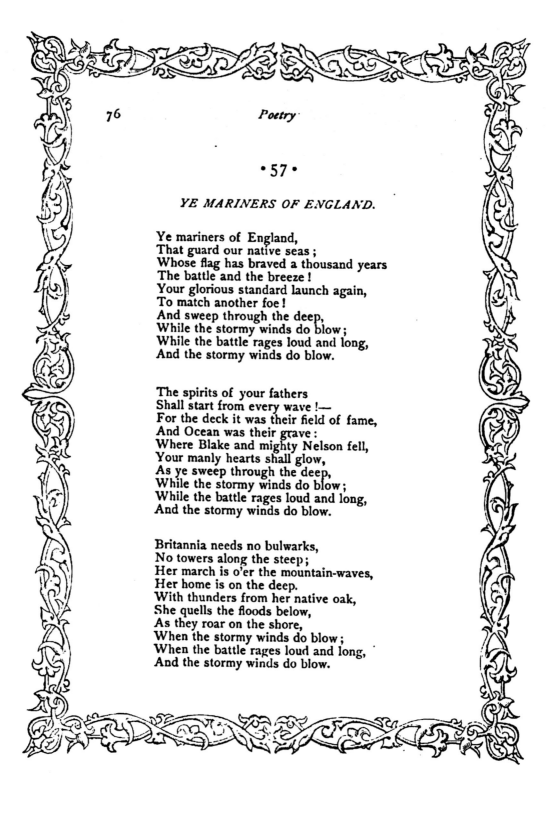

• 57 •

YE MARINERS OF ENGLAND.

Ye mariners of England,
That guard our native seas;
Whose flag has braved a thousand years
The battle and the breeze!
Your glorious standard launch again,
To match another foe!
And sweep through the deep,
While the stormy winds do blow;
While the battle rages loud and long,
And the stormy winds do blow.

The spirits of your fathers
Shall start from every wave!—
For the deck it was their field of fame,
And Ocean was their grave:
Where Blake and mighty Nelson fell,
Your manly hearts shall glow,
As ye sweep through the deep,
While the stormy winds do blow;
While the battle rages loud and long,
And the stormy winds do blow.

Britannia needs no bulwarks,
No towers along the steep;
Her march is o'er the mountain-waves,
Her home is on the deep.
With thunders from her native oak,
She quells the floods below,
As they roar on the shore,
When the stormy winds do blow;
When the battle rages loud and long,
And the stormy winds do blow.

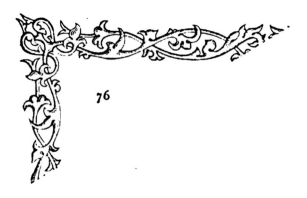

76

The meteor flag of England,
Shall yet terrific burn;
Till danger's troubled night depart,
And the star of peace return.
Then, then, ye ocean warriors!
Our song and feast shall flow
To the fame of your name,
When the storm has ceased to blow:
When the fiery fight is heard no more,
And the storm has ceased to blow.

Thos. Campbell.

• 58 •

JOHN GILPIN.

John Gilpin was a citizen
  Of credit and renown,
A train-band captain eke was he
  Of famous London Town.

John Gilpin's spouse said to her dear,
  "Though wedded we have been
These twice ten tedious years, yet we
  No holiday have seen.

"To-morrow is our wedding-day,
  And we will then repair
Unto the Bell at Edmonton,
  All in a chaise and pair.

"My sister and my sister's child,
  Myself and children three,
Will fill the chaise; so you must ride
  On horseback after we."

He soon replied, "I do admire
  Of woman kind but one,
And you are she, my dearest dear,
  Therefore it shall be done.

"I am a linen-draper bold,
  As all the world doth know,
And my good friend the Calender,
  Will lend his horse to go."

Quoth Mrs. Gilpin, "That's well said;
  And for that wine is dear,
We will be furnished with our own,
  Which is both bright and clear."

John Gilpin kissed his loving wife;
  O'erjoyed was he to find
That, though on pleasure she was bent,
  She had a frugal mind.

The morning came, the chaise was brought,
  But yet was not allowed
To drive up to the door, lest all
  Should say that she was proud.

So three doors off the chaise was stayed,
  Where they did all get in,
Six precious souls, and all agog
  To dash through thick and thin.

Smack went the whip, round went the wheels,
  Were never folk so glad:
The stones did rattle underneath,
  As if Cheapside were mad.

John Gilpin, at his horse's side,
  Seized fast the flowing mane,
And up he got in haste to ride,
  But soon came down again;

For saddle-tree scarce reached had he
  His journey to begin,
When, turning round his head, he saw
  Three customers come in.

So down he came; for loss of time,
　Although it grieved him sore,
Yet loss of pence, full well he knew,
　Would trouble him much more.

'Twas long before the customers
　Were suited to their mind,
When Betty, screaming, came down stairs,
　" The wine is left behind ! "

" Good lack ! " quoth he, " yet bring it me,
　My leathern belt likewise,
In which I bear my trusty sword
　When I do exercise."

Now mistress Gilpin, careful soul !
　Had two stone bottles found,
To hold the liquor that she loved,
　And keep it safe and sound.

Each bottle had a curling ear,
　Through which the belt he drew,
And hung a bottle on each side,
　To make his balance true.

Then over all, that he might be
　Equipped from top to toe,
His long red cloak, well brushed and neat,
　He manfully did throw.

Now see him mounted once again
　Upon his nimble steed,
Full slowly pacing o'er the stones,
　With caution and good heed.

But finding soon a smoother road
　Beneath his well-shod feet,
The snorting beast began to trot,
　Which galled him in his seat.

So, "Fair and softly," John he cried,
  But John he cried in vain,
That trot became a gallop soon,
  In spite of curb and rein.

So stooping down, as needs he must
  Who cannot sit upright,
He grasped the mane with both his hands,
  And eke with all his might.

His horse, who never in that sort
  Had handled been before,
What thing upon his back had got
  Did wonder more and more.

Away went Gilpin, neck or nought;
  Away went hat and wig;
He little dreamed, when he set out,
  Of running such a rig.

The wind did blow, the cloak did fly,
  Like streamer long and gay,
Till, loop and button failing both,
  At last it flew away.

Then might all people well discern
  The bottles he had slung;
A bottle swinging at each side,
  As hath been said or sung.

The dogs did bark, the children screamed,
  Up flew the windows all;
And every soul cried out, "Well done!"
  As loud as he could bawl.

Away went Gilpin—who but he?
  His fame soon spread around,
"He carries weight! he rides a race!
  'Tis for a thousand pound!"

" ' T was wonderful to view
How in a trice the turnpike men
Their gates wide open threw."—*p. 80.*

And still as fast as he drew near,
  'Twas wonderful to view
How in a trice the turnpike men
  Their gates wide open threw.

And now, as he went bowing down
  His reeking head full low,
The bottles twain behind his back
  Were shattered at a blow.

Down ran the wine into the road,
  Most piteous to be seen,
Which made his horse's flanks to smoke
  As they had basted been.

But still he seemed to carry weight,
  With leathern girdle braced ;
For all might see the bottle necks
  Still dangling at his waist.

Thus all through merry Islington
  These gambols he did play,
Until he came unto the Wash
  Of Edmonton so gay ;

And there he threw the Wash about
  On both sides of the way,
Just like unto a trundling mop,
  Or a wild goose at play.

At Edmonton his loving wife
  From the balcony espied
Her tender husband, wondering much
  To see how he did ride.

"Stop, stop, John Gilpin !—Here's the house "—
  They all aloud did cry ;
" The dinner waits, and we are tired ; "
  Said Gilpin, " So am I ! "

But yet his horse was not a whit
  Inclined to tarry there;
For why? his owner had a house
  Full ten miles off at Ware.

So like an arrow swift he flew,
  Shot by an archer strong;
So did he fly—which brings me to
  The middle of my song.

Away went Gilpin, out of breath,
  And sore against his will,
Till at his friend the Calender's,
  His horse at last stood still.

The Calender, amazed to see
  His neighbor in such trim,
Laid down his pipe, flew to the gate,
  And thus accosted him:

"What news? what news? your tidings tell,
  Tell me you must and shall—
Say, why bare-headed you are come,
  Or why you come at all?"

Now Gilpin had a pleasant wit,
  And loved a timely joke;
And thus, unto the Calender,
  In merry guise he spoke:

"I came because your horse would come,
  And if I well forbode,
My hat and wig will soon be here,—
  They are upon the road."

The Calender, right glad to find
  His friend in merry pin,
Returned him not a single word,
  But to the house went in;

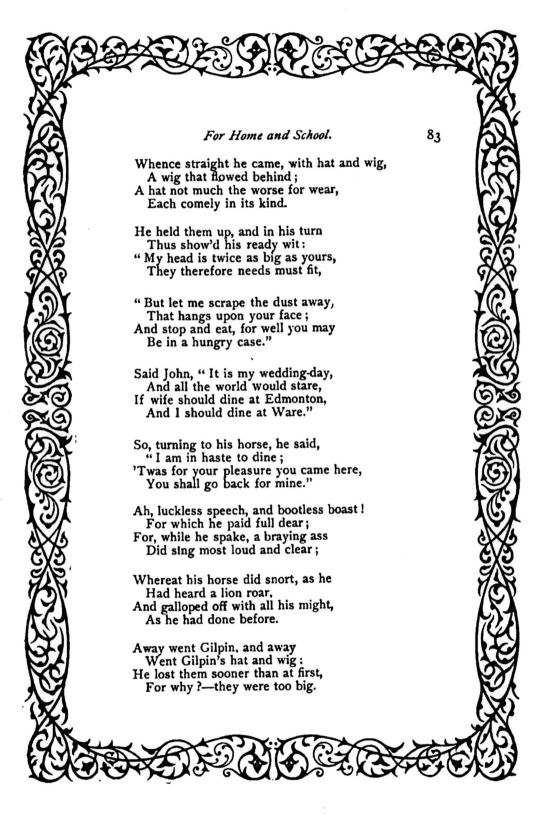

Whence straight he came, with hat and wig,
　A wig that flowed behind ;
A hat not much the worse for wear,
　Each comely in its kind.

He held them up, and in his turn
　Thus show'd his ready wit :
" My head is twice as big as yours,
　They therefore needs must fit,

" But let me scrape the dust away,
　That hangs upon your face ;
And stop and eat, for well you may
　Be in a hungry case."

Said John, " It is my wedding-day,
　And all the world would stare,
If wife should dine at Edmonton,
　And I should dine at Ware."

So, turning to his horse, he said,
　" I am in haste to dine ;
'Twas for your pleasure you came here,
　You shall go back for mine."

Ah, luckless speech, and bootless boast !
　For which he paid full dear ;
For, while he spake, a braying ass
　Did sing most loud and clear ;

Whereat his horse did snort, as he
　Had heard a lion roar,
And galloped off with all his might,
　As he had done before.

Away went Gilpin, and away
　Went Gilpin's hat and wig :
He lost them sooner than at first,
　For why ?—they were too big.

Now Mrs. Gilpin, when she saw
  Her husband posting down .
Into the country far away,
  She pulled out half-a-crown ;

And thus unto the youth she said,
  That drove them to the Bell,
" This shall be yours, when you bring back
  My husband safe and well."

The youth did ride, and soon did meet
  John coming back amain ;
Whom in a trice he tried to stop,
  By catching at his rein ;

But not performing what he meant,
  And gladly would have done,
The frighted steed he frighted more,
  And made him faster run.

Away went Gilpin, and away
  Went postboy at his heels,
The postboy's horse right glad to miss
  The rumbling of the wheels.

Six gentlemen upon the road
  Thus seeing Gilpin fly,
With postboy scampering in the rear,
  They raised a hue and cry :—

" Stop thief !—stop thief !—a highwayman !"
  Not one of them was mute ;
And all and each that passed that way
  Did join in the pursuit.

And now the turnpike gates again
  Flew open in short space :
The toll-men thinking as before,
  That Gilpin rode a race.

And so he did, and won it too,
   For he got first to town;
Nor stopped till where he had got up
   He did again get down.

Now let us sing, Long live the king,
   And Gilpin, long live he;
And, when he next doth ride abroad,
   May I be there to see.
                  William Cowper.

• 59 •

COUNTRY SCENES IN OLD DAYS.

Daybreak.

See the day begins to break,
And the light shoots like a streak
Of subtle fire; the wind blows cold
While the morning doth unfold;
Now the birds begin to rouse,
And the squirrel from the boughs
Leaps, to get him nuts and fruit;
The early lark, that erst was mute,
Carols to the rising day
Many a note and many a lay.

Unfolding the Flocks.

Shepherds, rise, and shake off sleep—
See the blushing morn doth peep
Through the windows, while the sun
To the mountain-tops is run,
Gilding all the vales below
With his rising flames, which grow
Greater by his climbing still.—
Up! ye lazy swains! and fill

Bag and bottle for the field ;
Clasp your cloaks fast, lest they yield
,To the bitter north-east wind.
Call the maidens up, and find
Who lies longest, that she may
Be chidden for untimed delay,
Feed your faithful dogs, and pray
Heaven to keep you from decay ;
So unfold, and then away.

Evening.

Shepherds all, and maidens fair,
Fold your flocks up, for the air
'Gins to thicken, and the sun
Already his great course hath run.
See the dew-drops how they kiss
Every little flower that is ;
Hanging on their velvet heads,
Like a rope of crystal beads.
See the heavy clouds low falling,
And bright Hesperus down calling
The dead night from underground ;
At whose rising, mists unsound,
Damps and vapors fly apace,
Hovering o'er the wanton face
Of t ese pastures, where they come
Striking dead both bud and bloom.
Therefore from such danger lock
Every one his lovèd flock ;
And let your dogs lie loose without,
Lest the wolf come, as a scout
From the mountain, and ere day
Bear a kid or lamb away ;
Or the crafty thievish fox
Break upon your simple flocks.
To secure yourselves from these,
Be not too secure in ease.
So shall you good shepherds prove,

And deserve you master's love.
Now, good night! may sweetest slumbers
And soft silence fall in numbers
On your eyelids! so farewell;
Thus I end my evening knell.

J. Fletcher.

* 60 *

THE SINGING LESSON.

A nightingale made a mistake;
    She sang a few notes out of tune;
Her heart was ready to break,
    And she hid from the moon.
She wrung her claws, poor thing,
    But was far too proud to speak;
She tucked her head under her wing,
    And pretended to be asleep.

A lark, arm-in-arm with a thrush,
    Came sauntering up to the place;
The nightingale felt herself blush,
    Though feathers hid her face;
She knew they had heard her song,
    She felt them snicker and sneer;
She thought this life was too long,
    And wished she could skip a year.

" Oh nightingale!" cooed a dove;
    " Oh nightingale! what's the use;
You bird of beauty and love,
    Why behave like a goose?
Don't skulk away from our sight,
    Like a common, contemptible fowl;
You bird of joy and delight,
    Why behave like an owl?

"Only think of all you have done;
　Only think of all you can do;
A false note is really fun
　From such a bird as you!
Lift up your proud little crest;
　Open your musical beak;
Other birds have to do their best,
　You need only to speak."

The nightingale shyly took
　Her head from under her wing,
And giving the dove a look,
　Straightway began to sing.
There was never a bird could pass;
　The night was divinely calm;
And the people stood on the grass
　To hear that wonderful psalm!

The nightingale did not care,
　She only sang to the skies;
Her song ascended there,
　And there she fixed her eyes.
The people that stood below
　She knew but little about;
And this story's a moral, I know,
　If you'll try to find it out!

Jean Ingelow.

• 61 •

ARIEL'S SONGS.

I.

Come unto these yellow sands,
And then take hands;
　Court'sied when you have, and kiss'd,
　The wild waves whist!
Foot it featly here and there;
And, sweet sprites, the burden bear.

"Where the bee sucks, there suck I;
In the cowslip's bell I lie.—*p. 89.*

Hark, hark!
Bow-wow.
The watch-dogs bark—
Bow-wow.
Hark, hark! I hear
The strain of strutting chanticleer
Cry Cock-a-doodle-doo.

II.

Full fathom five thy father lies;
Of his bones are coral made;
Those are pearls that were his eyes;
Nothing of him that doth fade
But doth suffer a sea-change
Into something rich and strange;
Sea-nymphs hourly ring his knell;
Ding-dong,
Hark! now I hear them—ding, dong, bell!

III.

Where the bee sucks, there suck I;
In a cowslip's bell I lie;
There I couch when owls do cry;
On the bat's back I do fly
After summer merrily.
Merrily, merrily shall I live now,
Under the blossom that hangs on the bough.
William Shakespeare.

• 62 •

SONG OF THE FAIRY.

Over hill, over dale,
Thorough bush, thorough brier,
Over park, over pale,
Thorough flood, thorough fire,
I do wander every where,

Swifter than the moones sphère ;
  And I serve the fairy queen ;
  To dew her orbs upon the green ;
  The cowslips tall her pensioners be ;
  In their gold coats, spots you see ;
  These be rubies, fairy favors—
  In those freckles live their savors,
I must go seek some dew drops here,
And hang a pearl in every cowslip's ear.
William Shakespeare.

• 63 •

THE STORMY PETREL.

A thousand miles from land are we,
Tossing about on a stormy sea ;
From billow to bounding billow cast,
Like fleecy snow on the stormy blast ;
The sails are scattered abroad like weeds,
The strong masts shake like quivering reeds,
The mighty cables, and iron chains,
The hull which all earthly strength disdains,
They strain and they crack, and hearts like stone
Their natural hard, proud strength disown.

Up and down !   Up and down !
From the base of the wave to the billow's crown,
And amidst the flashing and feathery foam
The Stormy Petrel finds a home,—
A home, if such a place may be,
For her who lives on the wide, wide sea,
On the craggy ice, in the frozen air,
And only seeketh her rocky lair
To warm her young, and to teach them to spring
At once o'er the waves on their stormy wing !

O'er the Deep !   O'er the Deep !
Where the whale, and the shark, and the sword-fish sleep,
Out-flying the blast and the driving rain,

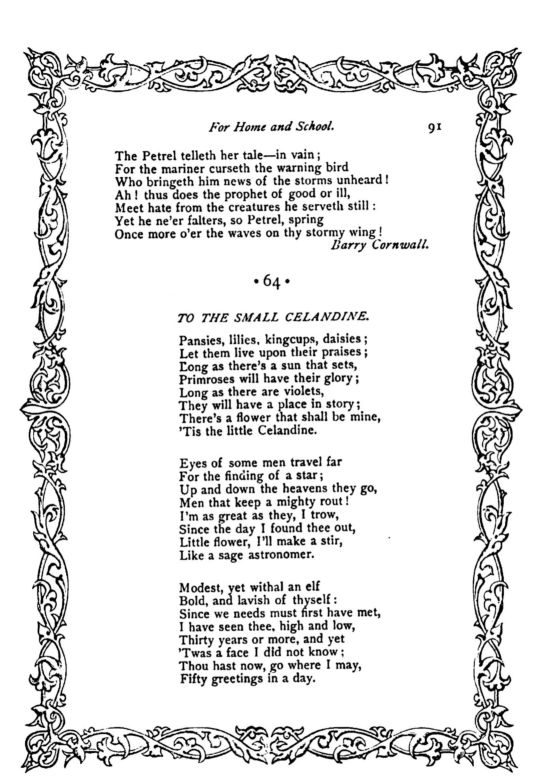

The Petrel telleth her tale—in vain;
For the mariner curseth the warning bird
Who bringeth him news of the storms unheard!
Ah! thus does the prophet of good or ill,
Meet hate from the creatures he serveth still:
Yet he ne'er falters, so Petrel, spring
Once more o'er the waves on thy stormy wing!
Barry Cornwall.

• 64 •

TO THE SMALL CELANDINE.

Pansies, lilies, kingcups, daisies;
Let them live upon their praises;
Long as there's a sun that sets,
Primroses will have their glory;
Long as there are violets,
They will have a place in story;
There's a flower that shall be mine,
'Tis the little Celandine.

Eyes of some men travel far
For the finding of a star;
Up and down the heavens they go,
Men that keep a mighty rout!
I'm as great as they, I trow,
Since the day I found thee out,
Little flower, I'll make a stir,
Like a sage astronomer.

Modest, yet withal an elf
Bold, and lavish of thyself:
Since we needs must first have met,
I have seen thee, high and low,
Thirty years or more, and yet
'Twas a face I did not know;
Thou hast now, go where I may,
Fifty greetings in a day.

Ere a leaf is on a bush,
In the time before the thrush
Has a thought about her nest,
Thou wilt come with half a call,
Spreading out thy glossy breast
Like a careless prodigal;
Telling tales about the sun,
When we've little warmth, or none.

Poets, vain men in their mood,
Travel with the multitude;
Never heed them; I aver
That they all are wanton wooers;
But the thrifty cottager,
Who stirs little out of doors,
Joys to spy thee near at home;
Spring is coming, thou art come!

Comfort have thou of thy merit,
Kindly, unassuming spirit!
Careless of thy neighborhood,
Thou dost show thy pleasant face
On the moor, and in the wood,
In the lane;—there's not a place,
Howsoever mean it be,
But 'tis good enough for thee.

Ill befall the yellow flowers,
Children of the flaring hours!
Buttercups that will be seen,
Whether we will see or no;
Others, too, of lofty mien;
They have done as worldlings do,
Taken praise that should be thine,
Little, humble Celandine.

Prophet of delight and mirth,
Ill-requited upon earth;
Herald of a mighty band,

Of a joyous train ensuing;
Serving at my heart's command,
Tasks that are no tasks renewing,
I will sing, as doth behoove,
Hymns in praise of what I love.
William Wordsworth.

· 65 ·

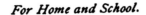

VIRTUE.

Sweet day, so cool, so calm, so bright,
  The bridal of the earth and sky!
The dew shall weep thy fall to-night;
  For thou must die.

Sweet rose, whose hue, angry and brave,
  Bids the rash gazer wipe his eye,
Thy root is ever in the grave,
  And thou must die.

Sweet spring, full of sweet days and roses,
  A box where sweets compacted lie,
Thy music shows ye have your closes,
  And all must die.

Only a sweet and virtuous soul,
  Like seasoned timber, never gives;
But, though the whole world turn to coal,
  Then chiefly lives.
George Herbert.

• 66 •

FRIENDS.

North Wind came whistling through the wood
  Where the tender, sweet things grew—
The tall, fair ferns and the maiden's-hair,
  And the gentle gentians blue.
" It's very cold—are we growing old?"
  They sighed, " What shall we do?"

The sigh went up to the loving leaves,—
  " We must help," they whispered low.
" They are frightened and weak, Oh, brave old trees!
  But we love you well, you know."
And the trees said, " We are strong—make haste!
  Down to the darlings go."

So the leaves went floating, floating down,
  All yellow and brown and red,
And the frail little trembling, thankful things
  Lay still and were comforted.
And the blue sky smiled through the bare old trees
  Down on their safe, warm bed.

L. G. Warner.

• 67 •

THE SOLDIER'S DREAM.

Our bugles sang truce, for the night-cloud had lowered,
  And the sentinel stars set their watch in the sky;
And thousands had sunk on the ground overpowered,
  The weary to sleep, and the wounded to die.

"I flew to the pleasant fields traversed so oft
In life's morning march, when my bosom was young."—*p. 95.*

When reposing that night on my pallet of straw
  By the wolf-scaring faggot that guarded the slain,
At the dead of the night a sweet Vision I saw;
  And thrice ere the morning I dreamed it again.

Methought from the battle-field's dreadful array
  Far, far, I had roamed on a desolate track;
'Twas Autumn,—and sunshine arose on the way
  To the home of my fathers, that welcomed me back.

I flew to the pleasant fields traversed so oft
  In life's morning march, when my bosom was young;
I heard my own mountain-goats bleating aloft,
  And knew the sweet strain that the corn-reapers sung.

Then pledged we the wine-cup, and fondly I swore
  From my home and my weeping friends never to part;
My little ones kissed me a thousand times o'er,
  And my wife sobbed aloud in her fulness of heart.

"Stay—stay with us!—rest!—thou art weary and worn!"—
  And fain was their war-broken soldier to stay;—
But sorrow returned with the dawning of morn,
  And the voice in my dreaming ear melted away,
                              Thomas Campbell.

• 68 •

THE PET LAMB.

The dew was falling fast, the stars began to blink;
I heard a voice; it said, "Drink, pretty creature, drink."
And looking o'er the hedge, before me I espied
A snow-white mountain lamb, with a maiden at its side.

No other sheep was near, the lamb was all alone,
And by a slender cord was tethered to a stone;
With one knee on the grass did the little maiden kneel,
While to that mountain lamb she gave its evening meal.

The lamb, while from her hand he thus his supper took,
Seemed to feast with head and ears, and his tail with
    pleasure shook ;
" Drink pretty creature, drink," she said, in such a tone,
That I almost received her heart into my own.

'Twas little Barbara Lethwaite, a child of beauty rare !
I watched them with delight, they were a lovely pair.
Now with her empty can the maiden turned away ;
But ere ten yards were gone, her footsteps she did stay.

Towards the lamb she looked ; and from that shady place
I unobserved could see the working of her face ;
If nature to her tongue could measured numbers bring,
Thus thought I, to her lamb that little maid might sing :

" What ails thee, young one ? what ? why pull so at thy cord ?
Is it not well with thee ? well both for bed and board ?
Thy plot of grass is soft, and green as grass can be ;
Rest, little young one rest ; what is't that aileth thee ?

" What is it thou wouldst seek ? What is wanting to thy heart ?
Thy limbs are they not strong ? And beautiful thou art.
This grass is tender grass ; these flowers they have no peers,
And that green corn all day is rustling in thy ears !

" If the sun be shining hot, do but stretch thy woolen
    chain,
This beech is standing by, its covert thou can'st gain ;
For rain and mountain storms—the like thou need'st not
    fear—
The rain and storms are things that scarcely can come here.

" Rest, little young one, rest ; thou hast forgot the day
When my father found thee first in places far away ;
Many flocks were on the hills, but thou wert owned by
    none,
And thy mother from thy side forevermore was gone

" He took thee in his arms, and in pity brought thee home;
O blessed day for thee ! then whither would'st thou roam?
A faithful nurse thou hast, the dam that did thee yean
Upon the mountain tops no kinder could have been.

"Thou know'st that twice a day I have brought thee in
   this can
Fresh water from the brook, as clear as ever ran ;
And twice in the day, when the ground is wet with dew,
I bring thee draughts of milk, warm milk it is and new.

"Thy limbs will shortly be twice as stout as they are
   now ;
Then I'll yoke thee to my cart, like a pony in a plough ;
My playmate thou shalt be ; and when the wind is cold
Our hearth shall be thy bed, our house shall be thy fold.

" Alas ! the mountain-tops that look so green and fair,
I've heard of fearful winds and darkness that come there ;
The little brooks that seem all pastime and all play,
When they are angry, roar like lions for their prey.

" Here thou need'st not dread the raven in the sky ;
Night and day thou art safe—our cottage is hard by.
Why bleat so after me ? Why pull so at thy chain ?
Sleep—and at break of day I will come to thee again."

As homeward through the lane I went, with lazy feet,
This song to myself did I oftentimes repeat ;
And it seemed as I retraced the ballad line by line,
That but half of it was hers, and one half of it was mine.

Again, and once again, did I repeat the song :
" Nay," said I, " more than half to the damsel must belong,
For she looked with such a look, and she spake with such a
   tone,
That I almost received her heart into my own."
      William Wordsworth.

• 69 •

THE BURIAL OF SIR JOHN MOORE AT CORUNNA.

Not a drum was heard, not a funeral note,
    As his corse to the rampart we hurried;
Not a soldier discharged his farewell shot
    O'er the grave where our hero we buried.

We buried him darkly at dead of night,
    The sods with our bayonets turning;
By the struggling moonbeam's misty light
    And the lantern dimly burning.

No useless coffin inclosed his breast,
    Nor in sheet nor in shroud we wound him;
But he lay like a warrior taking his rest
    With his martial cloak around him.

Few and short were the prayers we said,
    And we spoke not a word of sorrow;
But we steadfastly gazed on the face of the dead,
    And we bitterly thought of the morrow.

We thought as we hollowed his narrow bed
    And smoothed down his lonely pillow,
That the foe and the stranger would tread o'er his head,
    And we far away on the billow!

Lightly they'll talk of the spirit that's gone
    And o'er his cold ashes upbraid him,—
But little he'll reck, if they let him sleep on
    In the grave where a Briton has laid him.

But half of our heavy task was done
    When the clock tolled the hour for retiring;
And we heard the distant and random gun
    That the foe was sullenly firing.

Slowly and sadly we laid him down,
　From the field of his fame fresh and gory;
We carved not a line, and we raised not a stone—
　But we left him alone with his glory.

C. Wolfe.

• 70 •

THE BROOK.

I come from haunts of coot and hern,
　I make a sudden sally,
And sparkle out among the fern,
　To bicker down a valley.

By thirty hills I hurry down,
　Or slip between the ridges,
By twenty thorps, a little town,
　And half a hundred bridges.

Till last by Philip's farm I flow
　To join the brimming river,
For men may come, and men may go,
　But I go on forever.

I chatter over stony ways,
　In little sharps and trebles,
I bubble into eddying bays,
　I babble on the pebbles.

With many a curve my bank I fret
　By many a field and fallow,
And many a fairy foreland set
　With willow-weed and mallow.

I chatter, chatter as I flow
　To join the brimming river,
For men may come, and men may go,
　But I go on forever.

I wind about, and in and out,
 With here a blossom sailing,
And here and there a lusty trout,
 And here and there a grayling.

And here and there a foamy flake
 Upon me as I travel,
With many a silvery waterbreak
 Above the golden gravel.

And draw them all along, and flow
 To join the brimming river,
For men may come, and men may go,
 But I go on forever.

I steal by lawns and grassy plots,
 I slide by hazel covers,
I move the sweet forget-me-nots
 That grow for happy lovers.

I slip, I slide, I gloom, I glance,
 Among my skimming swallows;
I make the netted sunbeam dance
 Against my sandy shallows.

I murmur under moon and stars
 In brambly wildernesses;
I linger by my shingly bars;
 I loiter round my cresses.

And out again I curve and flow
 To join the brimming river,
For men may come, and men may go,
 But I go on forever.

                    Alfred Tennyson.

"I wind about and in and out."—*p. 100.*

· 71 ·

HOHENLINDEN.

On Linden, when the sun was low,
All bloodless lay the untrodden snow;
And dark as winter was the flow
    Of Iser, rolling rapidly.

But Linden saw another sight,
When the drum beat at dead of night,
Commanding fires of death to light
    The darkness of her scenery.

By torch and trumpet fast arrayed,
Each horseman drew his battle blade,
And furious every charger neighed
    To join the dreadful revelry.

Then shook the hills with thunder riven;
Then rushed the steed, to battle driven;
And louder than the bolts of Heaven
    Far flashed the red artillery.

But redder yet that fire shall glow
On Linden's hills of blood-stained snow;
And darker yet shall be the flow
    Of Iser, rolling rapidly.

'Tis morn; but scarce yon level sun
Can pierce the war-clouds, rolling dun,
Where furious Frank and fiery Hun
    Shout in their sulphurous canopy.

The combat deepens. On, ye brave
Who rush to glory, or the grave!
Wave, Munich, all thy banners wave,
    And charge with all thy chivalry!

Ah, few shall part, where many meet!
The snow shall be their winding-sheet,
And every turf beneath their feet
  Shall be a soldier's sepulchre.
                    Thomas Campbell.

• 72 •

THE REAPER.

Behold her, single in the field,
Yon solitary Highland Lass!
Reaping and singing by herself;
Stop here, or gently pass!
Alone she cuts and binds the grain,
And sings a melancholy strain;
O listen! for the vale profound
Is overflowing with the sound.

No nightingale did ever chant
More welcome notes to weary band
Of travellers, in some shady haunt
Among Arabian sands;
No sweeter voice was ever heard
In spring-time from the cuckoo-bird,
Breaking the silence of the seas
Among the farthest Hebrides.

Will no one tell me what she sings?
Perhaps the plaintive numbers flow
For old, unhappy, far-off things,
And battles long ago:
Or is it some more humble lay,
Familiar matter of to-day?
Some natural sorrow, loss or pain
That has been, and may be again?

"'Tis morn ; but scarce yon level sun
Can pierce the war-clouds, rolling dun."—*p. 101.*

Whate'er the theme, the maiden sang
As if her song could have no ending;
I saw her singing at her work,
And o'er the sickle bending;
I listen'd till I had my fill;
And as I mounted up the hill
The music in my heart I bore
Long after it was heard no more.
William Wordsworth.

· 73 ·

THE INCHCAPE ROCK.

No stir in the air, no stir in the sea,
The ship was as still as she could be,
Her sails from heaven received no motion,
Her keel was steady in the ocean.

Without either sign or sound of their shock
The waves flowed over the Inchcape Rock;
So little they rose, so little they fell,
They did not move the Inchcape Bell.

The good old Abbot of Aberbrothok
Had placed that bell on the Inchcape Rock;
On a buoy in the storm it floated and swung,
And over the waves its warning rung.

When the rock was hid by the surges' swell,
The Mariners heard the warning bell;
And then they knew the perilous rock,
And blessed the Abbot of Aberbrothok.

The sun in heaven was shining gay,
All things were joyful on that day;
The sea-birds screamed as they wheeled around,
And there was joyance in their sound.

The buoy of the Inchcape Bell was seen,
A darker speck on the ocean green;
Sir Ralph the Rover walked his deck,
And he fixed his eye on the darker speck.

He felt the cheering power of spring,
It made him whistle, it made him sing;
His heart was mirthful to excess,
But the Rover's mirth was wickedness.

His eye was on the Inchcape float;
Quoth he, "My men, put out the boat,
And row me to the Inchcape rock,
And I'll plague the abbot of Aberbrothok."

The boat is lowered, the boatmen row,
And to the Inchcape rock they go;
Sir Ralph bent over from the boat,
And he cut the bell from the Inchcape float.

Down sank the bell with a gurgling sound,
The bubbles rose and burst around;
Quoth Sir Ralph, "The next who comes to the rock
Won't bless the Abbot of Aberbrothok."

Sir Ralph the Rover sailed away,
He scoured the seas for many a day,
And now grown rich with plundered store,
He steers his course for Scotland's shore.

So thick a haze o'erspreads the sky
They cannot see the sun on high;
The wind hath blown a gale all day.
At evening it hath died away.

On the deck the Rover takes his stand,
So dark it is, they see no land.
Quoth Sir Ralph, "It will be lighter soon,
For there is the dawn of the rising moon."

"Can'st hear," said one, "the breakers roar?
For methinks we should be near the shore;
Now where we are, I cannot tell,
But I wish I could hear the Inchcape Bell."

They hear no sound, the swell is strong;
Though the wind hath fallen, they drift along,
Till the vessel strikes with a shivering shock;
O death! "It is the Inchcape Rock!

Sir Ralph the Rover tore his hair,
He cursed himself in his despair;
The waves rush in on every side,
The ship is sinking beneath the tide.

But even in his dying fear
One dreadful sound could the Rover hear,
A sound as if with the Inchcape Bell,
The fiends below were ringing his knell.
Robert Southey.

• 74 •

THE WRECK OF THE HESPERUS.

It was the schooner Hesperus,
　That sailed the wintry sea;
And the skipper had taken his little daughter,
　To bear him company.

Blue were her eyes as the fairy flax,
　Her cheeks like the dawn of day,
And her bosom white as the hawthorn buds,
　That ope in the month of May.

The skipper he stood beside the helm,
　With his pipe in his mouth,
And watched how the veering flaw did blow
　The smoke now West, now South.

Then up and spake an old sailor,
    Had sailed the Spanish Main,
"I pray thee, put into yonder port,
    For I fear a hurricane.

"Last night the moon had a golden ring,
    And to-night no moon we see!"
The skipper, he blew a whiff from his pipe
    And a scornful laugh laughed he.

Colder and louder blew the wind,
    A gale from the North-East;
The snow fell hissing in the brine,
    And the billows froth'd like yeast.

Down came the storm, and smote amain
    The vessel in its strength;
She shuddered and paused, like a frighted steed,
    Then leaped her cable's length.

"Come hither! come hither! my little daughter,
    And do not tremble so!
For I can weather the roughest gale,
    That ever wind did blow."

He wrapped her warm in his seaman's coat
    Against the stinging blast;
He cut a rope from a broken spar,
    And bound her to the mast.

"O father! I hear the church-bells ring,
    O say, what may it be?"
"'Tis a fog bell on a rock-bound coast!"—
    And he steered for the open sea.

"O father! I hear the sound of guns,
    O say, what may it be?"
"Some ship in distress that cannot live
    In such an angry sea!"

"Like a sheeted ghost, the vessel swept
Towards the reef of Norman's woe."—*p. 107.*

"O father! I see a gleaming light,
  O say, what may it be?"
But the father answered never a word,—
  A frozen corpse was he.

Lashed to the helm, all stiff and stark,
  With his face turned to the skies,
The lantern gleamed through the gleaming snow,
  On his fixed and glassy eyes.

The maiden clasped her hands and prayed
  That savèd she might be;
And she thought of Christ, who stilled the waves
  On the Lake of Galilee.

And fast through the midnight dark and drear,
  Through the whistling sleet and snow,
Like a sheeted ghost, the vessel swept
  Towards the reef of Norman's Woe.

And ever the fitful gusts between
  A sound came from the land;
It was the sound of the trampling surf,
  On the rocks and the hard sea-sand.

The breakers were right beneath her bows,
  She drifted a dreary wreck,
And a whooping billow swept the crew
  Like icicles from her deck.

She struck where the white and fleecy waves
  Looked soft as carded wool,
But the cruel rocks, they gored her sides
  Like the horns of an angry bull.

Her rattling shrouds, all sheathed in ice,
  With the masts went by the board;
Like a vessel of glass she stove and sank,
  Ho! ho! the breakers roared.

At day-break on the bleak sea-beach
　A fisherman stood aghast,
To see the form of a maiden fair
　Lashed close to a drifting mast.

The salt sea was frozen on her breast,
　The salt tears in her eyes;
And he saw her hair like the brown sea weed
　On the billows fall and rise.

Such was the wreck of the Hesperus,
　In the midnight and the snow;
Christ, save us all from a death like this
　On the reef of Norman's woe.
　　　　　　　Henry W. Longfellow.

• 75 •

CHORUS OF FLOWERS.

We are the sweet flowers,
　Born of sunny showers,
Think, whene'er you see us, what our beauty saith,
　Utterance, mute and bright,
　Of some unknown delight,
We fill the air with pleasure by our simple breath:
　All who see us love us—
　We befit all places;
Unto sorrow we give smiles—and unto graces, graces.

Mark our ways how noiseless
　All, and sweetly voiceless,
Though the March winds pipe to make our passage clear;
　Not a whisper tells
　Where our small seed dwells,
Nor is known the moment green when our tips appear
　We thread the earth in silence,
　In silence build our bowers,
And leaf by leaf in silence show, till we laugh a-top,
　sweet flowers.

"She struck where the white and fleecy waves
Looked soft as carded wool."—*p. 107.*

The dear lumpish baby,
Humming with the May-bee,
Hails us with his bright eye, stumbling through the grass;
The honey-dropping moon,
On a night in June,
Kisses our pale pathway leaves, that felt the bridegroom
pass.
Age, the withered clinger,
On us mutely gazes,
And wraps the thought of his last bed in his childhood's
daisies.

See and scorn all duller
Taste, how Heaven loves color;
How great Nature, clearly, joys in red and green;
What sweet thoughts she thinks
Of violets and pinks,
And a thousand flushing hues made solely to be seen;
See her whitest lilies
Chill the silver showers,
And what a red mouth is the rose, the woman of her flowers.

Uselessness divinest
Of a use the finest,
Painteth us, the teachers of the end of use;
Travellers, weary-eyed,
Bless us, far and wide;
Unto sick and prisoned thoughts, we give a sudden truce;
Not a poor town window
Loves its sickliest planting,
But its wall speaks loftier truth than Babylonian vaunting.

Sagest yet the uses
Mixed with our sweet juices,
Whether man or May-fly profit by the balm;
As fair fingers healed
Knights from the olden field,
We hold cups of the mightiest force to give the wildest,
calm.
Even the terror, poison,
Hath its plea for blooming;

Life it gives to reverent lips, though death to the presum-
ing.
And, oh! our sweet soul-taker,
The thief, the honey-maker,
What a house hath he by the thymy glen!
In his talking rooms
How the feasting fumes
Till the gold cups overflow to the mouths of men!
The butterflies come aping
Those fine thieves of ours,
And flutter round our rifled tops like tickled flowers with
flowers.

See those tops, how beauteous!
What fair service duteous
Round some idol waits, as on their lord, the Nine.
Elfin court 'twould seem,
And taught, perchance, that dream
Which the old Greek mountain dreamed upon nights divine.
To expound such wonder
Human speech avails not,
Yet there dies no poorest weed, that such a glory exhales
not.

Think of all these treasures,
Matchless works and pleasures,
Every one a marvel, more than thought can say;
Then think in what bright showers
We thicken fields and bowers,
And with what heaps of sweetness half stifle wanton May;
Think of the mossy forests
By the bee-birds haunted,
And all those Amazonian plains, lone-lying as enchanted.

Trees themselves are ours;
Fruits are born of flowers;
Peach, and roughest nut were blossoms in the Spring;
The lusty bee knows well
The news, and comes pell-mell
And dances in the gloomy thicks with darksome anthem-
ing;

Beneath the very burden
Of planet pressing ocean,
We wash our smiling cheeks in peace, a thought for meek
devotion,

Tears of Phœbus, missings
Of Cytherea's kissings,
Have in us been found, and wise men find them still;
Drooping grace unfurls
Still Hyacinthus' curls,
And Narcissus loves himself in the selfish rill;
Thy red lip, Adonis,
Still is wet with morning;
And the step that bled for thee, the rosy brier adorning.

Oh! true things are fables,
Fit for sagest tables,
And the flowers are true things—yet no fables they;
Fables were not more
Bright, nor loved of yore—
Yet they grew not, like the flowers, by every old pathway;
Grossest hand can test us—
Fools can prize us never—
Yet we rise, and rise, and rise—marvels sweet forever.

Who shall say that flowers
Dress not Heavens own bowers?
Who its love, without us, can fancy,—or sweet floor?
Who shall even dare
To say we sprang not there—
And came not down that love might bring one piece of
Heaven the more?
Oh pray believe that angels
From those blue dominions
Brought us in their white laps down, 'twixt their golden
pinions.

Leigh Hunt.

• 76 •

THE MILLER OF DEE.

There dwelt a miller, hale and bold,
　Beside the river Dee;
He worked and sang from morn till night,
　No lark more blithe than he;
And this the burden of his song
　Forever used to be,
" I envy nobody—no, not I,
　And nobody envies me."

"Thou'rt wrong, my friend," said good king Hal;
　" As wrong as wrong can be;
For could my heart be light as thine,
　I'd gladly change with thee:
And tell me now, what makes thee sing,
　With voice so loud and free,
While I am sad, though I'm the king,
　Beside the river Dee."

The miller smiled and doffed his cap,
　" I earn my bread," quoth he;
" I love my wife, I love my friend,
　I love my children three;
I owe no penny I can not pay;
　I thank the river Dee,
That turns the mill that grinds the corn
　That feeds my babes and me."

" Good friend," said Hal, and sighed the while,
　" Farewell, and happy be :
But say no more, if thou'dst be true,
　That no one envies thee:
Thy mealy cap is worth my crown;
　Thy mill, my kingdom's fee ;
Such men as thou are England's boast,
　O Miller of the Dee."

Chas. Mackay

• 77 •

ROBERT OF LINCOLN.

Merrily swinging on briar and weed,
Near to the nest of his little dame,
Over the mountain-side or mead,
Robert of Lincoln is telling his name :
Bob-o'-link, bob-o'-link,
Spink, spank, spink,
Snug and safe is this nest of ours,
Hidden among the summer flowers.
Chee, chee, chee.

Robert of Lincoln is gaily dressed,
Wearing a bright black wedding-coat ;
White are his shoulders, and white his crest,
Hear him call in his merry note :
Bob-o'-link, bob-o'-link,
Spink, spank, spink,
Look, what a nice new coat is mine ;
Sure there was never a bird so fine.
Chee, chee, chee.

Robert of Lincoln's Quaker wife,
Pretty and quiet, with plain brown wings,
Passing at home a patient life,
Broods in the grass while her husband sings :
Bob-o'-link, bob-o'-link,
Spink, spank, spink,
Brood, kind creature ; you need not fear
Thieves and robbers while I am here.
Chee, chee, chee.

Modest and shy as a nun is she ;
One weak chirp is her only note ;
Braggart and prince of braggarts is he,
Pouring boasts from his little throat :
Bob-o-link, bob-o'-link,

Spink, spank, spink,
Never was I afraid of man,
Catch me, cowardly knaves, if you can.
Chee, chee, chee.

Six white eggs on a bed of hay,
Flecked with purple, a pretty sight:
There as the mother sits all day,
Robert is singing with all his might:
Bob-o'-link, bob-o'-link,
Spink, spank, spink,
Nice good wife that never goes out,
Keeping house while I frolic about.
Chee, chee, chee.

Soon as the little ones chip the shell,
Six wide mouths are open for food;
Robert of Lincoln bestirs him well,
Gathering seeds for the hungry brood:
Bob-o'-link, bob-o'-link,
Spink, spank, spink,
This new life is likely to be
Hard for a gay young fellow like me.
Chee, chee, chee.

Robert of Lincoln at length is made
Sober with work, and silent with care,
Off is his holiday garment laid,
Half forgotten that merry air:
Bob-o'-link, bob-o'-link,
Spink, spank, spink,
Nobody knows but my mate and I,
Where our nest and our nestlings lie.
Chee, chee, chee.

Summer wanes: the children are grown:
Fun and frolic no more he knows;
Robert of Lincoln's a humdrum crone;
Off he flies, and we sing as he goes:

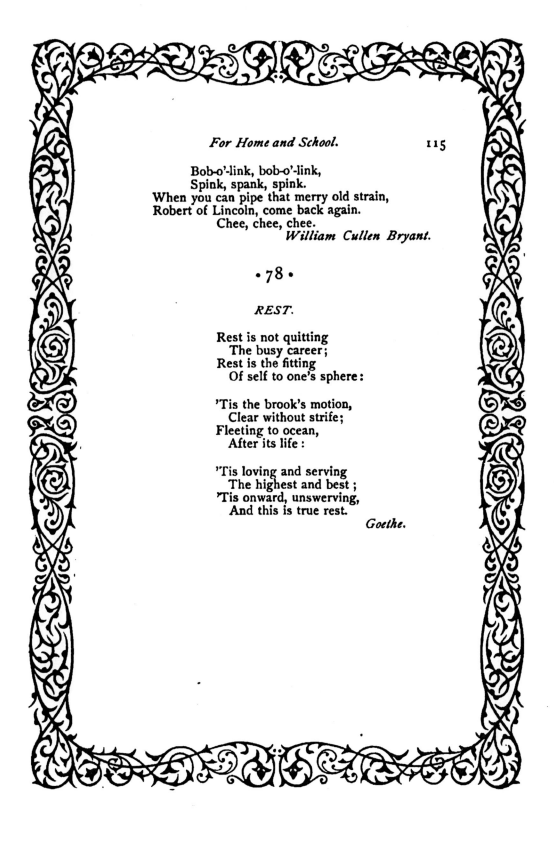

Bob-o'-link, bob-o'-link,
Spink, spank, spink.
When you can pipe that merry old strain,
Robert of Lincoln, come back again.
Chee, chee, chee.
William Cullen Bryant.

• 78 •

REST.

Rest is not quitting
The busy career;
Rest is the fitting
Of self to one's sphere :

'Tis the brook's motion,
Clear without strife;
Fleeting to ocean,
After its life :

'Tis loving and serving
The highest and best ;
'Tis onward, unswerving,
And this is true rest.

Goethe.

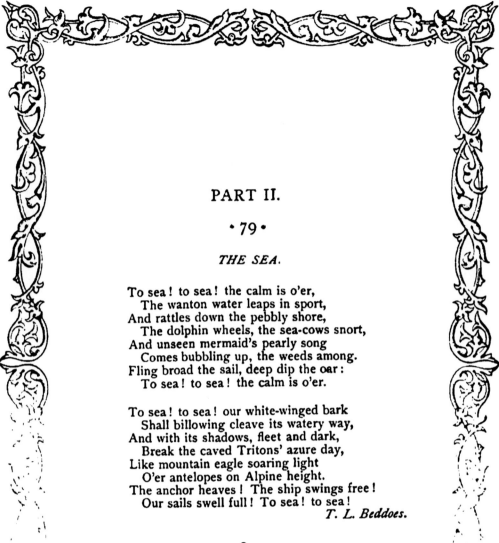

PART II.

• 79 •

THE SEA.

To sea! to sea! the calm is o'er,
  The wanton water leaps in sport,
And rattles down the pebbly shore,
  The dolphin wheels, the sea-cows snort,
And unseen mermaid's pearly song
  Comes bubbling up, the weeds among.
Fling broad the sail, deep dip the oar:
  To sea! to sea! the calm is o'er.

To sea! to sea! our white-winged bark
  Shall billowing cleave its watery way,
And with its shadows, fleet and dark,
  Break the caved Tritons' azure day,
Like mountain eagle soaring light
  O'er antelopes on Alpine height.
The anchor heaves! The ship swings free!
  Our sails swell full! To sea! to sea!
                    T. L. Beddoes.

• 80 •

BURIAL OF THE MINNISINK.

On sunny slope and beechen swell
The shadowed light of evening fell;
And, where the maple's leaf was brown,

With soft and silent lapse came down
The glory that the wood receives
At sunset, in its brazen leaves.

Far upward in the mellow light
Rose the blue hills.   One cloud of white,
Around a far uplifted cone,
In the warm blush of evening shone ;
An image of the silver lakes
By which the Indian's soul awakes.

But soon a funeral hymn was heard
Where the soft breath of evening stirred
The tall, gray forest ; and a band
Of stern in heart, and strong in hand,
Came winding down beside the wave,
To lay the red chief in his grave.

They sang, that by his native bowers
He stood, in the last moon of flowers,
And thirty snows had not yet shed
Their glory on the warrior's head ;
But, as the summer fruit decays,
So died he in those naked days.

A dark cloak of the roebuck's skin
Covered the warrior, and within
Its heavy folds the weapons, made
For the hard toils of war, were laid ;
The cuirass, woven of plaited reeds.
And the broad belt of shells and beads.

Before, a dark-haired virgin train
Chanted the death-dirge of the slain ;
Behind, the long procession came
Of hoary men and chiefs of fame,
With heavy hearts, and eyes of grief,
Leading the war-horse of their chief.

Stripped of his proud and martial dress,
Uncurbed, unreined, and riderless,
With darting eye, and nostril spread,
And heavy and impatient tread,
He came; and oft that eye so proud
Asked for his rider in the crowd.

They buried the dark chief; they freed
Beside the grave his battle steed;
And swift an arrow cleaved its way
To his stern heart! One piercing neigh
Arose,—and, on the dead man's plain,
The rider grasps his steed again.
H. W. Longfellow.

· 81 ·

HELVELLYN.

I climbed the dark brow of the mighty Helvellyn,
Lakes and mountains beneath me gleamed misty and wide,
All was still, save by fits, when the eagle was yelling,
And starting around me the echoes replied.
On the right, Striden-edge round the Red tarn was bend-
ing,
And Catchedicam its left verge was defending,
One huge nameless rock in the front was ascending,
When I marked the sad spot where the wanderer had died.

Dark green was the spot, 'mid the brown mountain heather,
Where the pilgrim of nature lay stretched in decay,
Like the corpse of an outcast abandoned to weather,
Till the mountain winds wasted the tenantless clay.
Nor yet quite deserted, though lonely extended,
For, faithful in death, his mute favorite attended,
The much-loved remains of her master defended,
And chased the hill-fox and the raven away.

How long did'st thou think that his silence was slumber?
When the wind waved his garment, how oft didst thou
        start,
How many long days and long weeks didst thou number,
Ere he faded before thee, the friend of thy heart?
And, O, was it meet, that,—no requiem read o'er him,
No mother to weep, and no friend to deplore him.
And thou, little guardian, alone stretched before him—
Unhonored the pilgrim from life should depart?

When a prince to the fate of a peasant has yielded
The tapestry waves dark round the dim-lighted hall;
With scutcheons of silver the coffin is shielded,
And pages stand mute by the canopied pall:
Through the courts, at deep midnight, the torches are glea
        ming,
In the proudly-arched chapel the banners are beaming,
Far adown the long aisle sacred music is streaming,
Lamenting a chief of the people should fall.

But meeter for thee, gentle lover of nature,
To lay down thy head like the meek mountain lamb:
When, wildered, he drops from some rock huge in stature,
And draws his last sob by the side of his dam:
And more stately thy couch by this desert lake lying,
Thy obsequies sung by the gray plover flying,
With one faithful friend but, to witness thy dying,
In the arms of Helvellyn and Catchedicam.

                Walter Scott.

· 82 ·

THE GRASSHOPPER.

Happy insect! what can be
In happiness compared to thee?
Fed with nourishment divine,
The dewy morning's gentle wine!

Nature waits upon thee still
And thy verdant cup doth fill;
'Tis filled wherever thou dost tread,
Nature's self's thy Ganymede.
Thou dost drink, and dance and sing,
Happier than the happiest king!
All the fields which thou dost see,
All the plants belong to thee,
All that summer hours produce,
Fertile made with early juice;
Man for thee does sow and plough;
Farmer he and landlord thou!
Thou dost innocently joy,
Nor doth thy luxury destroy.
The shepherd gladly heareth thee,
More harmonious than he.
Thee, country hinds with gladness hear,
Prophet of the ripened year:
Thee, Phœbus loves and doth inspire;
Phœbus is himself thy sire.
To thee of all things upon earth,
Life is no longer than thy mirth.
Happy insect! happy thou,
Dost neither age nor winter know:
But when thou'st drunk, and danced, and sung
Thy fill, the flowery leaves among,
Voluptuous and wise withal,
Epicurean animal,
Sated with the summer feast
Thou retir'st to endless rest.

Abraham Cowley.

• 83 •

TO DAFFODILS.

Fair daffodils, we weep to see
    You haste away so soon;
As yet the early rising sun
    Has not attain'd his noon:

Stay, stay,
Until the hastening day
Has run
But to the even-song;
And having prayed together, we
Will go with you along.

We have short time to stay as you;
We have as short a spring:
As quick a growth to meet decay
As you, or any thing:
We die,
As your hours do; and dry
Away.
Like to the summer's rain,
Or as the pearls of morning dew,
Ne'er to be found again.

Robert Herrick.

• 84 •

THE FIFTIETH BIRTHDAY OF AGASSIZ.

May 28, 1857.

It was fifty years ago
In the pleasant month of May,
In the beautiful *Pays de Vaud*,
A child in its cradle lay.

And Nature, the old nurse, took
The child upon her knee,
Saying: "Here is a story-book
Thy Father has written for thee."

"Come, wander with me," she said,
"Into regions yet untrod;
And read what is still unread
In the manuscripts of God."

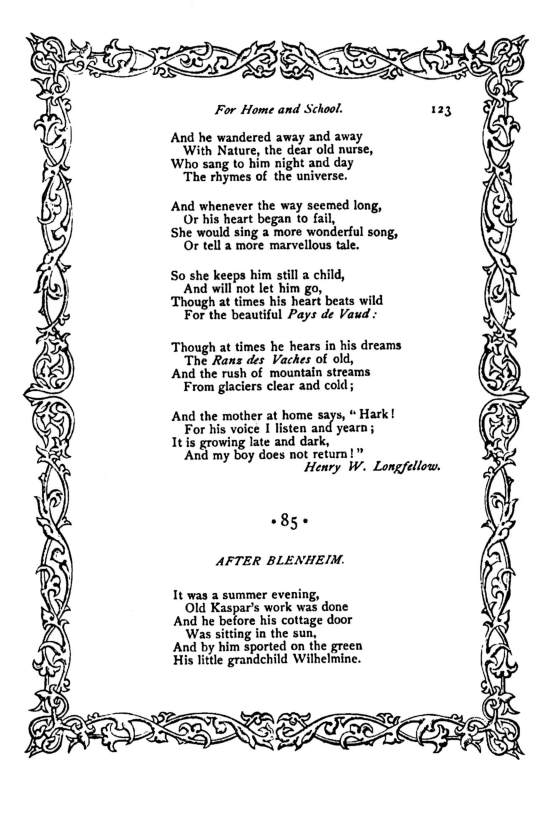

And he wandered away and away
  With Nature, the dear old nurse,
Who sang to him night and day
  The rhymes of the universe.

And whenever the way seemed long,
  Or his heart began to fail,
She would sing a more wonderful song,
  Or tell a more marvellous tale.

So she keeps him still a child,
  And will not let him go,
Though at times his heart beats wild
  For the beautiful *Pays de Vaud :*

Though at times he hears in his dreams
  The *Ranz des Vaches* of old,
And the rush of mountain streams
  From glaciers clear and cold;

And the mother at home says, " Hark !
  For his voice I listen and yearn ;
It is growing late and dark,
  And my boy does not return ! "
             Henry W. Longfellow.

• 85 •

AFTER BLENHEIM.

It was a summer evening,
  Old Kaspar's work was done
And he before his cottage door
  Was sitting in the sun,
And by him sported on the green
His little grandchild Wilhelmine.

She saw her brother Peterkin
　Roll something large and round,
Which he beside the rivulet
　In playing there had found;
He came to ask what he had found
That was so large, and smooth, and round.

Old Kaspar took it from the boy
　Who stood expectant by;
And then the old man shook his head,
　And with a natural sigh—
"'Tis some poor fellow's skull," said he,
"Who fell in the great victory."

"I find them in the garden,
　For there's many here about;
And often when I go to plough,
　The ploughshare turns them out.
For many a thousand men," said he,
"Were slain in that great victory."

"Now tell us what 'twas all about,
　Young Peterkin he cries;
And little Wilhelmine looks up
　With wonder-waiting eyes;
"Now tell us all about the war,
And what they fought each other for."

"It was the English," Kaspar cried,
　"Who put the French to rout;
But what they fought each other for,
　I could not well make out.
But everybody said," quoth he,
"That 'twas a famous victory."

"My father lived at Blenheim then,
　Yon little stream hard by;
They burnt his dwelling to the ground,
　And he was forced to fly:
So with his wife and child he fled,
Nor had he where to rest his head.

"With fire and sword the country round
   Was wasted far and wide,
And many a childing mother then
   And new-born baby died;
But things like that, you know, must be
At every famous victory.

" They say it was a shocking sight
   After the field was won;
For many thousand bodies here
   Lay rotting in the sun;
But things like that, you know, must be
After a famous victory.

" Great praise the Duke of Marlbro' won,
   And our good Prince Eugene;"
" Why 'twas a very wicked thing!"
   Said little Wilhelmine;
" Nay, nay, my little girl,"quoth he,
" It was a famous victory.

" And everybody praised the Duke
   Who this great fight did win."
" But what good came of it at last?"
   Quoth little Peterkin,
" Why that I cannot tell," said he,
" But 'twas a famous victory."
                Robert Southey.

• 86 •

THE PIED PIPER OF HAMELIN.

Hamelin Town's in Brunswick,
By famous Hanover city;
   The river Weser deep and wide
   Washes its walls on the southern side;
   A pleasanter spot you never spied;

But, when begins my ditty,
        Almost five hundred years ago,
        To see the townsfolk suffer so
From vermin, was a pity.

        Rats!
They fought the dogs and killed the cats,
        And bit the babies in their cradles,
And ate the cheeses out of the vats,
        And licked the soup from the cook's own ladles
Split open the kegs of salted sprats,
Made nests inside men's Sunday hats,
And even spoiled the women's chats
        By drowning their speaking
        With shrieking and squeaking
In fifty different sharps and flats.

At last the people in a body
To the Town-hall came flocking;
"'Tis clear," cried they, "our Mayor's a noddy;
And as for our Corporation—shocking!
To think we buy gowns lined with ermine
For dolts that can't or won't determine
What's best to rid us of our vermin!
You hope, because you're old and obese,
To find in the furry civic robe, ease!
Rouse up Sirs! Give your brains a racking.
To find the remedy we're lacking,
Or, sure as fate, we'll send you packing!"
At this the Mayor and Corporation
Quaked with a mighty consternation.

An hour they sat in council,
        At length the Mayor broke silence:
"For a guilder I'd my ermine gown sell;
        I wish I were a mile hence!
It's easy to bid one rack one's brain—
I'm sure my poor head aches again,
I've scratched it so, and all in vain.
Oh, for a trap, a trap, a trap!"

Just as he said this, what should hap
At the chamber door, but a gentle tap?
"Bless us," cried the Mayor, "what's that?
Anything like the sound of a rat
Makes my heart go pit-a-pat!

"Come in!" the Mayor cried, looking bigger:
And in did come the strangest figure!
His queer long coat from heel to head
Was half of yellow and half of red;
And he himself was tall and thin,
With sharp blue eyes each like a pin,
And light loose hair, yet swarthy skin,
No tuft on cheek, nor beard on chin,
But lips where smiles went out and in—
There was no guessing his kith and kin!
And nobody could enough admire
The tall man and his quaint attire;
Quoth one, "It's as if my great grandsire,
Starting up at the trump of Doom's tone,
Had walked this way from his painted tombstone!"

He advanced to the council table;
And, "Please your honours," said he, "I'm able,
By means of a secret charm, to draw
All creatures living beneath the sun,
That creep, or swim, or fly, or run,
After me so as you never saw!
And I chiefly use my charm
On creatures that do people harm,
The mole, the toad, the newt, the viper
And people call me the Pied Piper.
Yet," said he, "poor piper as I am,
In Tartary I freed the Cham,
Last June, from his huge swarm of gnats;
I eased in Asia the Nizam
Of a monstrous brood of vampyre bats;
And as for what your brain bewilders,
If I can rid your town of rats,

Will you give me a thousand guilders ? "
" One ? fifty thousand ! " was the exclamation
Of the astonished Mayor and Corporation.

Into the street the Piper stept,
  Smiling first a little smile,
As if he knew what magic slept
  In his quiet pipe the while ;
Then like a musical adept,
To blow the pipe his lips he wrinkled,
And green and blue his sharp eyes twinkled,
Like a candle flame where salt is sprinkled ;
And ere three shrill notes the pipe had uttered,
You heard as if an army muttered ;
And the muttering grew to a grumbling ;
And the grumbling grew to a mighty rumbling ;
And out of the houses the rats came tumbling—
Great rats, small rats, lean rats, brawny rats,
Brown rats, black rats, grey rats, tawny rats,
Grave old plodders, gay young friskers,
  Fathers, mothers, uncles, cousins,
Cocking tails and pricking whiskers,
  Families by tens and dozens.
Brothers, sisters, husbands, wives,—
Followed the Piper for their lives.
From street to street he piped, advancing,
And step for step they followed, dancing,
Until they came to the river Weser
Wherein all plunged and perished.
Save one, who stout as Julius Cæsar,
Swam across, and lived to carry,—
As he the manuscript he cherished—
To Rat-land home his commentary,
Which was, " At the first shrill notes of the pipe,
I heard a sound as of scraping tripe,
And putting apples wondrous ripe
Into a cider press's gripe ;
And a moving away of pickle-tub boards,
And a leaving ajar of conserve cupboards,
And a drawing the corks of train-oil flasks,

And a breaking the hoops of butter casks;
And it seemed as if a voice
Sweeter far than by harp or by psaltery
Is breathed—called out, Oh rats, rejoice!
The world is grown to one vast drysaltery!
So munch on, crunch on, take your nuncheon,
Breakfast, dinner, supper, luncheon!
And just as a bulky sugar puncheon,
All ready staved, like a great sun shone
Glorious, scarce an inch before me,
Just as methought it said, "Come, bore me!"
—I found the Weser rolling o'er me.
You should have heard the Hamelin people
Ringing the bells till they rocked the steeple;
"Go," cried the Mayor, "and get long poles!
Poke out the nests, and block up the holes!
Consult with carpenters and builders,
And leave in our town not even a trace
Of the rats!" When suddenly up the face
Of the Piper perked in the market-place,
With a " First, if you please, my thousand guilders!"

A thousand guilders! The Mayor looked blue,
So did the Corporation too.
For council dinners made rare havock
With Claret, Moselle, Vin-de-Grave, Hock;
And half the money would replenish
Their cellar's biggest butt with Rhenish.
To pay this sum to a wandering fellow
With a gipsy coat of red and yellow!
"Besides," quoth the Mayor, with a knowing wink,
"Our business was done at the river's brink;
We saw with our eyes the vermin sink,
And what's dead can't come to life, I think.
So friend, we're not the folks to shrink
From the duty of giving you something to drink,
And a matter of money to put in your poke;
But, as for the guilders, what we spoke
Of them, as you very well know, was in joke—
Besides, our losses have made us thrifty:
A thousand guilders! come take fifty!"

The piper's face fell, and he cried,
" No trifling ! I can't wait ! Beside,
I've promised to visit by dinner-time
Bagdad, and accept the prime
Of the head cook's pottage, all he's rich in,
For having left in the caliph's kitchen,
Of a nest of scorpions no survivor.
With him I proved no bargain driver,
With you, don't think I'll bate a stiver !
And folks who put me in a passion
May find me pipe to another fashion."

"How ? " cried the Mayor, "d'ye think I'll brook
Being worse treated than a cook ?
Insulted by a lazy ribald
With idle pipe and vesture piebald ?
You threaten us, fellow ? Do your worst,
Blow your pipe there till you burst."

Once more he stepped into the street,
And to his lips again
Laid his long pipe of smooth, straight cane ;
And ere he blew three notes—such sweet
Soft notes as yet musician's cunning
Never gave the enraptured air—
There was a rustling that seemed like a bustling
Of merry crowds justling at pitching and hustling,
Small feet were pattering, wooden shoes clattering,
Little hands clapping and little tongues chattering,
And like fowls in a farmyard when barley is scattering
Out came the children running :
All the little boys and girls,
With rosy cheeks and flaxen curls,
And sparkling eyes and teeth like pearls,
Tripping and skipping, ran merrily after
The wonderful music with shouting and laughter.

The Mayor was dumb, and the Council stood
As if they were changed into blocks of wood,
Unable to move a step, or cry

To the children merrily skipping by—
And could only follow with the eye
The joyous crowd at the piper's back.
And now the Mayor was on the rack,
And the wretched Council's bosoms beat,
As the Piper turned from the High Street
To where the Weser rolled its waters
Right in the way of their sons and daughters!
However he turned from south to west,
And to Koppelberg Hill his steps addressed.
And after him the children pressed;
Great was the joy in every breast.
"He never can cross that mighty top;
He's forced to let the piping drop,
And we shall see our children stop!"
When, lo! as they reached the mountain's side,
A wondrous portal opened wide,
As if a cavern was suddenly hollowed;
And the piper advanced, and the children followed;
And when all were in to the very last,
The door in the mountain side shut fast.
Did I say all? No! One was lame,
And could not dance the whole of the way:
And in after years, if you would blame
His sadness, he was used to say,—
"It's dull in our town since my playmates left!
I can't forget that I'm bereft
Of all the pleasant sights they see,
Which the piper also promised me:
For he led us, he said, to a joyous land,
Joining the town and just at hand,
Where waters gushed and fruit trees grew,
And flowers put forth a fairer hue,
And everything was strange and new;
The sparrows were brighter then peacocks here,
And their dogs outran our fallow-deer,
And honey-bees had lost their stings,
And horses were born with eagles' wings;
And just as I became assured
My lame foot would be speedily cured,
The music stopped and I stood still,

And found myself outside the hill,
Left alone against my will,
To go now limping as before,
And never hear of that country more!"

The Mayor sent east, west, north, and south,
To offer the piper by word of mouth,
Wherever it was man's lot to find him,
Silver and gold to his heart's content,
If he'd only return the way he went,
And bring the children behind him.
But when they saw 'twas a lost endeavor,
And Piper and dancers were gone forever,
They made a decree that lawyers never
Should think their records dated duly,
If after the day of the month and year
These words did not as well appear.
" And so long after what happened here
On the twenty-second of July,
Thirteen hundred and seventy six :"
And the better in memory to fix
The place of the children's last retreat,
They called it, the Pied Piper's Street—
Where any one playing on pipe or tabor,
Was sure for the future to lose his labor.
Nor suffered they hostelry or tavern
To shock with mirth a street so solemn ;
But opposite the place of the cavern
They wrote the story on a column,
And on the great church window painted
The same, to make the world acquainted
How their children were stolen away ;
And there it stands to this very day.
And I must not omit to say
That in Transylvania there's a tribe
Of alien people, that ascribe
The outlandish ways and dress
On which their neighbors lay such stress,
To their fathers' and mothers' having risen
Out of some subterraneous prison,

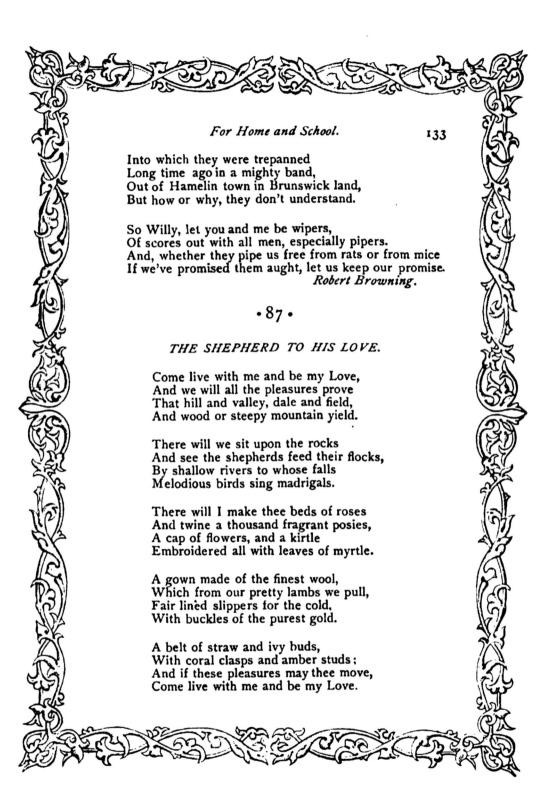

Into which they were trepanned
Long time ago in a mighty band,
Out of Hamelin town in Brunswick land,
But how or why, they don't understand.

So Willy, let you and me be wipers,
Of scores out with all men, especially pipers.
And, whether they pipe us free from rats or from mice
If we've promised them aught, let us keep our promise.
Robert Browning.

· 87 ·

THE SHEPHERD TO HIS LOVE.

Come live with me and be my Love,
And we will all the pleasures prove
That hill and valley, dale and field,
And wood or steepy mountain yield.

There will we sit upon the rocks
And see the shepherds feed their flocks,
By shallow rivers to whose falls
Melodious birds sing madrigals.

There will I make thee beds of roses
And twine a thousand fragrant posies,
A cap of flowers, and a kirtle
Embroidered all with leaves of myrtle.

A gown made of the finest wool,
Which from our pretty lambs we pull,
Fair lined slippers for the cold,
With buckles of the purest gold.

A belt of straw and ivy buds,
With coral clasps and amber studs;
And if these pleasures may thee move,
Come live with me and be my Love.

Thy silver dishes for thy meat
As precious as the gods do eat,
Shall on an ivory table be
Prepared each day for thee and me.

The shepherd swains shall dance and sing
For thy delight each May-morning:
If these delights thy mind may move,
Come live with me and be my Love.
                                    Christopher Marlowe.

• 88 •

THE NYMPH'S REPLY.

If that the world and love were young,
And truth on every shepherd's tongue,
These pretty pleasures might me move
To live with thee and be thy Love.

But time drives flocks from field to fold,
When rivers rage, and rocks grow cold;
And Philomel becometh dumb,
And all complain of cares to come.

The flowers do fade, and wanton fields
To wayward winter reckoning yields;
A honey tongue, a heart of gall,
Is fancy's spring, but sorrow's fall.

Thy gowns, thy shoes, thy beds of roses,
Thy cap, thy kirtle, and thy posies
Soon break, soon wither, soon forgotten—
In folly ripe, in reason rotten.

Thy belt of straw and ivy buds
Thy coral clasps and amber studs—
All these in me no means can move
To come to thee and be thy Love.

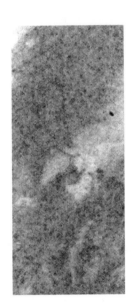

But could youth last, and love still breed,
Had joys no date, nor age no need,
Then those delights my mind might move
To live with thee and be thy Love.
Walter Raleigh.

• 89 •

ROBIN HOOD AND ALLAN A DALE.

Come listen to me, you gallants so free,
　All you that love mirth for to hear,
And I will tell you of a bold outlaw
　That lived in Nottinghamshire.

As Robin Hood in the forest stood,
　All under the greenwood tree,
There he was aware of a brave young man
　As fine as fine might be.

The youngster was clothed in scarlet red,
　In scarlet fine and gay ;
And he did frisk it over the plain,
　And chanted a roundelay.

As Robin Hood next morning stood
　Amongst the leaves so gay,
There did he espy the same young man
　Come drooping along the way.

The scarlet he wore the day before
　It was clean cast away ;
And at every step he fetched a sigh,
　" Alack and a well-a-day ! "

Then stepped forth brave Little John,
　And Midge, the miller's son,
Which made the young man bend his bow,
　When as he saw them come.

" Stand off, stand off ! " the young man said,
  " What is your will with me ? "
" You must come before our master straight,
  Under yon greenwood tree."

And when he came bold Robin before,
  Robin asked him courteously,
" O, hast thou any money to spare
  For my merry men and me ? "

" I have no money," the young man said,
  " But five shillings and a ring :
And that I have kept this seven long years,
  To have it at my wedding.

" Yesterday I should have married a maid,
  But she soon from me was ta'en
And chosen to be an old knight's delight,
  Whereby my poor heart is slain."

" What is thy name ? " then said Robin Hood,
  " Come tell me without any fail : "
" By the faith of my body ! " Then said the young
                man,
  " My name it is Allan a Dale."

" What wilt thou give me ? " said Robin Hood,
  " In ready gold or fee,
To help thee to thy true love again,
  And deliver her unto thee ? "

" I have no money," then quoth the young man,
  " No ready gold or fee,
But I will swear upon a book
  Thy true servant for to be ! "

" How many miles is it to thy true love ?
  Come tell me without guile : "
" By the faith of my body ! " then said the young man,
  " It is but five little mile."

Then Robin he hasted over the plain,
  He did neither stint nor lin,
Until he came unto the church,
  Where Allan should keep his wedding.

"What hast thou here?" the bishop then said,
  " I· prithee now tell unto me : "
" I am a bold harper," quoth Robin Hood,
  " And the best in the north country."

" O welcome, O welcome," the bishop he said,
  " That music best pleaseth me ; "
" You shall have no music," quoth Robin Hood,
  " Till the bride and the bridegroom I see."

With that came in a wealthy knight,
  Which was both grave and old,
And after him a finikin lass,
  Did shine like the glistering gold.

" This is not a fit match," quoth bold Robin Hood,
  " That you do seem to make here,
For since we are come into the church
  The bride shall choose her own dear."

Then Robin Hood put his horn to his mouth,
  And blew blasts two or three ;
When four and twenty bowmen bold
  Came leaping over the lea.

And when they came into the churchyard,
  Marching all on a row,
The very first man was Allan a Dale,
  To give bold Robin his bow.

" This is thy true love," Robin he said,
  " Young Allan as I hear say ;
And you shall be married at this same time,
  Before we depart away."

"That shall not be," the bishop he said,
 "For thy word shall not stand:
They shall be three times asked in the church,
 As the law is of our land."

Robin Hood pulled off the bishop's coat,
 And put it upon Little John;
"By the faith of my body," then Robin said,
 "This cloth doth make thee a man."

When Little John went into the choir,
 The people began to laugh;
He asked them seven times in the church,
 Lest three times should not be enough.

"Who gives me this maid?" said Little John;
 Quoth Robin Hood, "That do I,
And he that takes her from Allan a Dale,
 Full dearly he shall her buy."

And thus having end of this merry wedding,
 The bride looked like a queen;
And so they returned to the merry greenwood,
 Amongst the leaves so green.

• 90 •

THE LOSS OF THE ROYAL GEORGE.

Toll for the brave!
 The brave that are no more!
All sunk beneath the wave,
 Fast by their native shore!

Eight hundred of the brave,
 Whose courage well was tried,
Had made the vessel heel,
 And laid her on her side.

A land breeze shook the shrouds,
  And she was overset;
Down went the Royal George,
  With all her crew complete.

Toll for the brave!
  Brave Kempenfelt is gone;
His last sea-fight is fought,
  His work of glory done.

It was not in the battle;
  No tempest gave the shock;
She sprang no fatal leak;
  She ran upon no rock.

His sword was in his sheath;
  His fingers held the pen,
When Kempenfelt went down,
  With twice four hundred men.

Weigh the vessel up,
  Once dreaded by our foes!
And mingle with our cup
  The tear that England owes.

Her timbers yet are sound,
  And she may float again,
Full charged with England's thunder,
  And plough the distant main.

But Kempenfelt is gone,
  His victories are o'er;
And he and his eight hundred
  Shall plough the wave no more.
                    William Cowper.

• 91 •

THE DESERTED HOUSE.

Life and Thought have gone away.
  Side by side,
Leaving door and windows wide,
  Careless tenants they!

All within is dark as night;
  In the windows is no light;
And no murmur at the door,
  So frequent on its hinge before.

Close the door, the shutters close,
  Or through the windows we shall see,
The nakedness and vacancy
  Of the dark, deserted house.

Come away; no more of mirth
  Is here or merry-making sound.
The house was builded of the earth,
  And shall fall again to ground.

Come away; for Life and Thought
  Here no longer dwell;
    But in a city glorious—
A great and distant city—have bought
  A mansion incorruptible,
    Would they could have stayed with us!
        Alfred Tennyson.

• 92 •

TO A MOUNTAIN DAISY

TURNED DOWN BY A PLOUGH.

Wee, modest, crimson tippéd flower,
Thou's met me in an evil hour;
For I maun crush amang the stoure

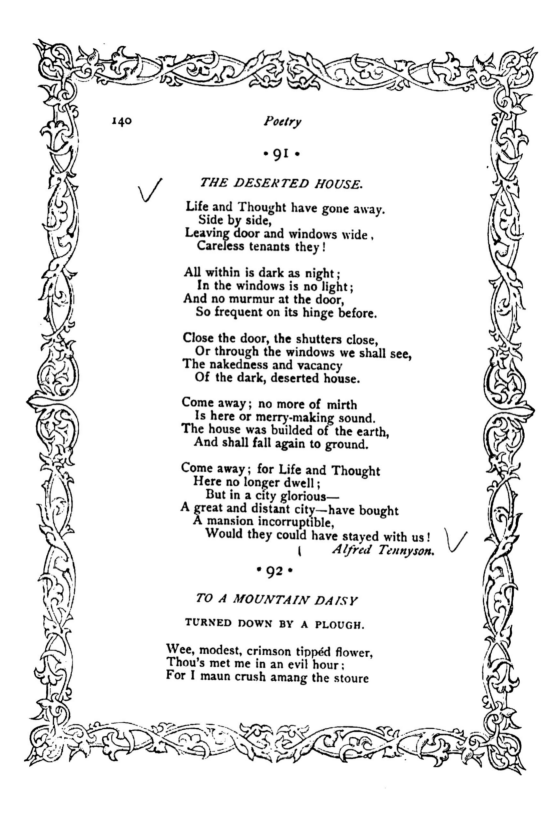

"Wee, modest, crimson-tippéd flower,
Thou 's met me in an evil hour."—*p. 140.*

Thy slender stem :
To spare thee now is past my power,
Thou bonnie gem!

Alas, it's not thy neebor sweet,
The bonnie lark, companion meet!
Bending thee 'mang the dewy weet!
Wi' speckled breast,
When upward springing, blythe, to greet
The purpling east.

Cauld blew the bitter, biting north
Upon thy early humble birth ;
Yet cheerfully thou glinted forth,
Amid the storm!
Scarce reared above the parent earth
Thy tender form.

The flaunting flowers our gardens yield,
High sheltering woods and wa's maun shield
But thou, beneath the random bield
O' clod or stane,
Adorns the histie stibble-field,
Unseen, alane.

There in thy scanty mantle clad,
Thy snawie bosom sunward spread,
Thou lifts thy unassuming head
In humble guise ;
But now the share uptears thy bed,
And low thou lies !

Such is the fate of simple bard,
On life's rough ocean luckless starred !
Unskilful he to note the card
Of prudent lore,
Till billows rage, and gales blow hard,
And whelm him o'er.

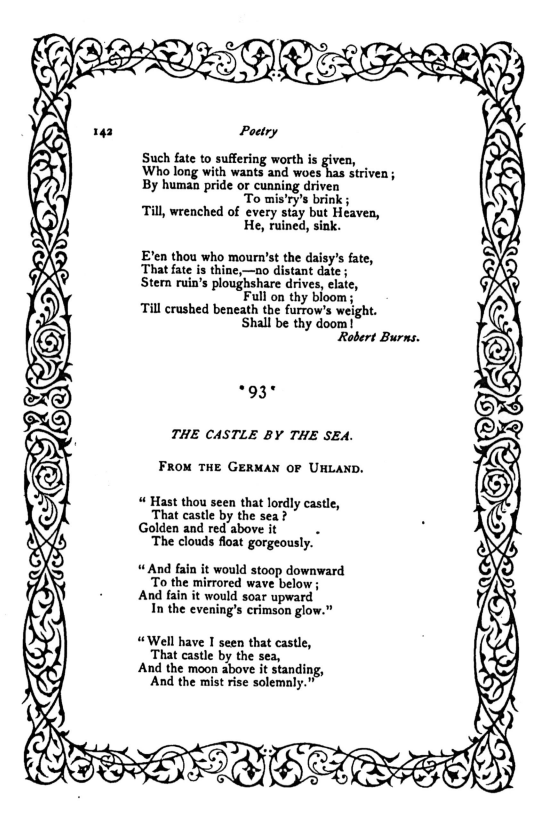

Such fate to suffering worth is given,
Who long with wants and woes has striven;
By human pride or cunning driven
          To mis'ry's brink;
Till, wrenched of every stay but Heaven,
          He, ruined, sink.

E'en thou who mourn'st the daisy's fate,
That fate is thine,—no distant date;
Stern ruin's ploughshare drives, elate,
          Full on thy bloom;
Till crushed beneath the furrow's weight.
          Shall be thy doom!

                    Robert Burns.

· 93 ·

THE CASTLE BY THE SEA.

FROM THE GERMAN OF UHLAND.

" Hast thou seen that lordly castle,
   That castle by the sea?
Golden and red above it
   The clouds float gorgeously.

"And fain it would stoop downward
   To the mirrored wave below;
And fain it would soar upward
   In the evening's crimson glow."

"Well have I seen that castle,
   That castle by the sea,
And the moon above it standing,
   And the mist rise solemnly."

"The winds and the waves of ocean,
  Had they a merry chime?
Didst thou hear, from those lofty chambers,
  The harp and the minstrel's rhyme?"

"The winds and the waves of ocean,
  They rested quietly;
But I heard on the gale a sound of wail,
  And tears came to mine eye."

"And sawest thou on the turrets
  The king and his royal bride?
And the wave of their crimson mantles?
  And the golden crown of pride?

"Led they not forth, in rapture,
  A beauteous maiden there,
Resplendent as the morning sun,
  Beaming with golden hair?"

"Well saw I the ancient parents,
  Without the crown of pride;
They were moving slow, in weeds of woe
  No maiden was by their side!"
                    Henry W. Longfellow.

• 94 •

PEACE OF MIND.

My mind to me a kingdom is;
  Such perfect joy therein I find
As far exceeds all earthly bliss
  That God or nature hath assigned:
Though much I want that most would have,
  Yet still my mind forbids to crave.

Content I live, this is my stay;
  I seek no more than may suffice:
I press to bear no haughty sway;

Look! what I lack, my mind supplies.
Lo! thus I triumph like a king,
    Content with that my mind doth bring.

I see how plenty surfeits oft,
    And hasty climbers soonest fall
I see that such as sit aloft
    Mishap doth threaten most of all;
These get with toil, and keep with fear;
    Such cares my mind could never bear.

No princely pomp, nor wealthy store,
    No force to win a victory,
No wily wit to salve a sore,
    No shape to win a lover's eye;
To none of these I yield as thrall,
    For why? My mind despiseth all.

Some have too much, yet still they crave;
    I little have, yet seek no more;
They are but poor, though much they have
    And I am rich with little store;
They poor, I rich; they beg, I give;
    They lack, I lend; they pine, I live.

I laugh not at another's loss,
    I grudge not at another's gain;
No worldly wave my mind can toss:
    I brook that is another's bane.
I fear no foe, nor fawn no friend;
    I loathe not life, nor dread mine end.

My wealth is health and perfect ease;
    My conscience clear my chief defence;
I never seek by bribes to please,
    Nor by desert to give offence;
Thus do I live, thus will I die;
    Would all did so as well as I!

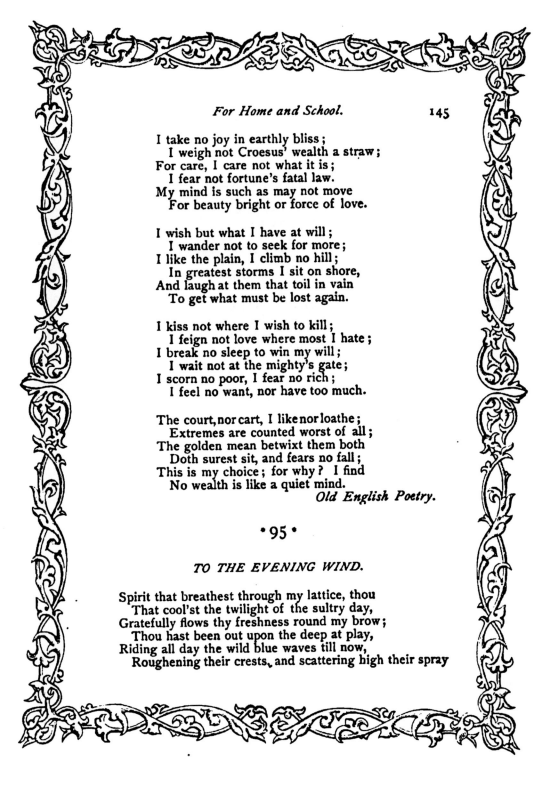

I take no joy in earthly bliss;
　　I weigh not Croesus' wealth a straw;
For care, I care not what it is;
　　I fear not fortune's fatal law.
My mind is such as may not move
　　For beauty bright or force of love.

I wish but what I have at will;
　　I wander not to seek for more;
I like the plain, I climb no hill;
　　In greatest storms I sit on shore,
And laugh at them that toil in vain
　　To get what must be lost again.

I kiss not where I wish to kill;
　　I feign not love where most I hate;
I break no sleep to win my will;
　　I wait not at the mighty's gate;
I scorn no poor, I fear no rich;
　　I feel no want, nor have too much.

The court, nor cart, I like nor loathe;
　　Extremes are counted worst of all;
The golden mean betwixt them both
　　Doth surest sit, and fears no fall;
This is my choice; for why? I find
　　No wealth is like a quiet mind.
　　　　　　　　　　Old English Poetry.

• 95 •

TO THE EVENING WIND.

Spirit that breathest through my lattice, thou
　　That cool'st the twilight of the sultry day,
Gratefully flows thy freshness round my brow;
　　Thou hast been out upon the deep at play,
Riding all day the wild blue waves till now,
　　Roughening their crests, and scattering high their spray

And swelling the white sail. I welcome thee
To the scorched land, thou wanderer of the sea.

Nor I alone ;—a thousand bosoms round
  Inhale thee in the fulness of delight;
And, languid forms rise up, and pulses bound
  Livelier at coming of the wind of night :
And languishing to hear thy grateful sound,
  Lies the vast inland stretched beyond the sight.
Go forth into the gathering shade ; go forth,
God's blessing breathed upon the fainting earth !

Go, rock the little wood-bird in his nest,
  Curl the still waters, bright with stars, and rouse
The wide old wood from his majestic rest,
  Summoning from the innumerable boughs
The strange deep harmonies that haunt his breast;
  Pleasant shall be thy way where meekly bows
The shutting flower, and darkling waters pass,
And where the o'ershadowing branches sweep the grass.

The faint old man shall lean his silver head
  To feel thee ; thou shalt kiss the child asleep,
And dry the moistened curls that overspread
  His temples, while his breathing grows more deep;
And they who stand about the sick man's bed
  Shall joy to listen to thy distant sweep,
And softly part his curtains to allow
Thy visit, grateful to his burning brow.

Go,—but the circle of eternal change,
  Which is the life of nature, shall restore,
With sounds and scents from all thy mighty range,
  Thee to thy birthplace of the deep once more, ;
Sweet odors in the sea-air, sweet and strange,
  Shall tell the homesick mariner of the shore ;
And, listening to thy murmur, he shall dream
He hears the rustling leaf and running stream.
                                    Wm. C. Bryant.

· 96 ·

TIMES GO BY TURNS.

The loppèd tree in time may grow again,
 Most naked plants renew both fruit and flower;
The sorriest wight may find release of pain;
 The driest soil suck up some moistening shower;
Times go by turns, and chances change by course,
From foul to fair, from better hap to worse.

The sea of fortune doth not ever flow;
 She draws her favors to the lowest ebb;
Her tides have equal times to come and go;
 Her loom doth weave the fine and coarsest web;
No joy so great but runneth to an end,
No hap so hard but may in fine amend.

Not always fall of leaf, nor ever spring;
 Not endless night, nor yet eternal day;
The saddest birds a season find to sing,
 The roughest storm, a calm may soon allay,
Thus with succeeding turns God tempereth all,
That man may hope to rise, yet fear to fall.

A chance may win that by mischance was lost;
 That net that holds no great, takes little fish;
In some things all, in all things none, are crossed;
 Few all they need, but none have all they wish.
Unmingled joys here to no man befall;
Who least, have some; who most, have never all.
Robert Southwell.

· 97 ·

ABOU BEN ADHEM.

Abou Ben Adhem—may his tribe increase—
Awoke one night from a deep dream of peace,
And saw, within the moonlight in his room,

Making it rich, and like a lily in bloom,
An angel, writing in a book of gold;
Exceeding peace had made Ben Adhem bold;
And to the presence in the room he said,
"What writest thou?"   The vision raised his head,
And with a look made all of sweet accord,
Answered, "The names of those who love the Lord."
"And is mine one?" said Abou.   "Nay not so,"
Replied the angel.   Abou spoke more low,
But cheerly still; and said, "I pray thee then,
Write me as one that loves his fellow-men."
The angel wrote and vanished.   The next night
He came again with great awakening light,
And showed the names whom love of God had blessed.
And lo! Ben Adhem's name led all the rest.

Leigh Hunt.

• 98 •

THE ISLES OF GREECE.

The isles of Greece! the isles of Greece!
  Where burning Sappho loved and sung,—
Where grew the arts of war and peace,—
  Where Delos rose and Phœbus sprung!
Eternal summer gilds them yet,
  But all, except their sun, is set.

The Scian and the Teian Muse,
  The hero's harp, the lover's lute,
Have found the fame your shores refuse;
  Their place of birth alone is mute
To sounds which echo farther west
  Than your sires' "Islands of the Blest."

The mountains look on Marathon,—
  And Marathon looks on the sea;
And musing there an hour alone,
  I dreamed that Greece might still be free;
For, standing on the Persians' grave,
  I could not deem myself a slave.

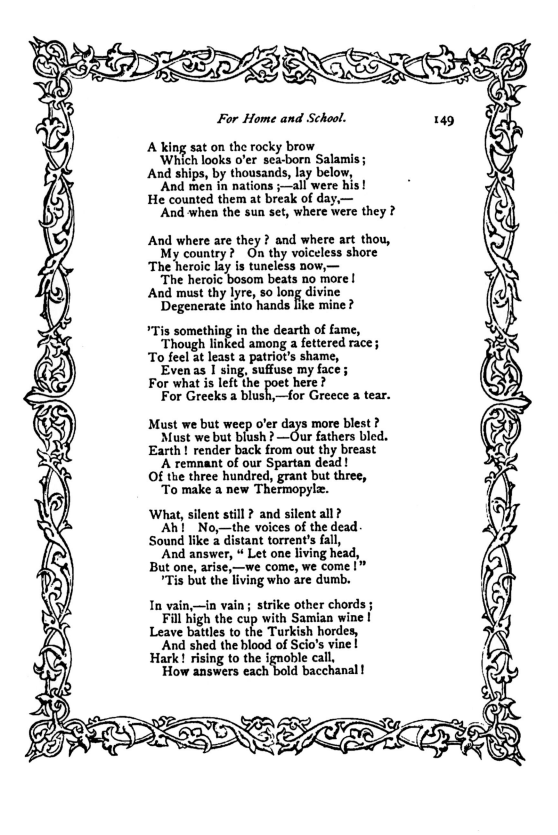

A king sat on the rocky brow
　　Which looks o'er sea-born Salamis;
And ships, by thousands, lay below,
　　And men in nations;—all were his!
He counted them at break of day,—
　　And when the sun set, where were they?

And where are they? and where art thou,
　　My country? On thy voiceless shore
The heroic lay is tuneless now,—
　　The heroic bosom beats no more!
And must thy lyre, so long divine
　　Degenerate into hands like mine?

'Tis something in the dearth of fame,
　　Though linked among a fettered race;
To feel at least a patriot's shame,
　　Even as I sing, suffuse my face;
For what is left the poet here?
　　For Greeks a blush,—for Greece a tear.

Must we but weep o'er days more blest?
　　Must we but blush?—Our fathers bled.
Earth! render back from out thy breast
　　A remnant of our Spartan dead!
Of the three hundred, grant but three,
　　To make a new Thermopylæ.

What, silent still? and silent all?
　　Ah! No,—the voices of the dead·
Sound like a distant torrent's fall,
　　And answer, " Let one living head,
But one, arise,—we come, we come!"
　　'Tis but the living who are dumb.

In vain,—in vain; strike other chords;
　　Fill high the cup with Samian wine!
Leave battles to the Turkish hordes,
　　And shed the blood of Scio's vine!
Hark! rising to the ignoble call,
　　How answers each bold bacchanal!

You have the Pyrrhic dance as yet,—
    Where is the Pyrrhic phalanx gone?
Of two such lessons, why forget
    The nobler and the manlier one?
You have the letters Cadmus gave,—
    Think ye he meant them for a slave?

Fill high the bowl with Samian wine!
    We will not think of themes like these!
It made Anacreon's song divine;
    He served—but served Polycrates—
A tyrant; but our masters then
    Were still, at least, our countrymen.

The tyrant of the Chersonese
    Was freedom's best and bravest friend;
That tyrant was Miltiades!
    O, that the present hour would lend
Another despot of the kind!
    Such chains as his were sure to bind.

Fill high the bowl with Samian wine!
    On Suli's rock, and Parga's shore,
Exists the remnant of a line
    Such as the Doric mothers bore;
And there perhaps some seed is sown,
    The Heracleidan blood might own.

Trust not for freedom to the Franks,—
    They have a king who buys and sells.
In native swords and native ranks
    The only hope of courage dwells;
But Turkish force and Latin fraud
    Would break your shield, however broad

Fill high the bowl with Samian wine!
    Our virgins dance beneath the shade,—
I see their glorious black eyes shine;
    But, gazing on each glowing maid,
My own the burning tear-drop laves,
    To think such breasts must suckle slaves.

Place me on Sunium's marbled steep,—
  Where nothing, save the waves and I,
May hear our mutual murmurs sweep;
  There, swan-like, let me sing and die,
A land of slaves shall ne'er be mine,—
  Dash down yon cup of Samian wine !

Byron.

• 99 •

THE NEW- YEAR.

Ring out, wild bells, to the wild sky,
  The flying cloud, the frosty light :
  The year is dying in the night;
Ring out, wild bells, and let him die.

Ring out the old, ring in the new,
  Ring, happy bells, across the snow :
  The year is going, let him go;
Ring out the false, ring in the true.

Ring out the grief that saps the mind,
  For those that here we see no more;
  Ring out the feud of rich and poor,
Ring in redress to all mankind.

Ring out a slowly dying cause,
  And ancient forms of party strife;
  Ring in the nobler modes of life,
With sweeter manners, purer laws.

Ring out the want, the care, the sin,
  The faithless coldness of the times;
  Ring out, ring out my mournful rhymes,
But ring the fuller minstrel in.

Ring out false pride in place and blood,
    The civic slander and the spite;
    Ring in the love of truth and right,
Ring in the common love of good.

Ring out old shapes of foul disease;
    Ring out the narrowing lust of gold;
    Ring out the thousand wars of old,
Ring in the thousand years of peace.

Ring in the valiant man and free,
    The larger heart, the kindlier hand;
    Ring out the darkness of the land,
Ring in the Christ that is to be.
                              Alfred Tennyson.

• 100 •

IL PENSEROSO.

Hence, vain deluding joys,
    The brood of Folly without father bred!
How little you bestead
    Or fill the fixèd mind with all your toys!
Dwell in some idle brain,
    And fancies fond with gaudy shapes possess
As thick and numberless
    As the gay motes that people the sunbeams,
Or likest hovering dreams
    The fickle pensioners of Morpheus' train.

But hail, thou goddess sage and holy,
Hail, divinest Melancholy!
Whose saintly visage is too bright
To hit the sense of human sight,
And therefore to our weaker view
O'erlaid with black, staid Wisdom's hue;
Black, but such as in esteem

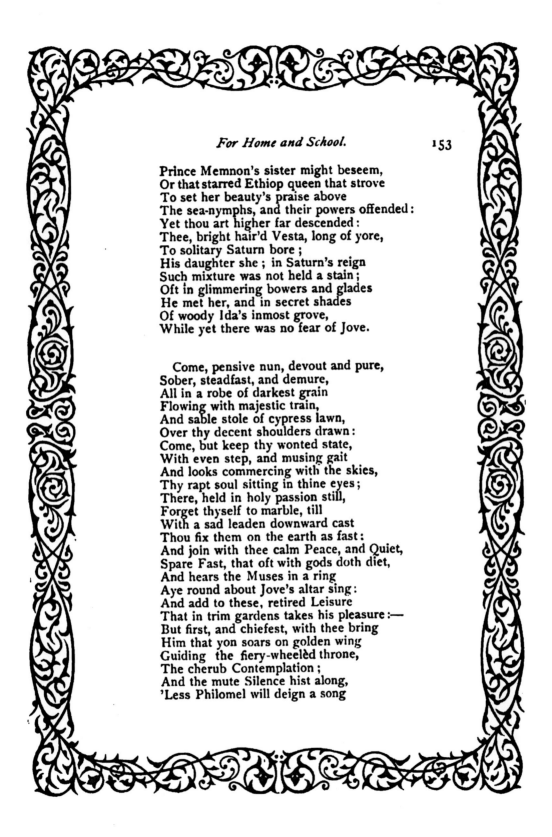

Prince Memnon's sister might beseem,
Or that starred Ethiop queen that strove
To set her beauty's praise above
The sea-nymphs, and their powers offended:
Yet thou art higher far descended:
Thee, bright hair'd Vesta, long of yore,
To solitary Saturn bore;
His daughter she; in Saturn's reign
Such mixture was not held a stain;
Oft in glimmering bowers and glades
He met her, and in secret shades
Of woody Ida's inmost grove,
While yet there was no fear of Jove.

Come, pensive nun, devout and pure,
Sober, steadfast, and demure,
All in a robe of darkest grain
Flowing with majestic train,
And sable stole of cypress lawn,
Over thy decent shoulders drawn:
Come, but keep thy wonted state,
With even step, and musing gait
And looks commercing with the skies,
Thy rapt soul sitting in thine eyes;
There, held in holy passion still,
Forget thyself to marble, till
With a sad leaden downward cast
Thou fix them on the earth as fast:
And join with thee calm Peace, and Quiet,
Spare Fast, that oft with gods doth diet,
And hears the Muses in a ring
Aye round about Jove's altar sing:
And add to these, retired Leisure
That in trim gardens takes his pleasure:—
But first, and chiefest, with thee bring
Him that yon soars on golden wing
Guiding the fiery-wheelèd throne,
The cherub Contemplation;
And the mute Silence hist along,
'Less Philomel will deign a song

In her sweetest, saddest plight,
Smoothing the rugged brow of Night,
While Cynthia checks her dragon yoke
Gently o'er the accustomed oak.

—Sweet bird that shunn'st the noise of folly,
Most musical, most melancholy!
Thee, chantress, oft, the woods among
I woo, to hear thy even-song;
And missing thee, I walk unseen
On the dry, smooth shaven green,
To behold the wandering Moon
Riding near her highest noon,
Like one that had been led astray
Through the heaven's wide pathless way,
And oft, as if her head she bowed,
Stooping through a fleecy cloud.

Oft, on a plat of rising ground
I hear the far off curfew sound
Over some wide-watered shore,
Swinging slow with sullen roar:
Or, if the air will not permit.
Some still removèd place will fit,
Where glowing embers through the room
Teach light to counterfeit a gloom;
Far from all resort of mirth,
Save the cricket on the hearth,
Or the bellman's drowsy charm
To bless the doors from nightly harm.

Or let my lamp at midnight hour
Be seen in some high lonely tower,
Where I may oft out-watch the Bear
With thrice-great Hermes, or unsphere
The spirit of Plato, to unfold
What worlds or what vast regions hold.
The immortal mind, that hath forsook
Her mansion in this fleshly nook;
And of those demons that are found

"Haste thee, Nymph, and bring with thee
Jest, and youthful jollity."—*p. 158.*

In fire, air, flood, or under ground,
Whose power hath a true consent
With planet, or with element.
Sometime let gorgeous Tragedy
In sceptered pall come sweeping by,
Presenting Thebes, or Pelops' line,
Or the tale of Troy divine ;
Or what, though rare, of later age
Ennobled hath the buskined stage.

But, O sad Virgin, that thy power
Might raise Musaeus from his bower,
Or bid the soul of Orpheus sing
Such notes as, warbled to the string,
Drew iron tears down Pluto's cheek,
And made Hell grant what Love did seek !
Or call up him that left half told
The story of Cambuscan bold,
Of Camball, and of Algarsife,
And who had Canacé to wife
That owned the virtuous ring and glass ·
And of the wondrous horse of brass
On which the Tartar King did ride :
And if aught else great bards beside
In sage and solemn tunes have sung
Of tourneys, and of trophies hung,
Of forests, and enchantments drear,
Where more is meant than meets the ear.

Thus, Night, oft see me in thy pale career,
Till civil suited Morn appear,
Not tricked and frounced as she was wont
With the Attic Boy to hunt,
But kercheeft in a comely cloud
While rocking winds are piping loud,
Or usher'd with a shower still,
When the gust hath blown his fill,
Ending on the rustling leaves
With minute drops from off the eaves.
And when the sun begins to fling

His flaring beams, me, goddess, bring
To archèd walks of twilight groves,
And shadows brown that Sylvan loves,
Of pine, or monumental oak,
Where the rude axe, with heavèd stroke
Was never heard the nymphs to daunt
Or fright them from their hallow'd haunt.
There in close covert by some brook
Where no profaner eye may look
Hide me from day's garish eye,
While the bee with honeyed thigh
That at her flowery work doth sing,
And the waters murmuring,
With such concert as they keep
Entice the dewy-feathered Sleep;
And let some strange mysterious dream
Wave at his wings in airy stream
Of lively portraiture displayed,
Softly on my eyelids laid;
And, as I wake, sweet music breathe
Above, about, or underneath,
Sent by some spirit to mortals good,
Or the unseen Genius of the wood.

But let my due feet never fail
To walk the studious cloister's pale,
And love the high embowèd roof,
With antique pillars massy proof,
And storied windows richly dight
Casting a dim religious light:
There let the pealing organ blow
To the full-voicèd choir below
In service high and anthems clear,
As may with sweetness, through mine ear
Dissolve me into ecstasies,
And bring all Heaven before mine eyes.

And may at last my weary age
Find out the peaceful hermitage,
The hairy gown and mossy cell

"Oft list'ning how the hounds and horn
Cheerly rouse the slumbering morn."—*p. 158.*

Where I may sit, and rightly spell
Of every star that heaven doth show,
And every herb that sips the dew;
Till old experience do attain
To something like prophetic strain.

These pleasures, Melancholy, give,
And I with thee will choose to live.
John Milton.

⋅ 101 ⋅

L'ALLEGRO.

Hence, loathed Melancholy,
Of Cerberus and blackest Midnight born
In Stygian cave forlorn
'Mongst horrid shapes, and shrieks, and sights unholy!
Find out some uncouth cell
Where brooding Darkness spreads his jealous wings
And the night raven sings;
There under ebon shades, and low-browed rocks
As ragged as thy locks,
In dark Cimmerian desert ever dwell.

But come, thou Goddess fair and free,
In heaven yclep'd Euphrosyne,
And by men, heart-easing Mirth,
Whom lovely Venus at a birth,
With two sister Graces more
To ivy-crowned Bacchus bore:
Or whether (as some sages sing)
The frolic wind that breathes the spring,
Zephyr, with Aurora playing,
As he met her once a-Maying—
There on beds of violets blue
And fresh-blown roses washed in dew
Filled her with thee, a daughter fair,

So buxom, blithe, and debonair.
   Haste thee, Nymph, and bring with thee
Jest, and youthful jollity,
Quips, and cranks, and wanton wiles,
Nods and becks, and wreathed smiles
Such as hang on Hebe's cheek,
And love to live in dimple sleek;
Sport that wrinkled Care derides,
And Laughter holding both his sides:—
Come, and trip it as you go
On the light fantastic toe;
And in thy right hand lead with thee
The mountain nymph, sweet Liberty;
And if I give thee honor due
Mirth, admit me of thy crew,
To live with her, and live with thee
In unreprovèd pleasures free;
To hear the lark begin his flight
And singing, startle the dull night
From his watch-tower in the skies,
Till the dappled dawn doth rise;
Then to come, in spite of sorrow,
And at my window bid good-morrow
Through the sweetbriar, or the vine,
Or the twisted eglantine;
While the cock with lively din
Scatters the rear of darkness thin,
And to the stack, or the barn-door,
Stoutly struts, his dames before:
Oft listening how the hounds and horn
Cheerly rouse the slumbering morn,
From the side of some hoar hill,
Through the high wood echoing shrill.
Sometimes walking not unseen,
By hedge-row elms, on hillocks green,
Right against the eastern gate
Where the great sun begins his state,
Robed in flames and amber light,
The clouds in thousand liveries dight;
While the ploughman, near at hand;
Whistles o'er the furrowed land,

" And the milkmaid singeth blithe,
And the mower whets his scythe."—*p. 159.*

And the milkmaid singeth blithe,
And the mower whets his scythe,
And every shepherd tells his tale
Under the hawthorn in the dale.
   Straight mine eye hath caught new pleasures
Whilst the landscape round, it measures
Russet lawns, and fallows gray,
Where the nibbling flocks do stray;
Mountains, on whose barren breast
The laboring clouds do often rest;
Meadows trim with daisies pied,
Shallow brooks, and rivers wide;
Towers and battlements it sees
Bosomed high in tufted trees,
Where perhaps some Beauty lies,
The cynosure of neighboring eyes.
   Hard by, a cottage chimney smokes
From betwixt two aged oaks,
Where Corydon and Thyrsis, met,
Are at their savory dinner set
Of herbs, and other country messes
Which the neat-handed Phillis dresses;
And then in haste her bower she leaves
With Thestylis to bind the sheaves;
Or, if the earlier season lead,
To the tanned haycock in the mead.
   Sometimes with secure delight
The upland hamlets will invite,
When the merry bells ring round,
And the jocund rebecks sound
To many a youth and many a maid,
Dancing in the chequered shade;
And young and old come forth to play
On a sunshine holiday,
Till the live-long day-light fail:
Then to the spicy nut brown ale,
With stories told of many a feat,
How fairy Mab the junkets eat;
She was pinched and pulled, she said;
And he, by friar's lantern led;
Tells how the drudging Goblin sweat

To earn his cream-bowl duly set.
When in one night ere glimpse of morn,
His shadowy flail hath threshed the corn
That ten day-laborers could not end;
Then lays him down the lubber fiend,
And, stretched out all the chimney's length
Basks at the fire his hairy strength;
And crop-full out of doors he flings,
Ere the first cock his matin rings.
    Thus done the tales, to bed they creep,
By whispering winds soon lulled asleep.
    Towered cities please us then
And the busy hum of men,
Where throngs of knights and barons bold,
In weeds of peace high triumphs hold,
With store of ladies, whose bright eyes
Rain influence, and judge the prize
Of wit or arms, while both contend
To win her grace whom all commend.
There let Hymen oft appear
In saffron robe, with taper clear,
And pomp, and feast, and revelry,
With mask, and antique pageantry;
Such sights as youthful poets dream
On summer eves by haunted stream.
Then to the well-trod stage anon,
If Jonson's learned sock be on,
Or sweetest Shakespeare, Fancy's child,
Warble his native wood notes wild.
    And ever against eating cares
Lap me in soft Lydian airs
Married to immortal verse,
Such as the meeting soul may pierce
In notes, with many a winding bout
Of linked sweetness long drawn out,
With wanton heed and giddy cunning,
The melting voice through mazes running,
Untwisting all the chains that tie
The hidden soul of harmony;
That Orpheus' self may heave his head
From golden slumber, on a bed

"Towers and battlements it sees
Bosomed high in tufted trees."—*p. 158.*

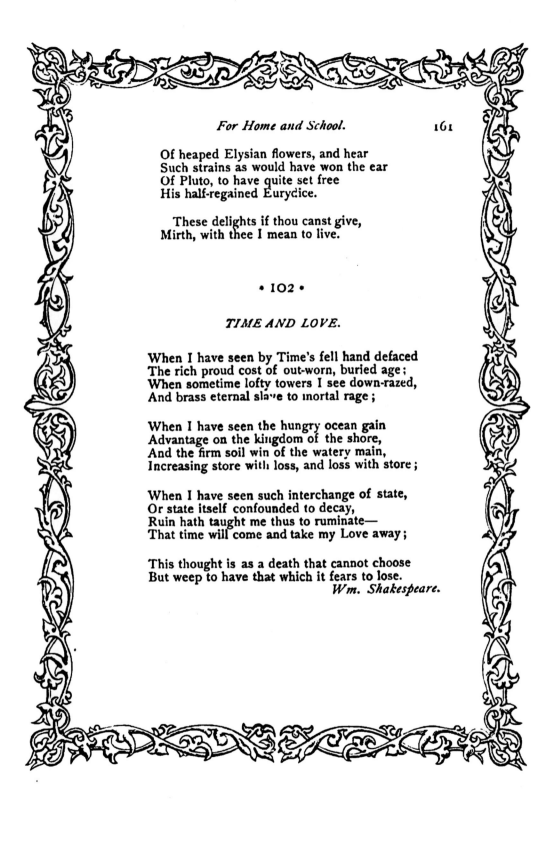

Of heaped Elysian flowers, and hear
Such strains as would have won the ear
Of Pluto, to have quite set free
His half-regained Eurydice.

These delights if thou canst give,
Mirth, with thee I mean to live.

• 102 •

TIME AND LOVE.

When I have seen by Time's fell hand defaced
The rich proud cost of out-worn, buried age;
When sometime lofty towers I see down-razed,
And brass eternal slave to mortal rage;

When I have seen the hungry ocean gain
Advantage on the kingdom of the shore,
And the firm soil win of the watery main,
Increasing store with loss, and loss with store;

When I have seen such interchange of state,
Or state itself confounded to decay,
Ruin hath taught me thus to ruminate—
That time will come and take my Love away;

This thought is as a death that cannot choose
But weep to have that which it fears to lose.
                    Wm. Shakespeare.

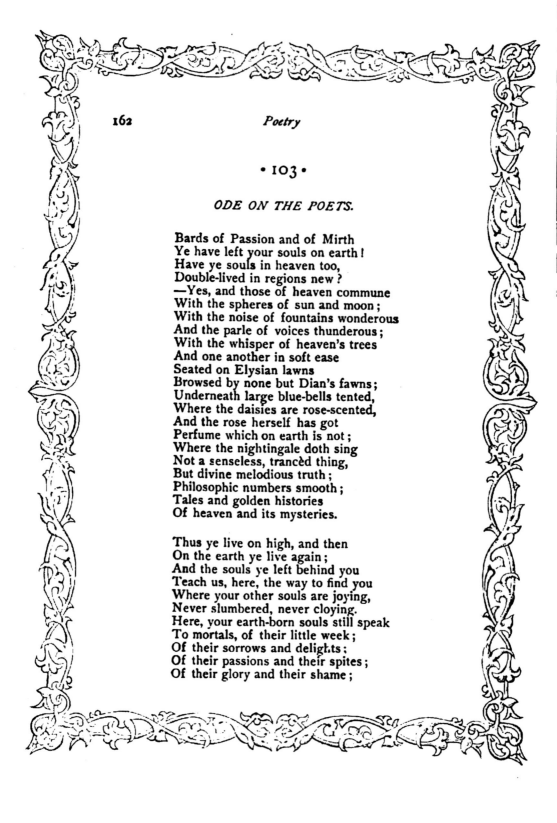

• 103 •

ODE ON THE POETS.

Bards of Passion and of Mirth
Ye have left your souls on earth!
Have ye souls in heaven too,
Double-lived in regions new?
—Yes, and those of heaven commune
With the spheres of sun and moon;
With the noise of fountains wonderous
And the parle of voices thunderous;
With the whisper of heaven's trees
And one another in soft ease
Seated on Elysian lawns
Browsed by none but Dian's fawns;
Underneath large blue-bells tented,
Where the daisies are rose-scented,
And the rose herself has got
Perfume which on earth is not;
Where the nightingale doth sing
Not a senseless, trancèd thing,
But divine melodious truth;
Philosophic numbers smooth;
Tales and golden histories
Of heaven and its mysteries.

Thus ye live on high, and then
On the earth ye live again;
And the souls ye left behind you
Teach us, here, the way to find you
Where your other souls are joying,
Never slumbered, never cloying.
Here, your earth-born souls still speak
To mortals, of their little week;
Of their sorrows and delights;
Of their passions and their spites;
Of their glory and their shame;

" Hard by, a cottage chimney smokes
From betwixt two aged oaks."—*p. 159.*

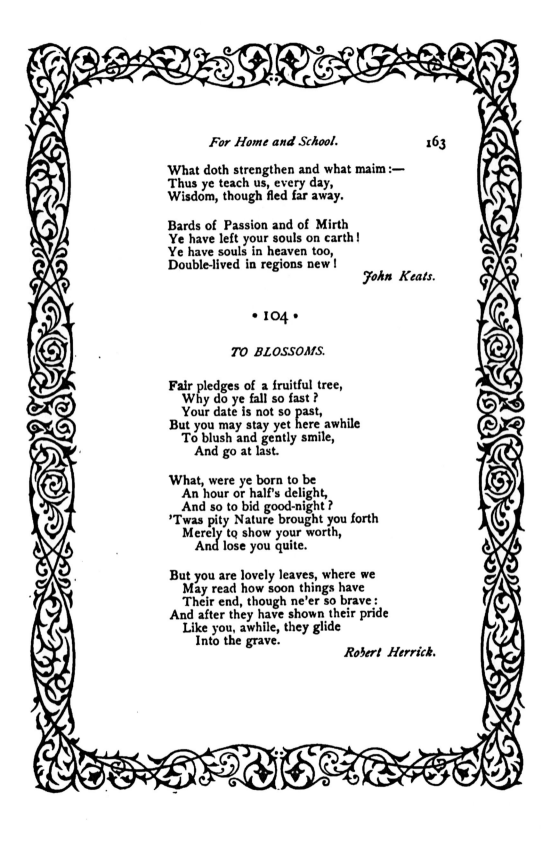

What doth strengthen and what maim :—
Thus ye teach us, every day,
Wisdom, though fled far away.

Bards of Passion and of Mirth
Ye have left your souls on earth!
Ye have souls in heaven too,
Double-lived in regions new!

John Keats.

• 104 •

TO BLOSSOMS.

Fair pledges of a fruitful tree,
  Why do ye fall so fast?
  Your date is not so past,
But you may stay yet here awhile
  To blush and gently smile,
    And go at last.

What, were ye born to be
  An hour or half's delight,
  And so to bid good-night?
'Twas pity Nature brought you forth
  Merely to show your worth,
    And lose you quite.

But you are lovely leaves, where we
  May read how soon things have
  Their end, though ne'er so brave:
And after they have shown their pride
  Like you, awhile, they glide
    Into the grave.

Robert Herrick.

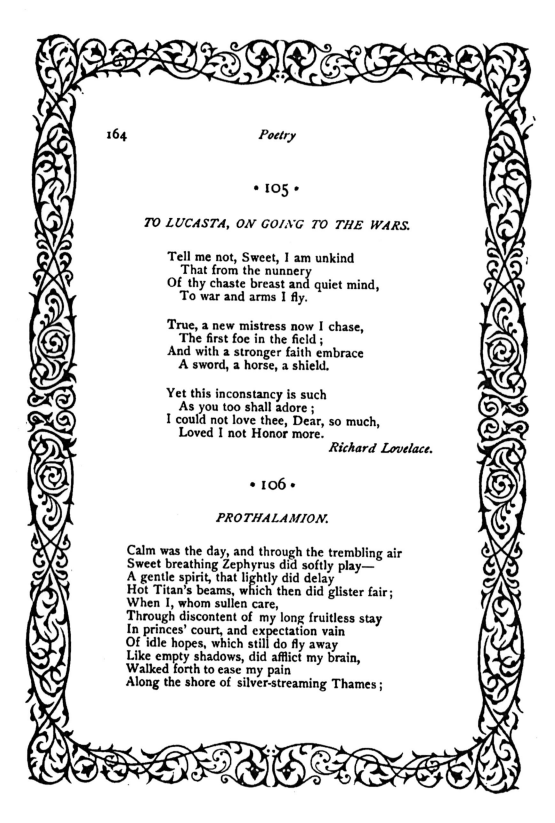

• 105 •

TO LUCASTA, ON GOING TO THE WARS.

Tell me not, Sweet, I am unkind
   That from the nunnery
Of thy chaste breast and quiet mind,
   To war and arms I fly.

True, a new mistress now I chase,
   The first foe in the field;
And with a stronger faith embrace
   A sword, a horse, a shield.

Yet this inconstancy is such
   As you too shall adore;
I could not love thee, Dear, so much,
   Loved I not Honor more.

                        Richard Lovelace.

• 106 •

PROTHALAMION.

Calm was the day, and through the trembling air
Sweet breathing Zephyrus did softly play—
A gentle spirit, that lightly did delay
Hot Titan's beams, which then did glister fair;
When I, whom sullen care,
Through discontent of my long fruitless stay
In princes' court, and expectation vain
Of idle hopes, which still do fly away
Like empty shadows, did afflict my brain,
Walked forth to ease my pain
Along the shore of silver-streaming Thames;

" And he, by friar's lantern led ;
   Tells how the drudging Goblin sweat
   To earn his cream-bowl duly set."—*p. 159.*

Whose rutty bank, the which his river hems,
Was painted all with variable flowers,
And all the meads adorn'd with dainty gems
Fit to deck maiden's bowers,
And crown their paramours
Against the bridal day, which is not long:
    Sweet Thames! run softly, till I end my song.

There in a meadow by the river's side,
A flock of nymphs I chancèd to espy,
All lovely daughters of the flood thereby,
With goodly greenish locks all loose untied
As each had been a bride;
And each one had a little wicker basket
Made of fine twigs, entrailèd curiously,
In which they gathered flowers to fill their flasket,
And with fine fingers cropped full feateously
The tender stalks on high.
Of every sort which in that meadow grew
They gathered some; the violet, pallid blue,
The little daisy that at evening closes,
The virgin lily and the primrose true;
With store of vermeil roses,
To deck their bridegrooms' posies
Against the bridal day, which was not long:
    Sweet Thames! run softly, till I end my song.

With that I saw two swans of goodly hue
Come softly swimming down along the lee;
Two fairer birds I yet did never see;
The snow which doth the top of Pindus strow
Did never whiter show,
Nor Jove himself, when he a swan would be
For love of Leda, whiter did appear;
Yet Leda was, they say, as white as he,
Yet not so white as these, nor nothing near;
So purely white they were
That even the gentle stream, the which them bare,
Seemed foul to them, and bade his billows spare
To wet their silken feathers, lest they might

Soil their fair plumes with water not so fair,
And mar their beauties bright
That shone as Heaven's light
Against their bridal day, which was not long:
　Sweet Thames! run softly, till I end my song.

Eftsoons the nymphs, which now had flowers their fill,
Ran all in haste to see that silver brood
As they came floating on the crystal flood;
Whom when they saw, they stood amazèd still
Their wondering eyes to fill;
Them seemed they never saw a sight so fair
Of fowls, so lovely, that they sure did deem
Them heavenly born, or to be that same pair
Which through the sky draw Venus' silver team;
For sure they did not seem
To be begot of any earthly seed,
But rather angels, or of angels' breed;
Yet were they bred of summer's heat, they say,
In sweetest season, when each flower and weed
The earth did fresh array;
So fresh they seemed as day,
Even as their bridal day, which was not long:
　Sweet Thames! run softly, till I end my song.

Then forth they all out of their baskets drew
Great store of flowers, the honor of the field,
That to the sense did fragrant odors yield,
All which upon those goodly birds they threw
And all the waves did strew,
That like old Peneus' waters they did seem,
When down along by pleasant Tempe's shore
Scattered with flowers, through Thessaly they stream,
That they appear, through lilies' plenteous store,
Like a bride's chamber-floor.
Two of those nymphs meanwhile two garlands bound
Of freshest flowers which in that mead they found,
The which presenting all in trim array,
Their snowy foreheads there withal they crowned,
Whilst one did sing this lay,

Prepared against that day,
Against their bridal day, which was not long;
　Sweet Thames! run softly, till I end my song.

"Ye gentle birds! the world's fair ornament,
And Heaven's glory, whom this happy hour
Doth lead unto your lovers' blissful bower,
Joy may you have, and gentle hearts content
Of your love's complement;
And let fair Venus, that is queen of love,
With her heart-quelling son upon you smile,
Whose smile, they say, hath virtue to remove
All love's dislike, and friendship's faulty guile
For ever to assoil.
Let endless peace your steadfast hearts accord,
And blessed plenty wait upon your board;
And let your bed with pleasures chaste abound,
That fruitful issue may to you afford,
Which may your foes confound,
And make your joys redound
Upon your bridal day, which is not long:
　Sweet Thames! run softly, till I end my song."

So ended she; and all the rest around
To her redoubled that her undersong,
Which said their bridal day should not be long,
And gentle Echo from the neighbor ground
Their accents did resound.
So forth those joyous birds did pass along
Adown the lee that to them murmured low,
As he would speak but that he lacked a tongue,
Yet did by signs his glad affection show,
　Making his stream run slow.
And all the fowl which in his flood did dwell
'Gan flock about these twain, that did excel
The rest, so far as Cynthia doth shend
The lesser stars.　So they, enrangèd well,
Did on those two attend,
And their best service lend
Against their wedding day, which was not long.
　Sweet Thames! run softly, till I end my song.

At length they all to merry London came,
To merry London, my most kindly nurse,
That to me gave this life's first native source,
Though from another place I take my name,
An house of ancient fame !
There when they came, whereas those bricky towers
The which on Thames' broad aged back do ride,
Where now the studious lawyers have their bowers,
There whilome wont the Templar-knights to bide,
Till they decayed through pride ;
Next whereunto there stands a stately place,
Where oft I gainèd gifts and goodly grace
Of that great lord, which therein wont to dwell,
Whose want too well now feels my friendless case ;
But ah ! here fits not well
Old woes, but joys, to tell
Against the bridal day, which is not long ;
  Sweet Thames ! run softly, till I end my song.

Yet therein now doth lodge a noble peer,
Great England's glory and the world's wide wonder;
Whose dreadful name late through all Spain did thunder
And Hercules' two pillars standing near
Did make to quake and fear :
Fair branch of honor, flower of chivalry !
That fillest England with thy triumphs' fame
Joy have thou of thy noble victory,
And endless happiness of thine own name
That promiseth the same ;
That through thy prowess and victorious arms
Thy country may be freed from foreign harms,
And great Eliza's glorious name may ring
Through all the world, filled with thy wide alarms
Which some brave Muse may sing
To ages following,
Upon the bridal day, which is not long ;
  Sweet Thames ! run softly, till I end my song.

From those high towers this noble lord issuing
Like radiant Hesper, when his golden hair
In th' ocean billows he hath bathèd fair,

Descended to the river's open viewing
With a great train ensuing.
Above the rest were goodly to be seen
Two gentle knights of lovely face and feature,
Beseeming well the bower of any queen,
With gifts of wit and ornaments of nature
Fit for so goodly stature,
That like the twins of Jove they seemed in sight,
Which deck the baldric of the Heavens bright;
They two, forth pacing to the river's side,
Received those two fair brides, their love's delight;
Which, at th' appointed tide,
Each one did make his bride
Against their bridal day, which is not long:
   Sweet Thames! run softly, till I end my song.
                   Edmund Spenser.

• 107 •

INCIDENT OF THE FRENCH CAMP.

You know, we French stormed Ratisbon:
   A mile or so away,
On a little mound, Napoleon
   Stood on our storming-day;
With neck out-thrust, you fancy how,
   Legs wide, arms locked behind,
As if to balance the prone brow,
   Oppressive with its mind.

Just as perhaps he mused, " My plans
   That soar, to earth may fall,
Let once my army-leader, Lannes,
   Waver at yonder wall,"—
Out 'twixt the battery-smokes there flew
   A rider, bound on bound
Full-galloping; nor bridle drew
   Until he reached the mound.

Then off there flung in smiling joy,
  And held himself erect,
By just his horse's mane, a boy:
  You hardly could suspect—
So tight he kept his lips compressed,
  Scarce any blood came through—
You looked twice ere you saw his breast
  Was all but shot in two.

"Well," cried he, "Emperor, by God's grace.
  We've got you Ratisbon!
The marshal's in the market-place,
  And you'll be there anon
To see your flag-bird flap his vans
  Where I, to heart's desire,
Perched him!" The chief's eye flashed; his plans
  Soared up again like fire.

The chief's eye flashed; but presently
  Softened itself, as sheathes
A film the mother eagle's eye
  When her bruised eaglet breathes:
"You're wounded!" "Nay," his soldier's pride
  Touched to the quick, he said:
"I'm killed, sire!" and, his chief beside,
Smiling, the boy fell dead.

Robert Browning

• 108 •

TO A SKY-LARK.

Hail to thee, blithe spirit!
  Bird thou never wert,
That from heaven, or near it,
  Pourest thy full heart
In profuse strains of unpremeditated art.

Higher still and higher
From the earth thou springest
Like a cloud of fire;
The blue deep thou wingest,
And singing still dost soar, and soaring ever singest.

In the golden lightning
Of the sunken sun
O'er which clouds are brightening,
Thou dost float and run,
Like an unbodied joy whose race is just begun.

The pale purple even
Melts around thy flight;
Like a star of heaven,
In the broad daylight
Thou art unseen, but yet I hear thy shrill delight.

Keen as are the arrows
Of that silver sphere,
Whose intense lamp narrows
In the white dawn clear,
Until we hardly see, we feel that it is there.

All the earth and air
With thy voice is loud,
As, when night is bare,
From one lonely cloud
The moon rains out her beams, and heaven is overflowed.

What thou art we know not;
What is most like thee?
From rainbow clouds there flow not
Drops so bright to see,
As from thy presence showers a rain of melody.

Like a poet hidden
In the light of thought,
Singing hymns unbidden,
Till the world is wrought
To sympathy with hopes and fears it heeded not;

Like a high-born maiden
In a palace tower,
Soothing her love-laden
Soul in secret hour
With music sweet as love, which overflows her bower;

Like a glow-worm golden
In a dell of dew,
Scattering unbeholden
Its ærial hue
Among the flowers and grass, which screen it from the view;

Like a rose embowered
In its own green leaves,
By warm winds deflowered
Till the scent it gives
Makes   faint   with   too   much   sweet   these   heavy-wingèd
thieves.

Sound of vernal showers
On the twinkling grass;
Rain awakened flowers,
All that ever was
Joyous, and clear, and fresh, thy music doth surpass.

Teach us, sprite or bird,
What sweet thoughts are thine;
I have never heard
Praise of love or wine
That panted forth a flood of rapture so divine.

Chorus hymeneal
Or triumphal chant
Matched with thine would be all
But an empty vaunt—
A thing wherein we feel there is some hidden want.

What objects are the fountains
Of thy happy strain?
What fields, or waves, or mountains?
What shapes of sky or plain?
What love of thine own kind? what ignorance of pain?

With thy clear keen joyance
    Languor cannot be :
Shadow of annoyance
    Never came near thee :
Thou lovest ; but ne'er knew love's sad satiety.

Waking or asleep,
    Thou of death must deem
Things more true and deep
    Than we mortals dream,
Or how could thy notes flow in such a crystal stream ?

We look before and after
    And pine for what is not,
Our sincerest laughter
    With some pain is fraught ;
Our sweetest songs are those that tell of saddest thought.

Yet if we could scorn
    Hate, and pride, and fear ;
If we were things born
    Not to shed a tear,
I know not how thy joy we ever should come near.

Better than all measures
    Of delightful sound.
Better than all treasures
    That in books are found,
Thy skill to poet were, thou scorner of the ground !

Teach me half the gladness
    That thy brain must know,
Such harmonious madness
    From my lips would flow,
The world should listen then, as I am listening now !
                    P. B. Shelley.

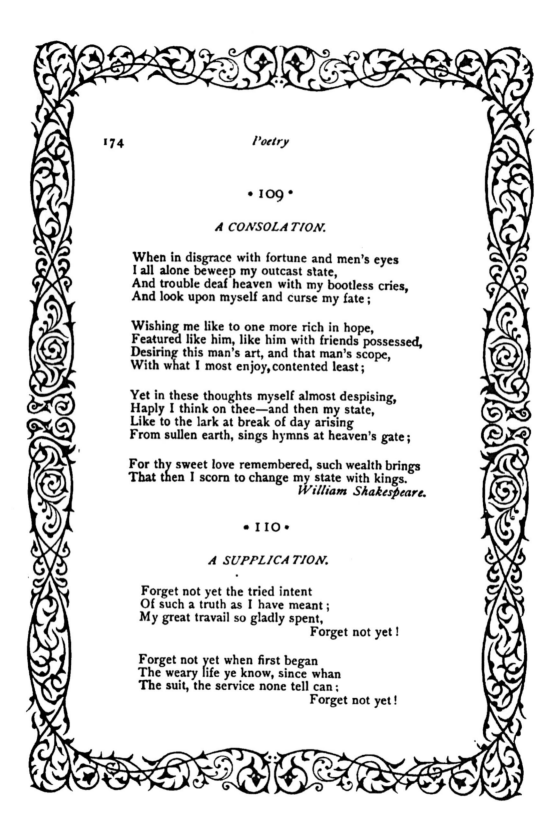

• 109 •

A CONSOLATION.

When in disgrace with fortune and men's eyes
I all alone beweep my outcast state,
And trouble deaf heaven with my bootless cries,
And look upon myself and curse my fate;

Wishing me like to one more rich in hope,
Featured like him, like him with friends possessed,
Desiring this man's art, and that man's scope,
With what I most enjoy, contented least;

Yet in these thoughts myself almost despising,
Haply I think on thee—and then my state,
Like to the lark at break of day arising
From sullen earth, sings hymns at heaven's gate;

For thy sweet love remembered, such wealth brings
That then I scorn to change my state with kings.
William Shakespeare.

• 110 •

A SUPPLICATION.

Forget not yet the tried intent
Of such a truth as I have meant;
My great travail so gladly spent,
      Forget not yet!

Forget not yet when first began
The weary life ye know, since whan
The suit, the service none tell can;
      Forget not yet!

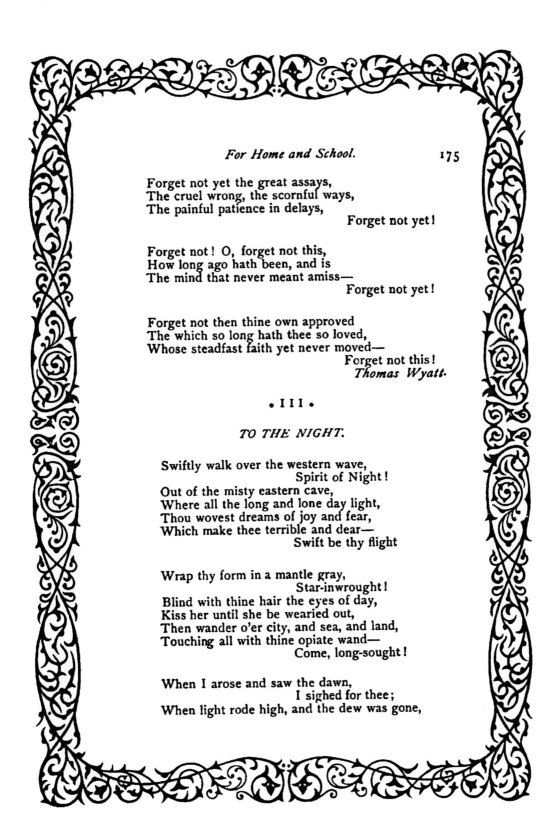

Forget not yet the great assays,
The cruel wrong, the scornful ways,
The painful patience in delays,
                    Forget not yet!

Forget not! O, forget not this,
How long ago hath been, and is
The mind that never meant amiss—
                    Forget not yet!

Forget not then thine own approved
The which so long hath thee so loved,
Whose steadfast faith yet never moved—
                    Forget not this!
                    Thomas Wyatt.

• I I I •

TO THE NIGHT.

Swiftly walk over the western wave,
                    Spirit of Night!
Out of the misty eastern cave,
Where all the long and lone day light,
Thou wovest dreams of joy and fear,
Which make thee terrible and dear—
                    Swift be thy flight

Wrap thy form in a mantle gray,
                    Star-inwrought!
Blind with thine hair the eyes of day,
Kiss her until she be wearied out,
Then wander o'er city, and sea, and land,
Touching all with thine opiate wand—
                    Come, long-sought!

When I arose and saw the dawn,
                    I sighed for thee;
When light rode high, and the dew was gone,

And noon lay heavy on flower and tree,
And the weary Day turned to his rest
Lingering like an unloved guest,
    I sighed for thee.

Thy brother Death came, and cried
    Wouldst thou me?
Thy sweet child Sleep, the filmy-eyed,
Murmured like a noon-tide bee,
Shall I nestle near thy side?
Wouldst thou me? And I replied
    No, not thee!

Death will come when thou art dead,
    Soon, too soon—
Sleep will come when thou art fled;
Of neither would I ask the boon
I ask of thee, beloved Night—
Swift be thine approaching flight,
    Come soon, soon!
      P. B. Shelley.

• 112 •

TO A FIELD MOUSE.

Wee, sleekit, cow'rin', tim'rous beastie,
O, what a panic's in thy breastie!
Thou need na start awa sae hasty,
Wi' bickering brattle!
I wad be laith to rin an' chase thee
Wi' murd'ring pattle!

I'm truly sorry man's dominion
Has broken nature's social union,
And justifies that ill opinion
Which makes thee startle
At me, thy poor earth-born companion,
And fellow-mortal!

I doubt na, whyles, but thou may thieve;
What then? poor beastie, thou maun live!

A daimen icker in a thrave
'S a sma' request :
I'll get a blessing wi' the lave,
And never miss't !

Thy wee bit housie too, in ruin !
Its silly wa's the win's are strewin' :
An' naething, now, to big a new ane,
O' foggage green !
An bleak December's winds ensuin'
Baith snell an' keen !

Thou saw the fields laid bare an' waste
An' weary winter comin' fast,
An' cozie here, beneath the blast,
Thou thought to dwell,
Till crash ! the cruel coulter past
Out thro' thy cell.

That wee bit heap o' leaves an' stibble
Has cost thee mony a weary nibble !
Now thou's turn'd out, for a' thy trouble,
But house or hald,
To thole the winter's sleety dribble
An' cranreuch cauld !

But mousie, thou art no thy lane
In proving foresight may be vain :
The best laid schemes o' mice an' men
Gang aft a-gley,
An' lea'e us nought but grief and pain,
For promised joy.

Still thou art blest, compared wi' me !
The present only toucheth thee :
But, och ! I backward cast my e'e
On prospects drear !
An' forward, tho' I canna see,
I guess an' fear.

Robert Burns.

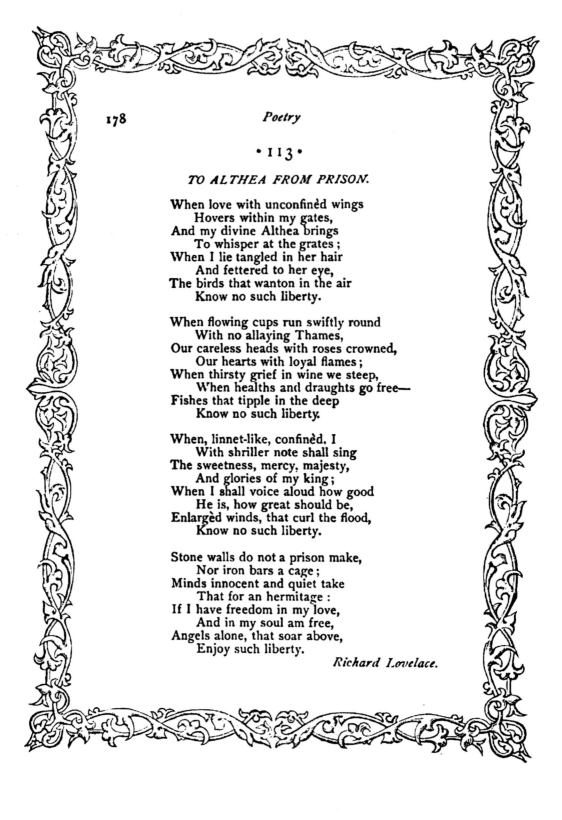

• 113 •

TO ALTHEA FROM PRISON.

When love with unconfinèd wings
   Hovers within my gates,
And my divine Althea brings
   To whisper at the grates ;
When I lie tangled in her hair
   And fettered to her eye,
The birds that wanton in the air
   Know no such liberty.

When flowing cups run swiftly round
   With no allaying Thames,
Our careless heads with roses crowned,
   Our hearts with loyal flames ;
When thirsty grief in wine we steep,
   When healths and draughts go free—
Fishes that tipple in the deep
   Know no such liberty.

When, linnet-like, confinèd, I
   With shriller note shall sing
The sweetness, mercy, majesty,
   And glories of my king ;
When I shall voice aloud how good
   He is, how great should be,
Enlargèd winds, that curl the flood,
   Know no such liberty.

Stone walls do not a prison make,
   Nor iron bars a cage ;
Minds innocent and quiet take
   That for an hermitage :
If I have freedom in my love,
   And in my soul am free,
Angels alone, that soar above,
   Enjoy such liberty.

Richard Lovelace.

• I I 4 •

ODE ON IMMORTALITY.

There was a time when meadow, grove, and stream,
The earth and every common sight
　　To me did seem
　　Apparelled in celestial light,
The glory and the freshness of a dream.
It is not now as it has been of yore ;—
　　Turn wheresoe'er I may,
　　By night or day,
The things which I have seen I now can see no more !

　　The rainbow comes and goes,
　　And lovely is the rose ;
　　The moon doth with delight
Look round her when the heavens are bare ;
　　Waters on a starry night
　　Are beautiful and fair ;
The sunshine is a glorious birth ;
But yet I know, where'er I go,
That there hath passed away a glory from the earth.

Now, while the birds thus sing a joyous song,
　　And while the young lambs bound
　　As to the tabor's sound,
To me alone there came a thought of grief :
A timely utterance gave that thought relief,
　　And I again am strong.
The cataracts blow their trumpets from the steep,—
No more shall grief of mine the season wrong ;
I hear the echoes through the mountains throng,
The winds come to me from the fields of sleep,
　　And all the earth is gay ;
　　Land and sea

Give themselves up to jollity,
And with the heart of May
Doth every beast keep holiday;
Thou child of joy
Shout round me, let me hear thy shouts, thou happy shep-
herd boy!

Ye blessed creatures, I have heard the call
Ye to each other make; I see
The heavens laugh with you in your jubilee;
My heart is at your festival,
My head hath its coronal,
The fulness of your bliss, I feel—I feel it all.
O evil day! if I were sullen
While earth herself is adorning
This sweet May morning;
And the children are pulling
On every side,
In a thousand valleys far and wide,
Fresh flowers; while the sun shines warm
And the babe leaps up on his mother's arm:
I hear, I hear, with joy I hear!
But there's a tree, of many, one,
A single field which I have looked upon,
Both of them speak of something that is gone:
The pansy at my feet
Doth the same tale repeat;
Whither is fled the visionary gleam?
Where is it now, the glory and the dream?

Our birth is but a sleep and a forgetting;
The soul that rises with us, our life's star,
Hath had elsewhere its setting
And cometh from afar;
Not in entire forgetfulness,
And not in utter nakedness,
But trailing clouds of glory do we come
From God, who is our home.
Heaven lies about us in our infancy!
Shades of the prison-house begin to close

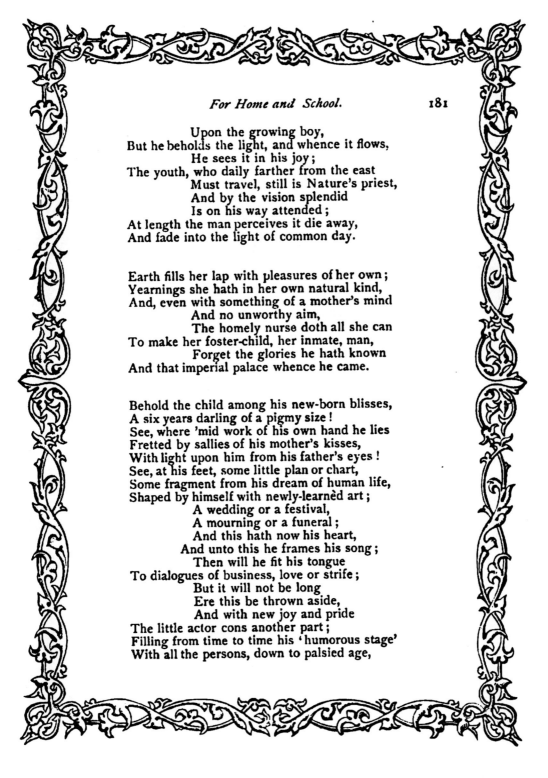

Upon the growing boy,
But he beholds the light, and whence it flows,
He sees it in his joy;
The youth, who daily farther from the east
Must travel, still is Nature's priest,
And by the vision splendid
Is on his way attended;
At length the man perceives it die away,
And fade into the light of common day.

Earth fills her lap with pleasures of her own;
Yearnings she hath in her own natural kind,
And, even with something of a mother's mind
And no unworthy aim,
The homely nurse doth all she can
To make her foster-child, her inmate, man,
Forget the glories he hath known
And that imperial palace whence he came.

Behold the child among his new-born blisses,
A six years darling of a pigmy size!
See, where 'mid work of his own hand he lies
Fretted by sallies of his mother's kisses,
With light upon him from his father's eyes!
See, at his feet, some little plan or chart,
Some fragment from his dream of human life,
Shaped by himself with newly-learnèd art;
A wedding or a festival,
A mourning or a funeral;
And this hath now his heart,
And unto this he frames his song;
Then will he fit his tongue
To dialogues of business, love or strife;
But it will not be long
Ere this be thrown aside,
And with new joy and pride
The little actor cons another part;
Filling from time to time his 'humorous stage'
With all the persons, down to palsied age,

That life brings with her in her equipage;
As if his whole vocation
Were endless imitation.

Thou, whose exterior semblance doth belie
Thy soul's immensity;
Thou best philosopher, who yet dost keep
Thy heritage, thou eye among the blind,
That, deaf and silent, read'st the eternal deep,
Haunted forever by the eternal mind,—
Mighty Prophet! Seer blest!
On whom those truths do rest
Which we are toiling all our lives to find;
Thou, over whom thy immortality
Broods like the day, a master o'er a slave,
A presence which is not to be put by;
Thou little child, yet glorious in the might
Of heaven-born freedom on thy being's height,
Why with such earnest pains dost thou provoke
The years to bring the inevitable yoke,
Thus blindly with thy blessedness at strife?
Full soon thy soul shall have her earthly freight,
And custom lie upon thee with a weight
Heavy as frost, and deep almost as life!

O joy! that in our embers
Is something that doth live,
That Nature yet remembers
What was so fugitive!
The thought of our past years in me doth breed
Perpetual benediction; not indeed
For that which is most worthy to be blest,
Delight and liberty, the simple creed
Of childhood, whether busy or at rest,
With new-fledged hope still fluttering in his breast,
Not for these I raise
The song of thanks and praise;
But for those obstinate questionings
Of sense and outward things,
Fallings from us, vanishings,

Blank misgivings of a creature
Moving about in worlds not realized,
High instincts, before which our mortal nature
Did tremble like a guilty thing surprised;
But for those first affections,
Those shadowy recollections,
Which be they what they may,
Are yet the fountain-light of all our day,
Are yet a master-light of all our seeing;
Uphold us—cherish—and have power to make
Our noisy years seem moments in the being
Of the eternal silence : truths that wake
To perish never;
Which neither listlessness nor mad endeavor
Nor man nor boy,
Nor all that is at enmity with joy,
Can utterly abolish or destroy !
Hence, in a season of calm weather
Though inland far we be,
Our souls have sight of that immortal sea
Which brought us hither;
Can in a moment travel thither—
And see the children sport upon the shore,
And hear the mighty waters rolling evermore.

Then sing ye birds, sing, sing a joyous song !
And let the young lambs bound
As to the tabor's sound !
We, in thought, will join your throng;
Ye that judge and ye that play,
Ye that through your hearts to-day
Feel the gladness of the May !
What though the radiance which was once so bright
Be now for ever taken from my sight,
Though nothing can bring back the hour
Of splendor in the grass, of glory in the flower;
We will grieve not, rather find
Strength in what remains behind,
In the primal sympathy
Which having been, must ever be.

In the soothing thoughts that spring
Out of human suffering,
In the faith that looks through death,
In years that bring the philosophic mind.

And O, ye fountains, meadows, hills, and groves,
Forbode not any severing of our loves !
Yet in my heart of hearts I feel your might ;
I only have relinquished one delight
To live beneath your more habitual sway ;
I love the brooks which down their channels fret
Even more than when I tripped lightly as they ;
The innocent brightness of a new-born day
Is lovely yet ;
The clouds that gather round the setting sun
Do take a sober coloring from an eye
That hath kept watch o'er man's mortality ;
Another race hath been, and other palms are won.
Thanks to the human heart by which we live,
Thanks to its tenderness, its joys, and fears,
To me the meanest flower that blows can give
Thoughts that do often lie too deep for tears.
                          William Wordsworth.

• 115 •

WINTER.

When icicles hang by the wall,
   And Dick the shepherd blows his nail,
And Tom bears logs into the hall,
   And milk comes frozen home in pail ;
When blood is nipped, and ways be foul,
   Then nightly sings the staring owl .
         Tuwhoo !
Tuwhit ! tuwhoo ! A merry note !
   While greasy Joan doth keel the pot.

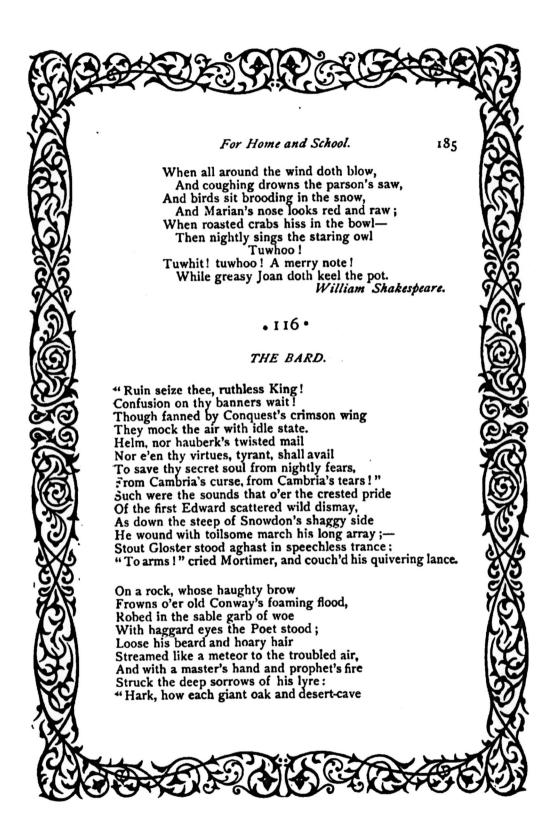

When all around the wind doth blow,
    And coughing drowns the parson's saw,
And birds sit brooding in the snow,
    And Marian's nose looks red and raw;
When roasted crabs hiss in the bowl—
    Then nightly sings the staring owl
        Tuwhoo!
Tuwhit! tuwhoo! A merry note!
    While greasy Joan doth keel the pot.
          William Shakespeare.

• 116 •

THE BARD.

"Ruin seize thee, ruthless King!
Confusion on thy banners wait!
Though fanned by Conquest's crimson wing
They mock the air with idle state.
Helm, nor hauberk's twisted mail
Nor e'en thy virtues, tyrant, shall avail
To save thy secret soul from nightly fears,
From Cambria's curse, from Cambria's tears!"
Such were the sounds that o'er the crested pride
Of the first Edward scattered wild dismay,
As down the steep of Snowdon's shaggy side
He wound with toilsome march his long array;—
Stout Gloster stood aghast in speechless trance:
"To arms!" cried Mortimer, and couch'd his quivering lance.

On a rock, whose haughty brow
Frowns o'er old Conway's foaming flood,
Robed in the sable garb of woe
With haggard eyes the Poet stood;
Loose his beard and hoary hair
Streamed like a meteor to the troubled air,
And with a master's hand and prophet's fire
Struck the deep sorrows of his lyre:
"Hark, how each giant oak and desert-cave

Sighs to the torrent's awful voice beneath !
O'er thee, O King ! their hundred arms they wave,
Revenge on thee in hoarser murmurs breathe :
Vocal no more, since Cambria's fatal day,
To high-born Hoel's harp, or soft Llewellyn's lay.

" Cold is Cadwallo's tongue,
That hushed the stormy main !
Brave Urien sleeps upon his craggy bed ;
Mountains, ye mourn in vain
Modred, whose magic song
Made huge Plinlimmon bow his cloud-topped head.
On dreary Arvon's shore they lie
Smeared with gore and ghastly pale ;
Far, far aloof the affrighted ravens sail ;
The famish'd eagle screams, and passes by.
Dear lost companions of my tuneful art,
Dear as the light that visits these sad eyes,
Dear as the ruddy drops that warm my heart,
Ye died amidst your dying country's cries—
No more I weep ; They do not sleep ;
On yonder cliffs, a grisly band,
I see them sit ; they linger yet,
Avengers of their native land ;
With me in dreadful harmony they join,
And weave with bloody hands the tissue of thy line.

" Weave the warp and weave the woof
The winding sheet of Edward's race ;
Give ample room and verge enough
The characters of hell to trace.
Mark the year and mark the night
When Severn shall re-echo with affright
The shrieks of death through Berkley's roof that ring,
Shrieks of an agonizing king !
She-wolf of France, with unrelenting fangs
That tear'st the bowels of thy mangled mate,
From thee be born, who o'er thy country hangs
The scourge of Heaven ! What terrors round him wait !
Amazement in his van, with Flight combined,
And Sorrow's faded form, and Solitude behind.

" Mighty victor, mighty lord,
Low on his funeral couch he lies!
No pitying heart, no eye, afford
A tear to grace his obsequies.
Is the sable warrior fled ?
Thy son is gone.   He rests among the dead.
The swarm that in thy noon-tide beam were born ?
Gone to salute the rising morn.
Fair laughs the Morn, and soft the zephyr blows,
While proudly riding o'er the azure realm
In gallant trim the gilded Vessel goes ;
Youth on the prow, and Pleasure at the helm ;
Regardless of the sweeping Whirlwind's sway,
That hushed in grim repose expects his evening prey.

" Fill high the sparkling bowl,
The rich repast prepare ;
Reft of a crown, he yet may share the feast ;
Close by the regal chair
Fell Thirst and Famine scowl
A baleful smile upon their baffled guest.
Heard ye the din of battle bray,
Lance to lance, and horse to horse ?
Long years of havoc urge their destined course,
And through the kindred squadrons mow their way.
Ye towers of Julius, London's lasting shame,
With many a foul and midnight murder fed,
Revere his consort's faith, his father's fame,
And spare the meek usurper's holy head !
Above, below, the rose of snow,
Twined with her blushing foe we spread ;
The bristled boar in infant gore
Wallows beneath the thorny shade.
Now, brothers, bending o'er the accursèd loom,
Stamp we our vengeance deep, and ratify his doom.

" Edward, lo ! to sudden fate
(Weave we the woof; The thread is spun ;)
Half of thy heart we consecrate.
(The web is wove; The work is done ;)
Stay, O stay ! nor thus forlorn

Leave me unblessed, unpitied here to mourn:
In yon bright track that fires the western skies
They melt, they vanish from my eyes,
But O! what solemn scenes on Snowdon's height
Descending slow, their glittering skirts unroll?
Visions of glory, spare my aching sight!
Ye unborn ages, crowd not on my soul!
No more our long-lost Arthur we bewail:—
All hail, ye genuine kings! Britannia's issue, hail!

"Girt with many a baron bold
Sublime their starry fronts they rear;
And gorgeous dames, and statesmen old
In bearded majesty, appear.
In the midst a form divine!
Her eye proclaims her of the Briton line:
Her lion port, her awe-commanding face
Attempered sweet to virgin grace.
What strings symphonious tremble in the air,
What strains of vocal transport round her play!
Hear from the grave, great Taliessin, hear;
They breathe a soul to animate thy clay.
Bright Rapture calls, and soaring as she sings,
Waves in the eye of Heaven her many-colored wings.

"The verse adorn again
Fierce War and faithful love
And Truth severe by fairy Fiction drest.
In buskined measures move
Pale Grief, and pleasing Pain,
With Horror, tyrant of the throbbing breast.
A voice as of the cherub-choir
Gales from blooming Eden bear,
And distant warblings lessen on my ear
That lost in long futurity expire.
Fond, impious man, think'st thou yon sanguine cloud,
Raised by thy breath, has quenched the orb of day?
To-morrow he repairs the golden flood
And warms the nations with redoubled ray.
Enough for me; with joy I see
The different doom our fates assign;

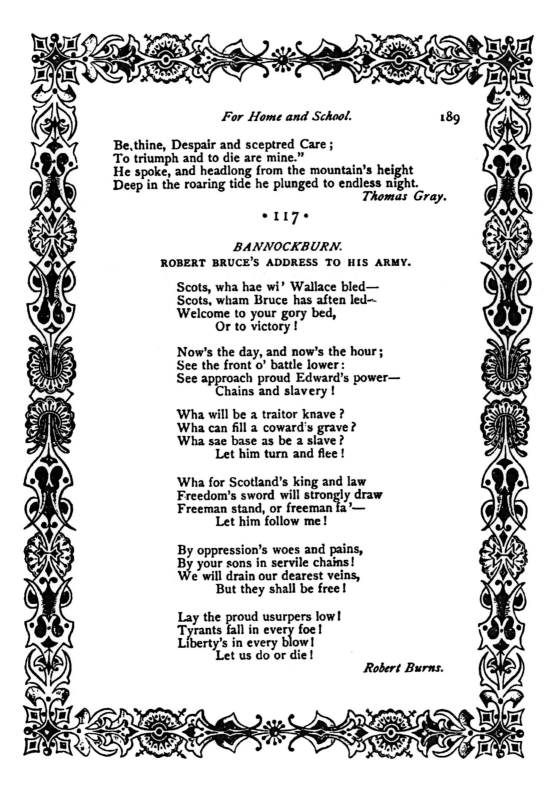

Be,thine, Despair and sceptred Care ;
To triumph and to die are mine."
He spoke, and headlong from the mountain's height
Deep in the roaring tide he plunged to endless night.
Thomas Gray.

• 117 •

BANNOCKBURN.
ROBERT BRUCE'S ADDRESS TO HIS ARMY.

Scots, wha hae wi' Wallace bled—
Scots, wham Bruce has aften led—
Welcome to your gory bed,
    Or to victory !

Now's the day, and now's the hour ;
See the front o' battle lower :
See approach proud Edward's power—
    Chains and slavery !

Wha will be a traitor knave ?
Wha can fill a coward's grave ?
Wha sae base as be a slave ?
    Let him turn and flee !

Wha for Scotland's king and law
Freedom's sword will strongly draw
Freeman stand, or freeman fa'—
    Let him follow me !

By oppression's woes and pains,
By your sons in servile chains !
We will drain our dearest veins,
    But they shall be free !

Lay the proud usurpers low !
Tyrants fall in every foe !
Liberty's in every blow !
    Let us do or die !

Robert Burns.

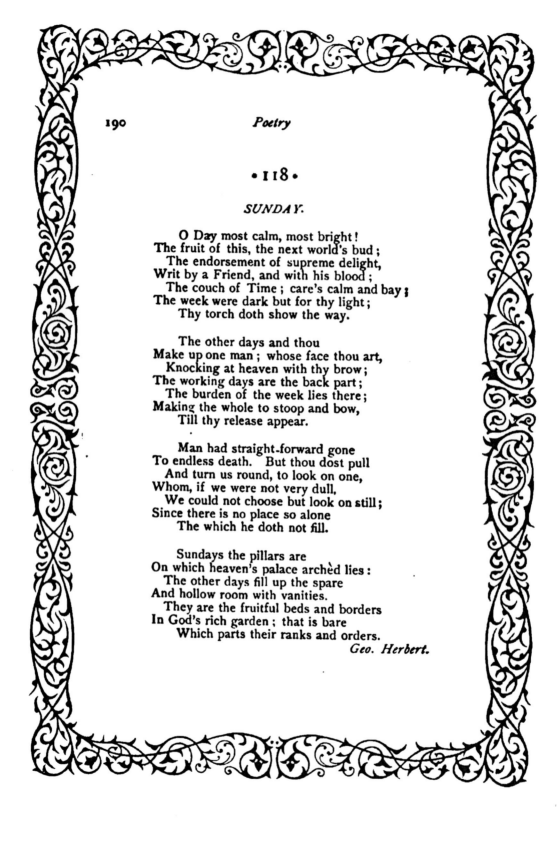

• 118 •

SUNDAY.

O Day most calm, most bright!
The fruit of this, the next world's bud ;
  The endorsement of supreme delight,
Writ by a Friend, and with his blood ;
  The couch of Time ; care's calm and bay ;
The week were dark but for thy light ;
    Thy torch doth show the way.

  The other days and thou
Make up one man ; whose face thou art,
  Knocking at heaven with thy brow ;
The working days are the back part ;
  The burden of the week lies there ;
Making the whole to stoop and bow,
    Till thy release appear.

  Man had straight-forward gone
To endless death. But thou dost pull
  And turn us round, to look on one,
Whom, if we were not very dull,
  We could not choose but look on still ;
Since there is no place so alone
    The which he doth not fill.

  Sundays the pillars are
On which heaven's palace archèd lies :
  The other days fill up the spare
And hollow room with vanities.
  They are the fruitful beds and borders
In God's rich garden ; that is bare
    Which parts their ranks and orders.
          Geo. Herbert.

"Liberty 's in every blow!
Let us do or die!"—*p. 189.*

•119•

THE GARDEN SONG.

Come into the garden, Maud,
  For the black bat, night, has flown,
Come into the garden, Maud,
  I am here at the gate alone;
And the woodbine spices are wafted abroad,
  And the musk of the roses blown.

For a breeze of morning moves,
  And the planet of love is on high,
Beginning to faint in the light that she loves,
  On a bed of daffodil sky,
To faint in the light of the sun she loves,
  To faint in his light, and to die.

All night have the roses heard
  The flute, violin, bassoon;
All night has the casement jessamine stirred
  To the dancers dancing in tune;
Till a silence fell with the waking bird,
  And a hush with the setting moon.

I said to the lily, "There is but one
  With whom she has heart to be gay.
When will the dancers leave her alone?
  She is weary of dance and play."
Now half to the setting moon are gone,
  And half to the rising day;
Low on the sand and loud on the stone
  The last wheel echoes away.

I said to the rose, "The brief night goes
  In babble and revel and wine.
O young lord-lover, what sighs are those,
  For one that will never be thine?

But mine, but mine," so I sware to the rose,
  "For ever and ever, mine."

And the soul of the rose went into my blood,
  As the music clashed in the hall;
And long by the garden lake I stood,
  For I heard your rivulet fall
From the lake to the meadow and on to the wood
  Our wood that is dearer than all;

From the meadow your walks have left so sweet
  That whenever a March wind sighs
He sets the jewel-print of your feet
  In violets blue as your eyes,
To the woody hollows in which we meet
  And the valleys of Paradise.

The slender acacia would not shake
  One long milk-bloom on the tree;
The white lake-blossom fell into the lake,
  As the pimpernel dozed on the lea;
But the rose was awake all night for your sake,
  Knowing your promise to me;
The lilies and roses were all awake,
  They sighed for the dawn and thee.

Queen rose of the rosebud garden of girls,
  Come hither, the dances are done,
In gloss of satin and glimmer of pearls,
  Queen lily and rose in one;
Shine out, little head, sunning over with curls,
  To the flowers, and be their sun.

There has fallen a splendid tear
  From the passion-flower at the gate.
She is coming, my dove, my dear;
  She is coming, my life, my fate;
The red rose cries, "She is near, she is near;"
  And the white rose weeps, "She is late;"
The larkspur listens, "I hear, I hear;"
  And the lily whispers, "I wait."

She is coming, my own, my sweet;
  Were it ever so airy a tread,
My heart would hear her and beat,
  Were it earth in an earthy bed;
My dust would hear her and beat,
  Had I lain for a century dead;
Would start and tremble under her feet,
  And blossom in purple and red.
                              Alfred Tennyson.

• 120 •

TELLING THE BEES.

Here is the place; right over the hill
  Runs the path I took;
You can see the gap in the old wall still,
  And the stepping-stones in the shallow brook.

There is the house, with the gate red-barred,
  And the poplars tall;
And the barn's brown length, and the cattle-yard,
  And the white horns tossing above the wall.

There are the bee-hives ranged in the sun;
  And down by the brink
Of the brook are her poor flowers, weed-o'errun,
  Pansy and daffodil, rose and pink.

A year has gone, as the tortoise goes,
  Heavy and slow;
And the same rose blows, and the same sun glows,
  And the same brook sings of a year ago.

There's the same sweet clover-smell in the breeze;
  And the June sun warm
Tangles his wings of fire in the trees,
  Setting as then, over Fernside farm.

I mind me how with a lover's care
  From my Sunday coat
I brushed off the burrs, and smoothed my hair,
  And cooled at the brook-side my brow and throat.

Since we parted, a month had passed,—
  To love, a year;
Down through the beeches I looked at last
  On the little red gate and the well sweep near.

I can see it all now,—the slantwise rain
  Of light through the leaves,
The sundown's blaze on her window-pane,
  The bloom of her roses under the eaves.

Just the same as a month before,—
  The house and the trees,
The barn's brown gable, the vine by the door,—
  Nothing changed but the hives of bees.

Before them under the garden wall,
  Forward and back,
Went drearily singing the chore-girl small,
  Draping each hive with a shred of black.

Trembling I listened; the summer sun
  Had the chill of snow;
For I knew she was telling the bees of one
  Gone on the journey we all must go!

Then I said to myself, "My Mary weeps
  For the dead to-day;
Haply her blind old grandsire sleeps
  The fret and pain of his age away."

But her dog whined low; on the doorway sill,
  With his cane to his chin
The old man sat; and the chore-girl still
  Sung to the bees stealing out and in.

And the song she was singing, ever since
  In my ear sounds on :—
"Stay at home, pretty bees, fly not hence!
  Mistress Mary is dead and gone!"
                                    John G. Whittier.

• 121 •

Flower in the crannied wall,
I pluck you out of the crannies;—
Hold you here, root and all, in my hand,
Little flower—but if I could understand
What you are, root and all, and all in all
I should know what God and man is.
                                    Alfred Tennyson.

• 122 •

ROBIN HOOD AND THE BISHOP OF HEREFORD.

Some will talk of bold Robin Hood,
  And some of barons bold;
But I'll tell you how he served the bishop of Hereford,
  When he robbed him of his gold.

As it befel in merry Barnsdale,
  All under the greenwood tree,
The bishop of Hereford was to come by,
  With all his company.

"Come kill me a ven'son," said bold Robin Hood,
  "Come kill me a good fat deer;
The bishop of Hereford is to dine with me to-day,
  And he shall pay well for his cheer."

"We'll kill a fat ven'son," said bold Robin Hood,
  "And dress it by the highway side;
And we will watch the bishop narrowly,
  Lest some other way he should ride."

Robin Hood dressed himself in shepherd's attire,
    With six of his men also;
And, when the bishop of Hereford came by,
    They about the fire did go.

"O what is the matter?" then said the bishop,
    "Or for whom do you make this ado?
Or why do you kill the king's ven'son,
    When your company is so few?"

"We are shepherds," said bold Robin Hood,
    "And we keep sheep all the year,
And we are disposed to be merry this day,
    And to kill of the king's fat deer."

"You are brave fellows," said the bishop,
    "And the king of your doings shall know;
Therefore make haste and come along with me,
    For before the king you shall go."

"O pardon, O pardon," said bold Robin Hood,
    "O pardon, I thee pray!
For it becomes not your lordship's coat
    To take so many lives away."

"No pardon, no pardon," said the bishop,
    "No pardon I thee owe;
Therefore make haste and come along with me,
    For before the king you shall go."

Then Robin set his back against a tree,
    And his foot against a thorn,
And from underneath his shepherd's coat.
    He pulled out a bugle horn.

He put the little end to his mouth,
    And a loud blast did he blow,
Till three score and ten of bold Robin's men
    Came running all in a row.

All making obeisance to bold Robin Hood;
  'Twas a comely sight for to see.
"What is the matter, master?" said Little John,
  "That you blow so hastily?"

"O here is the bishop of Hereford,
  And no pardon we shall have:"
"Cut off his head, master," said Little John,
  "And throw him into his grave."

"O pardon, O pardon," said the bishop,
  "O pardon, I thee pray!
For if I had known it had been you,
  I'd have gone some other way."

"No pardon, no pardon," said bold Robin Hood,
  "No pardon I thee owe;
Therefore make haste and come along with me
  For to merry Barnsdale you shall go."

Then Robin he took the bishop by the hand,
  And led him to merry Barnsdale;
He made him to stay and sup with him that night,
  And to drink wine, beer, and ale.

"Call in a reckoning," said the bishop,
  "For methinks it grows wondrous high:"
"Lend me your purse, master," said Little John,
  "And I'll tell you by and by."

Then Little John took the bishop's cloak,
  And spread it upon the ground,
And out of the bishop's portmanteau
  He took three hundred pound.

"Here's money enough, master," said Little John,
  "And a comely sight 'tis to see;
It makes me in charity with the bishop,
  Though he heartily loveth not me."

Robin Hood took the bishop by the hand,
  And he caused the music to play;
And he made the bishop to dance in his boots,
  And glad he could so get away.

                              Old Ballad.

• I 2 3 •

AN ELEGY ON THE DEATH OF A MAD DOG.

Good people all, of every sort
  Give ear unto my song;
And if you find it wondrous short,
  It cannot hold you long.

In Islington there lived a man,
  Of whom the world might say,
That still a goodly race he ran
  Whene'er he went to pray.

A kind and gentle heart he had,
  To comfort friends and foes;
The naked every day he clad,
  When he put on his clothes.

And in that town a dog was found,
  As many dogs there be,
Both mongrel, puppy, whelp, and hound,
  And curs of low degree.

This dog and man at first were friends;
  But when a pique began,
The dog, to gain his private ends,
  Went mad, and bit the man.

Around from all the neighboring streets,
  The wondering neighbors ran,
And swore the dog had lost his wits,
  To bite so good a man.

The wound it seemed both sore and sad
  To every Christian eye :
And while they swore the dog was mad,
  They swore the man would die.

But soon a wonder came to light,
  That showed the rogues they lied,
The man recovered of the bite,
  The dog it was that died.

Oliver Goldsmith.

• 124 •

THE APPROACH OF THE FAIRIES.

Now the hungry lion roars,
  And the wolf behowls the moon ;
Whilst the heavy ploughman snores,
  All with weary tasks foredone.
Now the wasted brands do glow,
  Whilst the scritch owl scritching loud,
Puts the wretch that lies in woe,
  In remembrance of a shroud.
Now it is the time of night
  That the graves, all gaping wide,
Every one lets forth his sprite,
  In the churchway paths to glide ;
And we fairies that do run,
  By the triple Hecate's team,
From the presence of the sun,
  Following darkness like a dream,
Now are frolic ; not a mouse
  Shall disturb this hallowed house ;
I am sent with broom before,
  To sweep the dust behind the door.

Through the house give glimmering light ;
  By the dead and drowsy fire,
Every elf and fairy sprite,
  Hop as light as bird from brier ;

And this ditty after me,
  Sing and dance it trippingly.
First rehearse this song by rote,
  To each word a warbling note,
Hand in hand, with fairy grace,
  We will sing, and bless this place.
Wm. Shakespeare.

• 125 •

BELSHAZZAR.

Belshazzar is king! Belshazzar is lord!
And a thousand dark nobles all bend at his board:
Fruits glisten, flowers blossom, meats steam, and a flood
Of the wine that man loveth, runs redder than blood;
Wild dancers are there, and a riot of mirth,
And the beauty that maddens the passions of earth:
    And the crowds all shout,
    Till the vast roofs ring,—
" All praise to Belshazzar, Belshazzar the king! "

" Bring forth," cries the Monarch, " the vessels of gold,
Which my father tore down from the temples of old ; —
Bring forth, and we'll drink, while the trumpets are blown,
To the gods of bright silver, of gold, and of stone ;
Bring forth !" and before him the vessels all shine,
And he bows unto Baal, and drinks the dark wine ;
    Whilst the trumpets bray,
    And the cymbals ring,—
" Praise, praise to Belshazzar, Belshazzar the king ! "

Now what cometh—look, look ! —without menace, or call?
Who writes, with the lightning's bright hand, on the wall?
What pierceth the king like the point of a dart ?
What drives the bold blood from his cheek to his heart?
"Chaldeans ! Magicians ! the letters expound ! "
They are read—and Belshazzar is dead on the ground!
    Hark !—the Persian is come
    On a conqueror's wing ;
And a Mede's on the throne of Belshazzar the king.
Barry Cornwall.

• 126 •

TRIUMPH OF CHARIS.

See the chariot at hand here of Love,
　　Wherein my lady rideth !
Each that draws is a swan, or a dove,
　　And well the car, Love guideth.
As she goes, all hearts do duty
　　　Unto her beauty,
And, enamored, do wish, so they might
　　　But enjoy such a sight,
That they still were to run by her side
Through swords, through seas, whither she would ride.

Do but look on her eyes ! they do light
　　All that Love's world compriseth;
Do but look on her hair ! it is bright
　　As Love's star when it riseth !
Do but mark—her forehead's smoother
　　　Than words that soothe her !
And from her arched brows such a grace
　　　Sheds itself through the face,
As alone there, triumphs to the life,
　　All the gain, all the good, of the elements' strife.

Have you seen but a bright lily grow,
　　Before rude hands have touched it ?
Have you marked but the fall of the snow,
　　Before the soil hath smutched it ?
Have you felt the wool of the beaver ?
　　　Or swan's down ever ?
Or have smelt o' the bud of the brier ?
　　　Or nard i' the fire ?
Or have tasted the bag of the bee ?
Oh, so white ! oh, so soft ! oh, so sweet, is she !
Ben. Jonson.

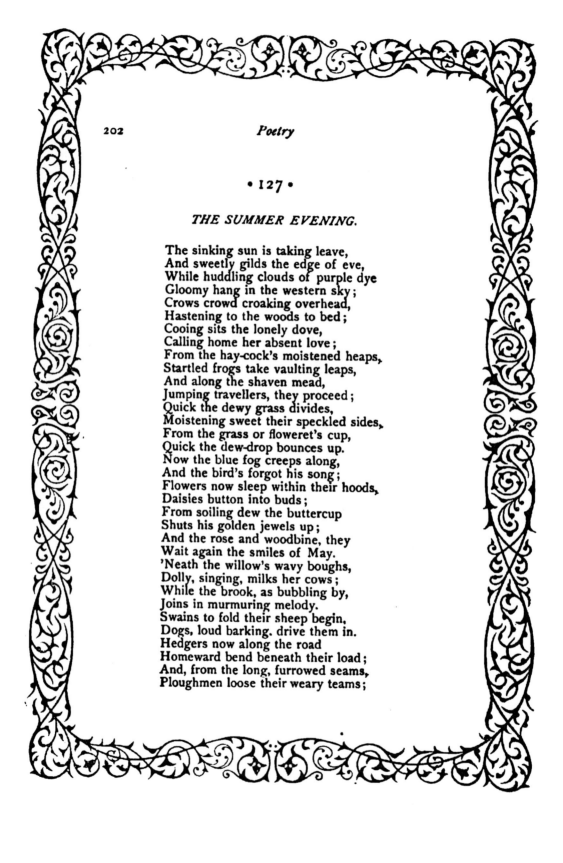

• 127 •

THE SUMMER EVENING.

The sinking sun is taking leave,
And sweetly gilds the edge of eve,
While huddling clouds of purple dye
Gloomy hang in the western sky;
Crows crowd croaking overhead,
Hastening to the woods to bed;
Cooing sits the lonely dove,
Calling home her absent love;
From the hay-cock's moistened heaps,
Startled frogs take vaulting leaps,
And along the shaven mead,
Jumping travellers, they proceed;
Quick the dewy grass divides,
Moistening sweet their speckled sides,
From the grass or floweret's cup,
Quick the dew-drop bounces up.
Now the blue fog creeps along,
And the bird's forgot his song;
Flowers now sleep within their hoods,
Daisies button into buds;
From soiling dew the buttercup
Shuts his golden jewels up;
And the rose and woodbine, they
Wait again the smiles of May.
'Neath the willow's wavy boughs,
Dolly, singing, milks her cows;
While the brook, as bubbling by,
Joins in murmuring melody.
Swains to fold their sheep begin,
Dogs, loud barking. drive them in.
Hedgers now along the road
Homeward bend beneath their load;
And, from the long, furrowed seams,
Ploughmen loose their weary teams;

Ball, with urging lashes mealed
Still so slow to drive afield,
Eager blundering from the plough,
Wants no whip to drive him now;
At the stable-door he stands,
Looking round for friendly hands
To loose the door its fastening pin,
And let him with his corn begin.
The night-wind now, with sooty wings,
In the cotter's chimney sings;
Now, as stretching o'er the bed,
Soft I raise my drowsy head,
Listening to the ushering charms
That shake the elm-tree's massy arms,
Till sweet slumbers stronger creep,
Deeper darkness stealing round;
Then, as rocked, I sink to sleep,
'Mid the wild wind's lulling sound.

John Clare.

• 128 •

THAT EACH THING IS HURT OF ITSELF.

Why fearest thou the outward foe,
  When thou thyself thy harm doth feed?
Of grief or hurt, of pain or woe,
  Within each thing is sown the seed.

So fine was never yet the cloth,
  No smith so hard his iron did beat,
But the one consumèd was by moth,
  T'other with canker all to fret.

The knotty oak and wainscot old,
  Within, doth eat the silly worm;
Even so a mind in envy rolled
  Always within itself doth burn.

Thus every thing that nature wrought
  Within itself its hurt doth bear;
No outward harm need to be sought,
  Where enemies be within so near.

Old English Poetry.

• 129 •

A DEWDROP FALLING.

A dewdrop falling on the wild sea wave,
Exclaimed in fear,—" I perish in this grave ! "
But, in a shell received, that drop of dew
Unto a pearl of marvellous beauty grew ;
And, happy now, the grace did magnify
Which thrust it forth, as it had feared to die ;—
Until again, " I perish quite " it said,
Torn by rude diver from its ocean bed ;
O unbelieving !—so it came to gleam
Chief jewel in a monarch's diadem.

Richard C Trench.

• 130 •

THE LADY OF SHALOTT.

PART I.

On either side the river lie
Long fields of barley and of rye,
That clothe the wold and meet the sky,
And through the field the road runs by
    To many-towered Camelot;
And up and down the people go,
Gazing where the lilies blow
Round an island there below,
    The island of Shalott.

Willows whiten, aspens quiver,
Little breezes dusk and shiver,
Through the wave that runs forever,
By the island in the river
      Flowing down to Camelot.
Four gray walls and four gray towers,
Overlook a space of flowers,
And the silent isle embowers
      The Lady of Shalott.

By the margin, willow-veiled,
Slide the heavy barges trailed
By slow horses ; and unhailed,
The shallop flitteth silken-sailed,
      Skimming down to Camelot ;
But who hath seen her wave her hand ?
Or at the casement seen her stand ?
Or is she known in all the land ?
      The Lady of Shalott.

Only reapers, reaping early
In among the bearded barley,
Hear a song that echoes cheerly
From the river winding clearly,
      Down to towered Camelot ;
And by the moon the reaper weary,
Piling sheaves in uplands airy,
Listening, whispers " 'Tis the fairy
      Lady of Shalott."

PART II.

There she weaves by night and day
A magic web with colors gay.
She has heard a whisper say,
A curse is on her if she stay
      To look down to Camelot.
She knows not what the curse may be,
And so she weaveth steadily,
And little other care hath she,
      The Lady of Shalott.

And moving through a mirror clear
That hangs before her all the year,
Shadows of the world appear.
There she sees the highway near
      Winding down to Camelot.
There the river eddy whirls,
And there the surly village churls,
And the red cloaks of market girls,
      Pass onward from Shalott.

Sometimes a troop of damsels glad,
An abbot on an ambling pad,
Sometimes a curly shepherd lad,
Or long-haired page in crimson clad,
      Goes by to towered Camelot.
And sometimes through the mirror blue
The knights come riding two and two;
She hath no loyal knight and true,
      The Lady of Shalott.

But in her web she still delights
To weave the mirror's magic sights,
For often through the silent nights
A funeral, with plumes and lights
      And music, went to Camelot.
Or when the moon was overhead
Came two young lovers lately wed;
 "I am half-sick of shadows," said
      The Lady of Shalott.

PART III.

A bow-shot from her bower eaves,
He rode between the barley sheaves,
The sun came dazzling through the leaves,
And flamed upon the brazen greaves
      Of bold Sir Lancelot.
A redcross knight forever kneeled
To a lady in his shield,
That sparkled on the yellow field,
      Beside remote Shalott.

" There she weaves by night and day
A magic web with colors gay."—*p. 205.*

The gemmy bridle glittered free,
Like to some branch of stars we see
Hung in the golden galaxy.
The bridle bells rang merrily,
   As he rode down to Camelot:
And from his blazoned baldric slung
A mighty silver bugle hung,
And as he rode his armor rung,
   Beside remote Shalott.

All in the blue unclouded weather
Thick jewelled shone the saddle leather,
The helmet and the helmet feather
Burned like one burning flame together,
   As he rode down to Camelot.
As often through the purple night,
Below the starry clusters bright,
Some bearded meteor, trailing light,
   Moves over still Shalott.

His broad clear brow in sunlight glowed;
On burnished hooves his war-horse trode;
From underneath his helmet flowed
His coal black curls as on he rode,
   As he rode down to Camelot.
From the bank and from the river
He flashed into the crystal mirror,
 "Tirra lirra," by the river
   Sang Sir Lancelot.

She left the web, she left the loom,
She made three paces through the room,
She saw the water-lily bloom,
She saw the helmet and the plume,
   She looked down to Camelot.
Out flew the web and floated wide;
The mirror cracked from side to side;
 "The curse is come upon me," cried
   The Lady of Shalott.

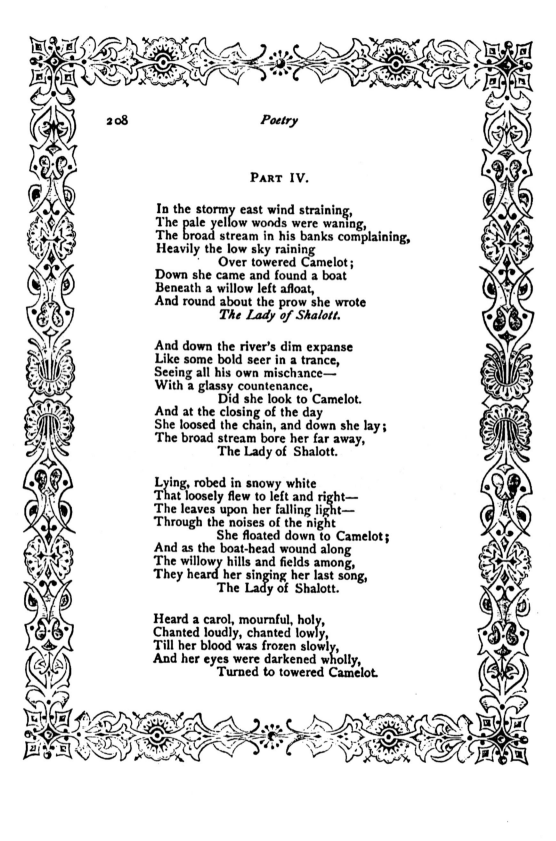

PART IV.

In the stormy east wind straining,
The pale yellow woods were waning,
The broad stream in his banks complaining,
Heavily the low sky raining
        Over towered Camelot;
Down she came and found a boat
Beneath a willow left afloat,
And round about the prow she wrote
    The Lady of Shalott.

And down the river's dim expanse
Like some bold seer in a trance,
Seeing all his own mischance—
With a glassy countenance,
        Did she look to Camelot.
And at the closing of the day
She loosed the chain, and down she lay;
The broad stream bore her far away,
        The Lady of Shalott.

Lying, robed in snowy white
That loosely flew to left and right—
The leaves upon her falling light—
Through the noises of the night
        She floated down to Camelot;
And as the boat-head wound along
The willowy hills and fields among,
They heard her singing her last song,
        The Lady of Shalott.

Heard a carol, mournful, holy,
Chanted loudly, chanted lowly,
Till her blood was frozen slowly,
And her eyes were darkened wholly,
        Turned to towered Camelot.

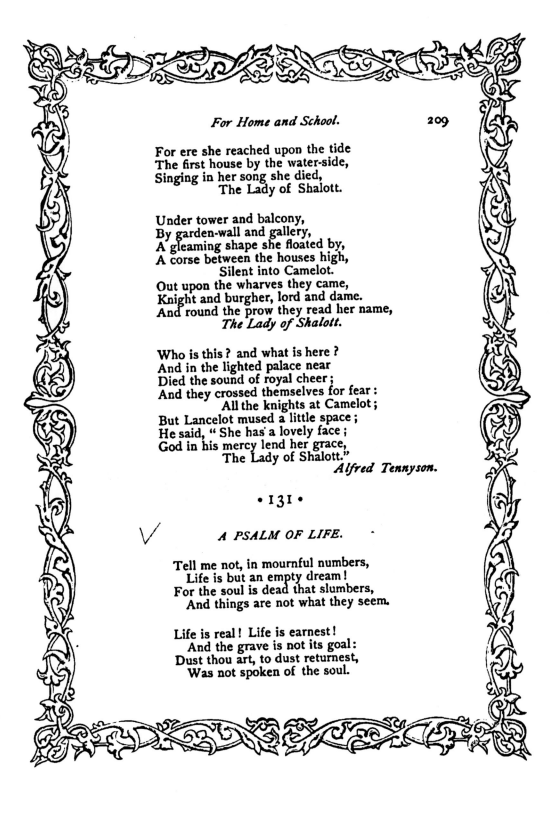

For ere she reached upon the tide
The first house by the water-side,
Singing in her song she died,
  The Lady of Shalott.

Under tower and balcony,
By garden-wall and gallery,
A gleaming shape she floated by,
A corse between the houses high,
  Silent into Camelot.
Out upon the wharves they came,
Knight and burgher, lord and dame.
And round the prow they read her name,
  The Lady of Shalott.

Who is this? and what is here?
And in the lighted palace near
Died the sound of royal cheer;
And they crossed themselves for fear:
  All the knights at Camelot;
But Lancelot mused a little space;
He said, " She has a lovely face;
God in his mercy lend her grace,
  The Lady of Shalott."
     Alfred Tennyson.

• 131 •

A PSALM OF LIFE.

Tell me not, in mournful numbers,
 Life is but an empty dream!
For the soul is dead that slumbers,
 And things are not what they seem.

Life is real! Life is earnest!
 And the grave is not its goal:
Dust thou art, to dust returnest,
 Was not spoken of the soul.

Not enjoyment, and not sorrow,
  Is our destined end or way;
But to act, that each to-morrow
  Find us farther than to-day.

Art is long, and Time is fleeting,
  And our hearts, though stout and brave
Still, like muffled drums, are beating
  Funeral marches to the grave.

In the world's broad field of battle,
  In the bivouac of Life,
Be not like dumb, driven cattle!
  Be a hero in the strife!

Trust no Future, howe'er pleasant!
  Let the dead Past bury its dead!
Act,—act in the living Present!
  Heart within, and God o'erhead!

Lives of great men all remind us
  We can make our lives sublime.
And, departing, leave behind us.
  Footprints on the sands of time :—

Footprints, that perhaps another,
  Sailing o'er life's solemn main,
A forlorn and shipwrecked brother,
  Seeing, shall take heart again.

Let us, then, be up and doing,
  With a heart for any fate;
Still achieving, still pursuing,
  Learn to labor and to wait.
            Henry W. Longfellow.

• 1 3 2 •

ODE TO THE NORTH-EAST WIND.

Welcome, wild North-easter!
　Shame it is to see
Odes to every zephyr;
　Ne'er a verse to thee.
Welcome, black North-easter!
　O'er the German foam;
O'er the Danish moorlands,
　From thy frozen home.
Tired we are of summer,
　Tired of gaudy glare,
Showers soft and steaming,
　Hot and breathless air.
Tired of listless dreaming,
　Through the lazy day;
Jovial wind of winter
　Turn us out to play!
Sweep the golden reed-beds;
　Crisp the lazy dyke;
Hunger into madness
　Every plunging pike.
Fill the lake with wild fowl;
　Fill the marsh with snipe;
While on dreary moorlands
　Lonely curlew pipe.
Through the black fir-forest
　Thunder harsh and dry,
Shattering down the snow-flakes
　Off the curdled sky.
Hark! the brave North-easter!
　Breast-high lies the scent,
On by holt and headland,
　Over heath and bent.
Chime ye dappled darlings,

Through the sleet and snow?
Who can over-ride you?
　Let the horses go!
Chime, ye dappled darlings,
　Down the roaring blast;
You shall see a fox die
　Ere an hour be past.
Go! and rest to-morrow,
　Hunting in your dreams,
While our skates are ringing
　O'er the frozen streams.
Let the luscious South-wind
　Breathe in lovers' sighs,
While the lazy gallants
　Bask in ladies' eyes.
What does he but soften
　Heart alike and pen?
'Tis the hard grey weather
　Breeds hard English men.
What's the soft South-wester?
　'Tis the ladies' breeze,
Bringing home their true loves
　Out of all the seas;
But the black North-easter,
　Through the snow-storm hurled,
Drives our English hearts of oak
　Seaward round the world!
Come! as came our fathers,
　Heralded by thee,
Conquering from the eastward,
　Lords by land and sea.
Come! and strong within us
　Stir the Vikings' blood;
Bracing brain and sinew;
　Blow, thou wind of God!

　　　　　　Charles Kingsley.

• 133 •

THE BUILDERS.

All are architects of Fate,
   Working in these walls of Time;
Some with massive deeds and great,
   Some with ornaments of rhyme.

Nothing useless is, or low;
   Each thing in its place is best;
And what seems but idle show
   Strengthens and supports the rest.

For the structure that we raise,
   Time is with materials filled;
Our to-days and yesterdays
   Are the blocks with which we build.

Truly shape and fashion these;
   Leave no yawning gaps between;
Think not because no man sees,
   Such things will remain unseen.

In the elder days of Art,
   Builders wrought with greatest care
Each minute and unseen part;
   For the Gods see everywhere.

Let us do our work as well,
   Both the unseen and the seen;
Make the house where Gods may dwell,
   Beautiful, entire and clean.

Else our lives are incomplete,
   Standing in these walls of Time,
Broken stairways, where the feet
   Stumble as they seek to climb.

Build to-day, then, strong and sure,
   With a firm and ample base ;
And ascending and secure
   Shall to-morrow find its place.

Thus alone can we attain
   To those turrets, where the eye
Sees the world as one vast plain,
   And one boundless reach of sky.
            Henry W. Longfellow.

• I 34 •

THE PROLOGUE.

Whanné that April with his shourés sote
The droughte of March hath percéd to the rote,
And bathéd every veine in swiche licour
Of which virtue engendred is the flour;
Whan Zephirus eké with his soté brethe
Enspiréd hath in every holt and hethe
The tender croppés, and the yongé sonne
Hath in the Ram his halfé cours yronne,
And smalé foulés maken melodie,
That slepen allé night with open eye,
So priketh hem nature in his corages ;
Than longen folk to gon on pilgrimages,
And palmeres for to seken strangé strondes
To servé halwes couthe in sondry londes ;
And specially, from every shirés ende
Of Englelond, to Canterbury they wende
The holy blisful martyr for to seke,
That hem hath holpén, when that they were seke.

Befelle, that, in that seson on a day,
In Southwerk at the Tabard as I lay,
Redy to wenden on my pilgrimage
To Canterbury with devoute corage,
At night was come into that hostelrie
Wel nine and twenty in a compagnie
Of sondry folk, by aventure yfalle
In felowship, and pilgrimes were they alle,
That toward Canterbury wolden ride ;
The chambres and the stables weren wide,
And wel we weren eséd até beste.

Geoffrey Chaucer.

• 135 •

SEVEN TIMES TWO, ROMANCE.

You bells in the steeple, ring, ring out your changes,
    How many soever they be,
And let the brown meadow lark's note as he ranges
    Come over, come over to me.

Yet birds, clearest carol by fall or by swelling
    No magical sense conveys,
And bells have forgotten their old art of telling
    The fortune of future days.

" Turn again, turn again," once they rang cheerily
    While a boy listened alone ;
Made his heart yearn again, musing so wearily
    All by himself on a stone.

Poor bells ! I forgive you ; your good days are over,
    And mine, they are yet to be ;
No listening, no longing shall aught, aught discover :
    You leave the story to me.

The foxglove shoots out of the green matted heather,
    And hangeth her hoods of snow ;
She was idle, and slept till the sunshiny weather ;
    O children take long to grow !

I wish, and I wish that the spring would go faster,
    Nor long summer bide so late ;
And I could grow on like the foxglove and aster,
    For some things are ill to wait.

I wait for the day when dear hearts shall discover,
    While dear hands are laid on my head ;
" The child is a woman. the book may close over,
    For all the lessons are said."

I wait for my story—the birds cannot sing it,
    Not one, as he sits on the tree ;
The bells cannot ring it, but long years, O, bring it !
    Such as I wish it to be !

                     Jean Ingelow.

· 136 ·

SONNET.

LIX.

Thrise happie she that is so well assured
Unto herselfe, and settled so in hart,
That neither will for better be allured,
Ne feard with worse to any chaunce to start ;
But, like a steddy ship, doth strongly part
The raging waves, and keepes her course aright ;
Ne aught for tempest doth from it depart,
Ne aught for fayrer weather's false delight.

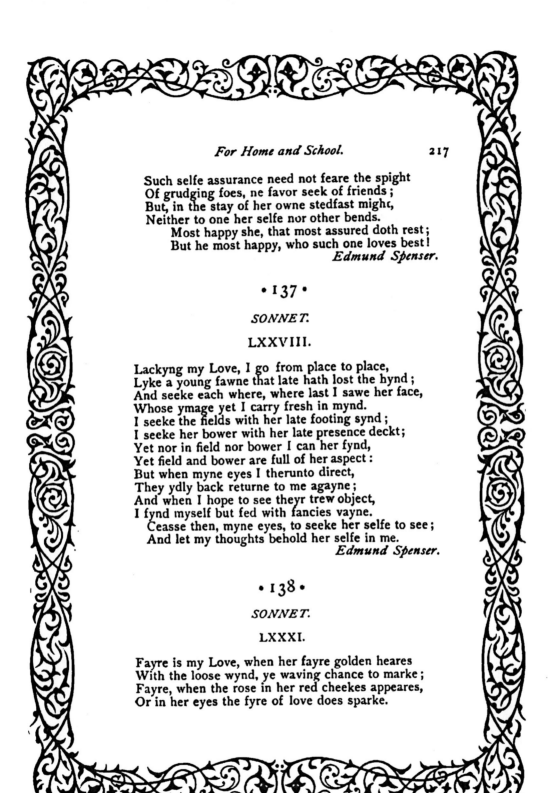

Such selfe assurance need not feare the spight
Of grudging foes, ne favor seek of friends;
But, in the stay of her owne stedfast might,
Neither to one her selfe nor other bends.
    Most happy she, that most assured doth rest;
    But he most happy, who such one loves best!
Edmund Spenser.

• 137 •

SONNET.

LXXVIII.

Lackyng my Love, I go from place to place,
Lyke a young fawne that late hath lost the hynd;
And seeke each where, where last I sawe her face,
Whose ymage yet I carry fresh in mynd.
I seeke the fields with her late footing synd;
I seeke her bower with her late presence deckt;
Yet nor in field nor bower I can her fynd,
Yet field and bower are full of her aspect:
But when myne eyes I therunto direct,
They ydly back returne to me agayne;
And when I hope to see theyr trew object,
I fynd myself but fed with fancies vayne.
    Ceasse then, myne eyes, to seeke her selfe to see;
    And let my thoughts behold her selfe in me.
Edmund Spenser.

• 138 •

SONNET.

LXXXI.

Fayre is my Love, when her fayre golden heares
With the loose wynd, ye waving chance to marke;
Fayre, when the rose in her red cheekes appeares,
Or in her eyes the fyre of love does sparke.

Fayre, when her breast, lyke a rich laden barke
With pretious merchandize, she forth doth lay;
Fayre, when that cloud of pryde, which oft doth dark
Her goodly light, with smiles she drives away;
But fayrest she, when so she doth display
The gate with pearls and rubyes richly dight;
Through which her words so wise do make their way
To beare the message of her gentle spright.
    The rest be works of natures wonderment;
    But this the worke of harts astonishment.

Edmund Spenser.

• 139 •

SONG OF THE SILENT LAND.

Into the Silent Land!
Ah! who shall lead us thither?
Clouds in the evening sky more darkly gather,
And shattered wrecks lie thicker on the strand.
Who leads us with a gentle hand
Thither, O thither,
Into the Silent Land?

Into the Silent Land!
To you, ye boundless regions
Of all perfection! Tender morning-visions
Of beauteous souls! The Future's pledge and band!
Who in life's battle firm doth stand,
Shall bear Hope's tender blossoms
Into the Silent Land!

O Land! O Land!
For all the broken-hearted
The mildest herald by our fate allotted,
Beckons and with inverted torch doth stand
To lead us with a gentle hand
To the land of the great Departed,
Into the Silent Land!

Uhland (Longfellow's Trans.).

• 140 •

TO A WATERFOWL.

Whither, 'midst falling dew,
While glow the heavens with the last steps of day,
Far through their rosy depths, dost thou pursue
    Thy solitary way ?

Vainly the fowler's eye
Might mark thy distant flight to do thee wrong,
As, darkly painted on the crimson sky,
    Thy figure floats along.

Seek'st thou the plashy brink
Of weedy lake, or marge of river wide,
Or where the rocking billows rise and sink
    On the chafed ocean side ?

There is a Power whose care
Teaches thy way along that pathless coast,—
The desert and illimitable air,—
    Lone wandering, but not lost.

All day thy wings have fanned,
At that far height, the cold, thin atmosphere,
Yet stoop not, weary, to the welcome land,
    Though the dark night is near.

And soon that toil shall end ;
Soon shalt thou find a summer home, and rest,
And scream among thy fellows ; reeds shall bend
    Soon o'er thy shelter'd nest.

Thou'rt gone ; the abyss of heaven
Hath swallowed up thy form ; yet on my heart
Deeply hath sunk the lesson thou hast given,
    And shall not soon depart.

He who from zone to zone,
Guides through the boundless sky thy certain flight
In the long way that I must tread alone
Will lead my steps aright.
　　　　　　　　　William C. Bryant.

• 141 •

HOW THEY BROUGHT THE GOOD NEWS FROM GHENT TO AIX.

I sprang to the stirrup, and Joris, and he ;
I galloped, Dirck galloped, we galloped all three ;
"Good speed !" cried the watch, as the gate-bolts undrew ;
"Speed," echoed the wall to us galloping through ;
Behind shut the postern, the lights sank to rest,
And into the midnight we galloped abreast.

Not a word to each other ; we kept the great pace
Neck by neck, stride by stride, never changing our place,
I turned in my saddle and made its girths tight,
Then shortened each stirrup and set the pique right,
Rebuckled the cheek-strap, chained slacker the bit,
Nor galloped less steadily Roland a whit.

'Twas moonset at starting ; but when we drew near
Lokeren, the cocks crew and twilight dawned clear ;
At Boom a great yellow star came out to see ;
At Duffeld, 'twas morning as plain as could be ;
And from Mechlen church-steeple we heard the half-chime,
So Joris broke silence with "Yet there is time !"

At Aerschot, up leaped of a sudden the sun,
And against him the cattle stood black every one,
To stare through the mist at us galloping past,
And I saw my stout galloper, Roland at last,
With resolute shoulders each butting away
The haze, as some bluff river headland, its spray :

And his low head and crest, just one sharp ear bent back
For my voice, and the other pricked out on his track;
And one eye's black intelligence—ever that glance
O'er its white edge at me, his own master, askance!
And the thick heavy spume-flakes which aye and anon
His fierce lips shook upwards in galloping on.

By Hasselt, Dirck groaned, and cried Joris "Stay spur!
Your Roos galloped bravely, the fault's not in her,
We'll remember at Aix"—for one heard the quick wheeze
Of her chest, saw the stretched neck, and staggering knees,
And sunk tail, and horrible heave of the flank,
As down on her haunches she shuddered and sank.

So we were left galloping, Joris and I,
Past Loos, and past Tongres, no cloud in the sky;
The broad sun above laughed a pitiless laugh.
'Neath our foot broke the brittle bright stubble like chaff;
Till over by Dalhem a dome-tower sprang white,
And "Gallop," cried Joris, "for Aix is in sight!"

"How they'll greet us!" and all in a moment his roan
Rolled neck and croup over, lay dead as a stone;
And there was my Roland to bear the whole weight,
Of the news which alone could save Aix from her fate,
With his nostrils like pits full of blood to the brim,
And with circles of red for his eye-sockets' rim.

Then I cast loose my buff-coat, each holster let fall,
Shook off both my jack-boots, let go belt and all,
Stood up in the stirrup, leaned, patted his ear,
Called my Roland his pet name, my horse without peer;
Clapped my hands, laughed and sang, any noise, bad or
            good,
Till at length into Aix, Roland galloped and stood.

And all I remember is, friends flocking round
As I sate with his head 'twixt my knees on the ground,

And no voice but was praising this Roland of mine,
As I poured down his throat our last measure of wine,
Which the burgesses voted, by common consent
Was no more than his due who brought good news from
    Ghent.

Robert Browning.

• 142 •

YOUNG LOCHINVAR.

O, young Lochinvar is come out of the West!
Through all the wide Border his steed is the best;
And save his good broadsword he weapon had none;
He rode all unarmed and he rode all alone.
So faithful in love, and so dauntless in war,
There never was knight like the young Lochinvar!

He stayed not for brake and he stopped not for stone;
He swam the Eske river where ford there was none;
But ere he alighted at Netherby gate,
The bride had consented; the gallant came late;
For a laggard in love and a dastard in war,
Was to wed the fair Ellen of brave Lochinvar.

So boldly he entered the Netherby Hall,
'mong bridesmen, and kinsmen, and brothers, and all;—
Then spake the bride's father, his hand on his sword,
For the poor craven bridegroom said never a word,
" O come ye in peace here, or come ye in war,
Or to dance at our bridal, young lord Lochinvar?"

" I long wooed your daughter, my suit you denied;
Love swells like the Solway, but ebbs like its tide;
And now I am come with this lost love of mine
To lead but one measure, drink one cup of wine.
There are maidens in Scotland more lovely by far,
That would gladly be bride to the young Lochinvar!"

The bride kissed the the goblet, the knight took it up,
He quaffed off the wine and he threw down the cup:
She looked down to blush, and she looked up to sigh,
With a smile on her lips and a tear in her eye.
He took her soft hand ere her mother could bar ;
" Now tread we a measure ! " said young Lochinvar.

So stately his form, and so lovely her face,
That never a hall such a galliard did grace ;—
While her mother did fret and her father did fume,
And the bridegroom stood dangling his bonnet and plume ;
And the bride-maidens whispered, " 'Twere better by far,
To have matched our fair cousin with young Lochinvar ! "

One touch to her hand and one word in her ear,
When they reached the hall door, and the charger stood
            near ;
So light to the croupe the fair lady he swung, .
So light to the saddle before her he sprung !
" She is won ! we are gone, over bank, bush and scaur,
They'll have fleet steeds that follow ! " cried young Lochinvar.

There was mounting 'mong Græmes of the Netherby clan ;
Forsters, Fenwicks, and Musgraves, they rode and they ran ;
There was racing and chasing on Cannobie lea ;
But the lost bride of Netherby ne'er did they see.
So daring in love, and so dauntless in war.
Have ye e'er heard of gallant like young Lochinvar ?
                                        Walter Scott.

• 143 •

THE DEATH OF THE FLOWERS.

The melancholy days have come, the saddest of the year,
Of wailing winds, and naked woods, and meadows brown
            and sear.
Heaped in the hollows of the grove, the withered leaves lie
            dead ;
They rustle to the eddying gust, and to the rabbit's tread.

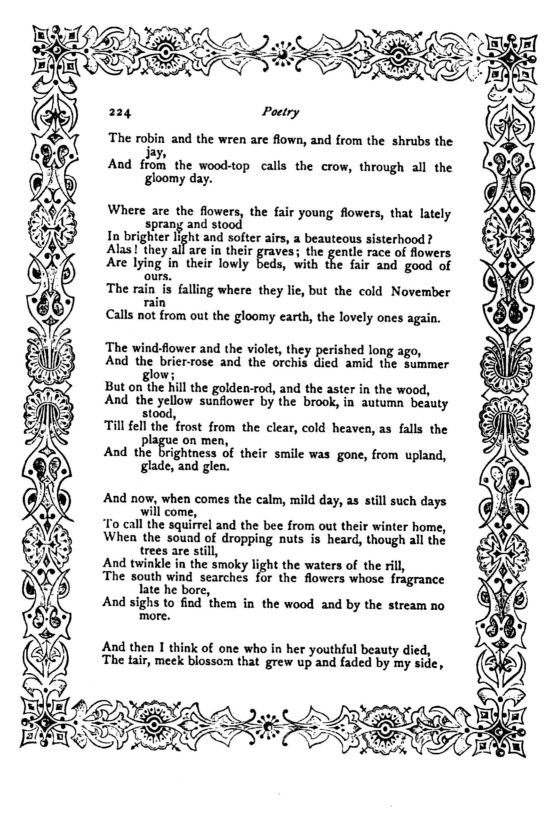

The robin and the wren are flown, and from the shrubs the
　　jay,
And from the wood-top calls the crow, through all the
　　gloomy day.

Where are the flowers, the fair young flowers, that lately
　　sprang and stood
In brighter light and softer airs, a beauteous sisterhood?
Alas! they all are in their graves; the gentle race of flowers
Are lying in their lowly beds, with the fair and good of
　　ours.
The rain is falling where they lie, but the cold November
　　rain
Calls not from out the gloomy earth, the lovely ones again.

The wind-flower and the violet, they perished long ago,
And the brier-rose and the orchis died amid the summer
　　glow;
But on the hill the golden-rod, and the aster in the wood,
And the yellow sunflower by the brook, in autumn beauty
　　stood,
Till fell the frost from the clear, cold heaven, as falls the
　　plague on men,
And the brightness of their smile was gone, from upland,
　　glade, and glen.

And now, when comes the calm, mild day, as still such days
　　will come,
To call the squirrel and the bee from out their winter home,
When the sound of dropping nuts is heard, though all the
　　trees are still,
And twinkle in the smoky light the waters of the rill,
The south wind searches for the flowers whose fragrance
　　late he bore,
And sighs to find them in the wood and by the stream no
　　more.

And then I think of one who in her youthful beauty died,
The fair, meek blossom that grew up and faded by my side,

In the cold, moist earth we laid her, when the forest cast
    the leaf,
And we wept that one so lovely should have a life so brief;
Yet not unmeet it was that one like that young friend of
    ours,
So gentle, and so beautiful, should perish with the flowers.
                      William C. Bryant.

• 144 •

IS THERE, FOR HONEST POVERTY.

Is there, for honest poverty,
    That hangs his head, and a' that!
The coward-slave, we pass him by,
    We dare be poor for a' that!
For a' that, and a' that,
    Our toil's obscure, and a' that;
The rank is but the guinea's stamp,
    The man 's the gowd for a' that!

What tho' on hamely fare we dine,
    Wear hodden gray, and a' that;
Gie fools their silks, and knaves their wine,
    A man's a man, for a' that!
For a' that, and a' that,
    Their tinsel show, and a' that,
The honest man, though e'er sae poor,
    Is king o' men for a' that!

Ye see yon birkie ca'd a lord,
    Wha struts, and stares, and a' that;
Though hundreds worship at his word,
    He's but a coof for a' that!
For a' that, and a' that,
    His riband, star, and a' that,
The man of independent mind,
    He looks and laughs at a' that!

A king can mak' a belted knight,
  A marquis, duke, and a' that;
But an honest man's aboon his might,
  Guid faith he manna fa' that!
For a' that, and a' that,
  Their dignities, and a' that,
The pith o' sense and pride o' worth
  Are higher ranks than a' that.

Then let us pray that come it may,—
  As come it will for a' that,—
That sense and worth o'er a' the earth,
  May bear the gree, and a' that!
For a' that, and a' that!
  It's comin' yet, for a' that,
That man to man, the warld o'er,
  Shall brothers be for a' that!

Robert Burns.

• 145 •

·ODE TO DUTY.

Stern daughter of the voice of God!
O Duty! if that name thou love
Who art a light to guide, a rod
To check the erring and reprove;
Thou who art victory and law
When empty terrors overawe;
From vain temptations dost set free
And calm'st the weary strife of frail humanity!

There are who ask not if thine eye
Be on them: who, in love and truth
Where no misgiving is, rely
Upon the genial sense of youth;
Glad hearts! without reproach or blot,
Who do thy work, and know it not
O, if through confidence misplaced,
They fail, thy saving arms, dread Power around them cast.

Serene will be our days and bright
And happy will our nature be
When love is an unerring light,
And joy its own security.
And they a blissful course may hold
Ev'n now who, not unwisely bold,
Live in the spirit of this creed ;
Yet find that other strength, according to their need.

I, loving freedom, and untried,
No sport of every random gust
Yet being to myself a guide,
Too blindly have reposed my trust ;
And oft, when in my heart was heard
Thy timely mandate, I deferred
The task, in smoother walks to stray ;
But thee I now would serve more strictly, if I may.

Through no disturbance of my soul
Or strong compunction in me wrought,
I supplicate for thy control,
But in the quietness of thought :
Me this unchartered freedom tires ;
I feel the weight of chance desires :
My hopes no more must change their name ;
I long for a repose which ever is the same.

Stern lawgiver ! yet thou dost wear
The Godhead's most benignant grace ;
Nor know we anything so fair
As is the smile upon thy face ;
Flowers laugh before thee on their beds,
And fragrance in thy footing treads :
Thou dost preserve the stars from wrong ;
And the most ancient heavens, through thee are fresh and
strong.

To humbler functions, awful power,
I call thee ! I myself commend
Unto thy guidance from this hour ;
O let my weakness have an end !

Give unto me, made lowly wise,
The spirit of self sacrifice ;
The confidence of reason give;
And in the light of truth thy bondman let me live.
                            William Wordsworth.

• 146 •

BLOW BUGLE.

The splendor falls on castle walls,
    And snowy summits old in story ;
The long light shakes across the lakes,
    And the wild cataract leaps in glory.
Blow, bugle, blow, set the wild echoes flying :
Blow, bugle ; answer, echoes, dying, dying, dying.

O hark, O hear ! how thin and clear,
    And thinner, clearer, further going ;
O sweet and far, from cliff and scar,
    The horns of Elfland faintly blowing !
Blow, let us hear the purple glens replying :
Blow, bugle ; answer, echoes, dying, dying, dying.

O love, they die in yon rich sky,
    They faint on hill or field or river:
Our echoes roll from soul to soul,
    And grow forever and forever.
Blow, bugle, blow, set the wild echoes flying,
And answer, echoes, answer, dying, dying, dying.
                            Alfred Tennyson.

• 147 •

TRUE LOVE.

Let me not to the marriage of true minds
Admit impediments. Love is not love
Which alters when it alteration finds,
Or bends with the remover to remove ;—

O no! It is an ever-fixèd mark
That looks on tempests, and is never shaken;
It is the star to every wandering bark
Whose worth's unknown, although his height be taken.

Love's not time's fool, though rosy lips and cheeks
Within his bending sickle's compass come;
Love alters not with his brief hours and weeks
But bears it out ev'n to the edge of doom:

If this be error, and upon me proved,
I never writ, nor no man ever loved.
William Shakespeare.

• 148 •

THE HOUSE.

There is no architect
    Can build as the Muse can;
She is skilful to select
    Materials for her plan;

Slow and warily to choose
    Rafters of immortal pine,
Or cedar incorruptible,
    Worthy her design.

She threads dark Alpine forests,
    Or valleys by the sea,
In many lands, with painful steps, ·
    Ere she can find a tree.

She ransacks mines and ledges,
    And quarries every rock,
To hew the famous adamant
    For each eternal block.

She lays her beams in music,
  In music every one,
To the cadence of the whirling world
  Which dances round the sun;

That so they shall not be displaced
  By lapses or by wars,
But, for the love of happy souls,
  Outlive the newest stars.
                    Ralph W. Emerson.

• 149 •

THE PASSIONS.

AN ODE FOR MUSIC.

When Music, heavenly maid, was young,
Wh'le yet in early Greece she sung,
The Passions oft, to hear her shell
Thronged around her magic cell
Exulting, trembling, raging, fainting,
Possessed beyond the Muse's painting ·
By turns they felt the glowing mind
Disturbed, delighted, raised, refined;
'Till once, 'tis said, when all were fired,
Filled with fury, rapt, inspired,
From the supporting myrtles round
They snatched her instruments of sound,
And, as they oft had heard apart
Sweet lessons of her forceful art,
Each, for Madness ruled the hour,
Would prove his own expressive power.

First Fear, his hand, its skill to try,
  Amid the chords bewildered laid,
And back recoiled, he knew not why,
  E'en at the sound himself had made.

Next Anger rushed; his eyes on fire,
    In lightnings owned his secret stings;
In one rude clash he struck the lyre
    And swept with hurried hand the strings.

With woeful measures wan Despair—
    Low sullen sounds his grief beguiled,
A solemn, strange, and mingled air,
    'Twas sad by fits, by starts 'twas wild.

But thou, O Hope, with eyès so fair,
    What was thy delighted measure?
Still it whispered promised pleasure
    And bade the lovely scenes at distance hail!
Still would her touch the strain prolong;
    And from the rocks, the woods, the vale
She called on Echo still through all the song;
    And where her sweetest theme she chose
    A soft responsive voice was heard at every close;
And Hope enchanted smiled, and waved her golden hair; —

And longer had she sung :—but with a frown
    Revenge impatient rose;
He threw his blood-stain'd sword in thunder down;
    And with a withering look
    The war-denouncing trumpet took;
And blew a blast so loud and dread,
Were ne'er prophetic sounds so full of woe.
    And ever and anon he beat
    The doubling drum with furious heat;
And though sometimes, each dreary pause between,
    Dejected Pity at his side
    Her soul-subduing voice applied,
    Yet still he kept his wild, unaltered mien,
While each strained ball of sight seemed bursting from his
    head.

Thy numbers, Jealousy, to nought were fixed:
    Sad proof of thy distressful state!
Of differing themes the veering song was mixed;
    And now it courted Love, now raving, called on Hate.

With eyes up-raised, as one inspired,
Pale Melancholy sat retired;
And from her wild sequestered seat,
In notes by distance made more sweet,
Poured through the mellow horn her pensive soul;
   And dashing soft from rocks around
Bubbling runnels joined the sound;
Through glades and glooms the mingled measure stole,
   Or, o'er some haunted stream, with fond delay,
   Round a holy calm diffusing,
   Love of peace, and lonely musing,
   In hollow murmurs died away.

But O! how altered was its sprightier tone
When Cheerfulness, a nymph of healthiest hue,
   Her bow across her shoulder flung,
   Her buskins gemmed with morning dew,
Blew an inspiring air, that dale and thicket rung,
   The hunter's call to Faun and Dryad known!
The oak-crown'd Sisters and their chaste-eyed Queen
   Satyrs and sylvan boys were seen
   Peeping from forth their alleys green;
Brown Exercise rejoiced to hear;
   And Sport leaped up, and seized his beechen Spear

Last came Joy's ecstatic trial:
He, with viny crown advancing,
   First to the lively pipe his hand addressed.
But soon he saw the brisk awakening viol
   Whose sweet entrancing voice he loved the best;
They would have thought who heard the strain
   They saw, in Tempe's vale, her native maids
   Amidst the festal-sounding shades
To some unwearied minstrel dancing;
While, as his flying fingers kissed the strings,
   Love framed with Mirth a gay fantastic round;
   Loose were her tresses seen, her zone unbound;
   And he, amidst his frolic play,
   As if he would the charming air repay,
Shook thousand odors from his dewy wings.

Oh Music! sphere-descended maid,
Friend of Pleasure, Wisdom's aid!
Why, goddess, why, to us denied,
Lay'st thou thy ancient lyre aside?
As in that loved Athenian bower
You learned an all-commanding power,
Thy mimic soul, Oh nymph endeared!
Can well recall what then it heard.
Where is thy native simple heart
Devote to Virtue, Fancy, Art?
Arise, as in that elder time,
Warm, energetic, chaste, sublime!
Thy wonders, in that god-like age,
Fill thy recording Sister's page;—
'Tis said, and I believe the tale,
Thy humblest reed could more prevail
Had more of strength, diviner rage,
Than all which charms this laggard age,
E'en all at once together found
Cecilia's mingled world of sound:—
O, bid our vain endeavors cease:
Revive the just designs of Greece:
Return in all thy simple state!
Confirm the tales her sons relate!

William Collins.

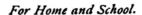

· 150 ·

LYCIDAS.

Yet once more, O ye laurels, and once more
Ye myrtles brown, with ivy never sere,
I come to pluck your berries harsh and crude,
And with forced fingers rude
Shatter your leaves before the mellowing year.

Bitter constraint, and sad occasion dear
Compels me to disturb your season due:
For Lycidas, is dead, dead ere his prime,
Young Lycidas, and hath not left his peer!
Who would not sing for Lycidas? he knew
Himself to sing, and build the lofty rhyme.
He must not float upon his watery bier
Unwept, and welter to the parching wind,
Without the meed of some melodious tear.

Begin then, Sisters of the sacred well
That from beneath the seat of Jove doth spring;
Begin, and somewhat loudly sweep the string.
Hence with denial vain and coy excuse;
So may some gentle Muse
With lucky words favor my destined urn;
And as he passes, turn
And bid fair peace be to my sable shroud.

For we were nursed upon the self-same hill,
Fed the same flock by fountain, shade, and rill.
Together both, ere the high lawns appeared
Under the opening eye-lids of the morn,
We drove afield, and both together heard
What time the gray fly winds her sultry horn,
Battening our flocks with the fresh dews of night;
Oft till the star, that rose at evening bright,
Toward heaven's descent had sloped his westering wheel.
Meanwhile the rural ditties were not mute,
Tempered to the oaten flute:
Rough Satyrs danced, and Fauns with cloven heel
From the glad sound would not be absent long,
And old Damoetas loved to hear our song.

But, O! the heavy change, now thou art gone,
Now thou art gone, and never must return!
Thee, Shepherd, thee the woods, and desert caves
With wild thyme and the gadding vine o'ergrown,

" Where were ye, Nymphs, when the remorseless deep
Closed o'er the head of your loved Lycidas ? "—*p. 235*.

And all their echoes, mourn :
The willows and the hazel copses green
Shall now no more be seen
Fanning their joyous leaves to thy soft lays ;—·
As killing as the canker to the rose,
Or taint-worm to the weanling herds that graze,
Or frost to flowers that their gay wardrobe wear
When first the white-thorn blows ;
Such Lycidas, thy loss to shepherd's ear.

Where were ye, Nymphs, when the remorseless deep
Closed o'er the head of your loved Lycidas ?
For neither were ye playing on the steep
Where your old bards, the famous Druids, lie,
Nor on the shaggy top of Mona high,
Nor yet where Deva spreads her wizard stream ;
Ay me ! I fondly dream—
Had ye been there—for what could that have done ?
What could the Muse herself that Orpheus bore,
The Muse herself, for her enchanting son,
Whom universal nature did lament,
When by the rout that made the hideous roar
His gory visage down the stream was sent,
Down the swift Hebrus to the Lesbian shore ?

Alas ! what boots it with incessant care
To tend the homely, slighted, shepherd's trade
And strictly meditate the thankless muse ?
Were it not better done, as others use,
To sport with Amaryllis in the shade,
Or with the tangles of Neaera's hair ?
Fame is the spur that the clear spirit doth raise—
That last infirmity of noble mind—
To scorn delights, and live laborious days ;
But the fair guerdon when we hope to find,
And think to burst out into sudden blaze,
Comes the blind Fury with the abhorrèd shears
And slits the thin-spun life. " But not the praise."
Phoebus replied, and touched my trembling ears :

" Fame is no plant that grows on mortal soil,
Nor in the glistering foil
Set off to the world, nor in broad rumor lies :
But lives and spreads aloft by those pure eyes
And perfect witness of all-judging Jove ;
As he pronounces lastly on each deed,
Of so much fame in heaven expect thy meed ! "

O fountain Arethuse, and thou honored flood,
Smooth-sliding Mincius, crowned with vocal reeds,
That strain I heard was of a higher mood ;
But now my oat proceeds,
And listens to the herald of the sea
That came in Neptune's plea ;
He asked the waves, and asked the felon winds,
What hard mishap hath doomed this gentle swain ?
And questioned every gust of rugged wings.
That blows from off each beakèd promontory :
They knew not of his story ;
And sage Hippotades their answer brings,
That not a blast was from his dungeon strayed ;
The air was calm and on the level brine
Sleek Panope with all her sisters played.
It was that fatal and perfidious bark
Built in the eclipse. and rigged with curses dark,
That sunk so low that sacred head of thine !

Next Camus, reverend sire. went footing slow,
His mantle hairy. and his bonnet sedge
Inwrought with figures dim, and on the edge
Like to that sanguine flower, inscribed with woe :
" Ah ! who hath reft, " quoth he, " my dearest pledge ! "
Last came, and last did go
The pilot of the Galilean lake ;
Two massy keys he bore of metals twain ;
—The golden opes. the iron shuts amain ;
He shook his mitred locks, and stern bespake :
" How well could I have spared for thee, young swain,
Enow of such, as for their bellies' sake.

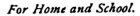

Creep, and intrude, and climb into the fold !
Of other care they little reckoning make
Than how to scramble at the shearer's feast,
And shove away the worthy bidden guest ;
Blind mouths ! that scarce themselves know how to hold
A sheep-hook, or have learned aught else the least
That to the faithful herdsman's art belongs !
What recks it them ? What need they ? They are sped ;
And when they list, their lean and flashy songs
Grate on their scrannel pipes of wretched straw ;
The hungry sheep look up, and are not fed ;
But swollen with wind and the rank mist they draw ;
Rot inwardly, and foul contagion spread ;
Besides what the grim wolf with privy paw
Daily devours apace, and nothing said :
But that two handed engine at the door
Stands ready to smite once, and smite no more."

    Return, Alpheus, the dread voice is past
That shrunk thy streams ; return, Sicilian Muse,
And call the vales, and bid them hither cast
Their bells and flowerets of a thousand hues.
Ye valleys low, where the mild whispers use
Of shades, and wanton winds, and gushing brooks
On whose fresh lap the swart star sparely looks ;
Throw hither all your quaint enamelled eyes
That on the green turf suck the honeyed showers
And purple all the ground with vernal flowers.
Bring the rathe primrose that forsaken dies,
The tufted crow-toe, and pale jessamine,
The white pink, and the pansy freaked with jet,
The glowing violet,
The musk-rose, and the well-attired woodbine,
With cowslips wan that hang the pensive head,
And every flower that sad embroidery wears :
Aid amaranthus all his beauty shed,
And daffodillies fill their cups with tears
To strew the laureate hearse where Lycid lies
For, so to interpose a little ease,
Let our frail thoughts dally with false surmise ;

Ay me! whilst thee the shores and sounding seas
Wash far away,—where'er thy bones are hurled,
Whether beyond the stormy Hebrides
Where thou perhaps, under the whelming tide,
Visit'st the bottom of the monstrous world;
Or whether thou, to our moist vows denied,
Sleep'st by the fable of Bellerus old,
Where the great vision of the guarded mount
Looks towards Namancos and Bayona's hold,
Look homeward, Angel, now, and melt with ruth:
And, O ye dolphins, waft the hapless youth!

Weep no more, woful shepherds, weep no more,
For Lycidas, your sorrow is not dead,
Sunk though he be beneath the watery floor;
So sinks the day-star in the ocean-bed,
And yet anon repairs his drooping head
And tricks his beams, and with new-spangled ore
Flames in the forehead of the morning sky;
So Lycidas sunk low, but mounted high
Through the dear might of Him that walked the waves;
Where, other groves and other streams along,
With nectar pure his oozy locks he laves,
And hears the unexpressive nuptial song.
In the blest kingdoms meek of joy and love,
There entertain him all the saints above
In solemn troops, and sweet societies,
That sing, and singing in their glory move,
And wipe the tears forever from his eyes.
Now, Lycidas, the shepherds weep no more;
Henceforth thou art the Genius of the shore
In thy large recompense, and shalt be good
To all that wander in that perilous flood.

Thus sang the uncouth swain to the oaks and rills,
While the still morn went out with sandals gray;
He touched the tender stops of various quills,
With eager thought warbling his Doric lay;

And now the sun had stretched out all the hills
And now was dropped into the western bay:
At last he rose, and twitched his mantle blue;
To-morrow to fresh woods, and pastures new.
John Milton.

• 151 •

HYMN BEFORE SUNRISE, IN THE VALE OF CHAMOUNI.

Hast thou a charm to stay the morning-star
In his steep course ? so long he seems to pause
On thy bald awful head, O sovran Blanc !
The Árvé and Arveiron at thy base
Rave ceaselessly ; but thou, most awful form,
Risest from forth thy silent sea of pines,
How silently ! Around thee and above
Deep is the air and dark, substantial, black,
An ebon mass : methinks thou piercest it,
As with a wedge ! But when I look again,
It is thy own calm home, thy crystal shrine,
Thy habitation from eternity !
Oh dread and silent mount ! I gazed upon thee,
Till thou, still present to the bodily sense,
Didst vanish from my thoughts : entranced in prayer
I worshipped the Invisible alone.

Yet, like some sweet, beguiling melody,
So sweet, we know not we are listening to it,
Thou the meanwhile, wast blending with my thought,
Yea, with my life and life's own secret joy :
Till the dilating soul, enrapped transfused,
Into the mighty vision passing,—there,
As in her natural form, swelled vast to heaven !

Awake, my soul! not only passive praise
Thou owest,—not alone these swelling tears,
Mute thanks, and secret ecstasy! Awake,
Voice of sweet song! Awake, my heart, awake!
Green vales and icy cliffs, all join my hymn!

Thou first and chief, sole sovran of the vale!
O, struggling with the darkness all the night,
And visited all night by troops of stars,
Or when they climb the sky or when they sink;
Companion of the morning-star at dawn,
Thyself earth's rosy star, and of the dawn
Co-herald! O, wake, and utter praise!
Who sank thy sunless pillars deep in earth?
Who filled thy countenance with rosy light?
Who made thee parent of perpetual streams?

And you, ye five wild torrents fiercely glad,
Who called you forth from night and utter death,
From dark and icy caverns called you forth,
Down those precipitous, black, jagged rocks,
For ever shattered and the same forever?
Who gave you your invulnerable life,
Your strength, your speed, your fury, and your joy,
Unceasing thunder and eternal foam?
And who commanded—and the silence came—
"Here let the billows stiffen, and have rest?"

Ye ice-falls! ye that from the mountain's brow
Adown enormous ravines slope amain,
Torrents, methinks, that heard a mighty voice,
And stopped at once amid their maddest plunge!
Motionless torrents! silent cataracts!
Who made you glorious as the gates of heaven
Beneath the keen, full moon? Who bade the sun
Clothe you with rainbows? Who, with living flowers
Of loveliest blue, spread garlands at your feet?
"God!" let the torrents, like a shout of nations,
Answer; and let the ice-plains echo, "God!"

"God!" sing, ye meadow-streams with gladsome voice!
Ye pine-groves, with your soft and soul-like sounds!
And they, too, have a voice, yon piles of snow,
And in their perilous fall shall thunder, "God!"

Ye living flowers, that skirt the eternal frost!
Ye wild goats, sporting round the eagle's nest!
Ye eagles, playmates of the mountain-storm!
Ye lightnings, the dread arrows of the clouds!
Ye signs and wonders of the elements!
Utter forth God, and fill the hills with praise!

Thou, too, hoar mount, with thy sky-pointing peaks!
Oft from whose feet the avalanche, unheard,
Shoots downward, glittering through the pure serene
Into the depths of clouds that veil thy breast,
Thou, too, again, stupendous mountain! thou
That as I raise my head, awhile bowed low
In adoration, upward from thy base
Slow travelling with dim eyes suffused with tears,
Solemnly seemest, like a vapory cloud,
To rise before me,—rise, O, ever rise,
Rise like a cloud of incense, from the earth!
Thou kingly spirit throned among the hills,
Thou dread ambassador from earth to heaven,
Great hierarch! tell thou the silent sky,
And tell the stars, and tell yon rising sun,
Earth, with her thousand voices praises God.
                              Samuel T. Coleridge.

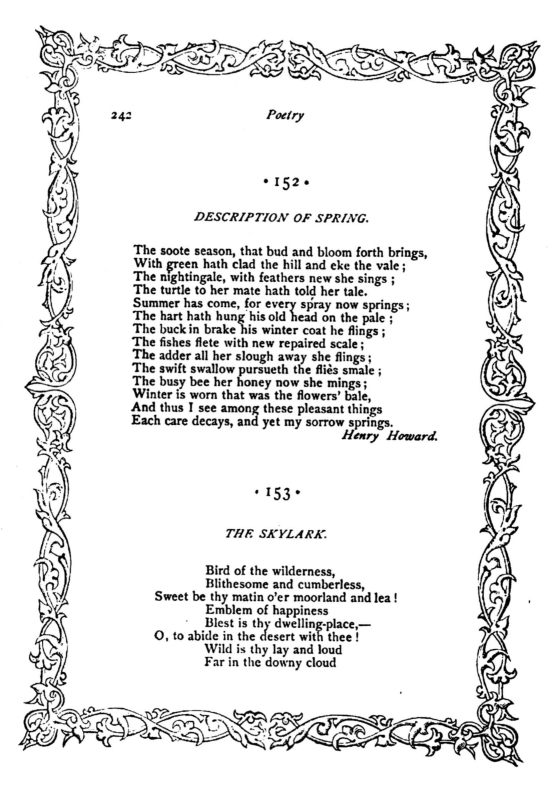

· 152 ·

DESCRIPTION OF SPRING.

The soote season, that bud and bloom forth brings,
With green hath clad the hill and eke the vale;
The nightingale, with feathers new she sings;
The turtle to her mate hath told her tale.
Summer has come, for every spray now springs;
The hart hath hung his old head on the pale;
The buck in brake his winter coat he flings;
The fishes flete with new repaired scale;
The adder all her slough away she flings;
The swift swallow pursueth the flies smale;
The busy bee her honey now she mings;
Winter is worn that was the flowers' bale,
And thus I see among these pleasant things
Each care decays, and yet my sorrow springs.

Henry Howard.

· 153 ·

THE SKYLARK.

Bird of the wilderness,
Blithesome and cumberless,
Sweet be thy matin o'er moorland and lea!
Emblem of happiness
Blest is thy dwelling-place,—
O, to abide in the desert with thee!
Wild is thy lay and loud
Far in the downy cloud

Love gives it energy, love gave it birth.
  Where, on the dewy wing,
  Where art thou journeying?
Thy lay is in heaven, thy love is on earth.
  O'er fell and fountain sheen,
  O'er moor and mountain green,
O'er the red streamer that heralds the day,
  Over the cloudlet dim,
  Over the rainbow's rim,
Musical cherub, soar, singing away!
  There, where the gloaming comes,
  Low in the heather blooms
Sweet will thy welcome and bed of love be;
  Emblem of happiness
  Blest is thy dwelling-place,—
O, to abide in the desert with thee!

                              James Hogg.

• 154 •

TURN, FORTUNE.

Turn, Fortune, turn thy wheel and lower the proud;
Turn thy wild wheel through sunshine, storm, and cloud;
Thy wheel and thee, we neither love nor hate.

Turn, Fortune, turn thy wheel with smile or frown;
With that wild wheel we go not up or down;
Our hoard is little, but our hearts are great.

Smile and we smile, the lords of many lands;
Frown and we smile, the lords of our own hands;
For man is man and master of his fate.

Turn, turn thy wheel above the staring crowd;
Thy wheel and thou are shadows in the cloud;
Thy wheel and thee we neither love nor hate.

                              Alfred Tennyson.

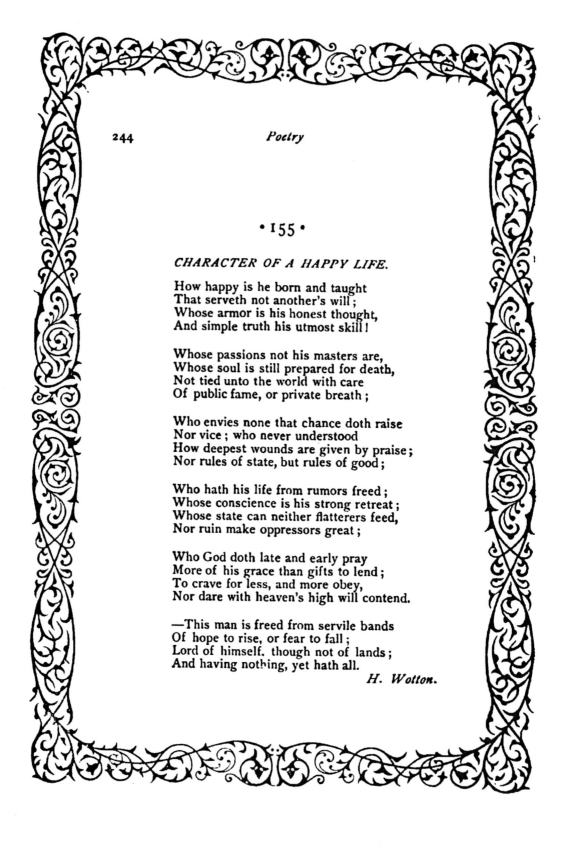

• 155 •

CHARACTER OF A HAPPY LIFE.

How happy is he born and taught
That serveth not another's will;
Whose armor is his honest thought,
And simple truth his utmost skill!

Whose passions not his masters are,
Whose soul is still prepared for death,
Not tied unto the world with care
Of public fame, or private breath;

Who envies none that chance doth raise
Nor vice; who never understood
How deepest wounds are given by praise;
Nor rules of state, but rules of good;

Who hath his life from rumors freed;
Whose conscience is his strong retreat;
Whose state can neither flatterers feed,
Nor ruin make oppressors great;

Who God doth late and early pray
More of his grace than gifts to lend;
To crave for less, and more obey,
Nor dare with heaven's high will contend.

—This man is freed from servile bands
Of hope to rise, or fear to fall;
Lord of himself. though not of lands;
And having nothing, yet hath all.

H. Wotton.

· 156 ·

ON HIS BLINDNESS.

When I consider how my light is spent
Ere half my days, in this dark world and wide,
And that one talent which is death to hide
Lodged with me useless, though my soul more bent
To serve therewith my Maker, and present
My true account, lest he returning chide,—
Doth God exact day-labor, light denied ?
I fondly ask :—But Patience, to prevent
That murmur, soon replies ; God doth not need
Either man's work, or his own gifts ; who best
Bear his mild yoke, they serve him best ; His state
Is kingly ; thousands at his bidding speed
And post o'er land and ocean without rest ;
They also serve who only stand and wait.

John Milton.

· 157 ·

ARETHUSA.

Arethusa arose
From her couch of snows,
In the Acroceraunian mountains,—
From cloud and from crag,
With many a jag,
Shepherding her bright fountains.
She leaped down the rocks
With her rainbow locks

Streaming among the streams;—
    Her steps paved with green
    The downward ravine
Which slopes to the western gleams;
    And gliding and springing
    She went, ever singing
In murmurs as soft as sleep;
    The Earth seemed to love her,
    And Heaven smiled above her,
As she lingered towards the deep.
    Then Alpheus bold,
    On his glacier cold,
With his trident the mountains strook.
    And opened a chasm
    In the rocks;—with a spasm
All Erymanthus shook :
    And the black south wind
    It concealed behind
The urns of the silent snow.
    And earthquake and thunder
    Did rend in sunder
The bars of the springs below:
    The beard and the hair
    Of the river-god were
Seen through the torrent's sweep,
    As he followed the light
    Of the fleet nymph's flight
To the brink of the Dorian deep.

    " O, save me ! O, guide me,
    And bid the deep hide me;
For he grasps me now by the hair !"
    The loud Ocean heard,
    To its blue depth stirred,
And divided at her prayer;
    And under the water
    The Earth's white daughter
Fled like a sunny beam;
    Behind her descended

Her billows unblended
With the brackish Dorian stream.
Like a gloomy stain
On the emerald main,
Alpheus rushed behind,—
As an eagle pursuing
A dove to its ruin
Down the streams of the cloudy wind.

Under the bowers
Where the Ocean Powers
Sit on their pearlèd thrones,—
Through the coral woods
Of the weltering floods,
Over heaps of unvalued stones,—
Through the dim beams
Which amid the streams
Weave a net-work of colored light,
And under the caves
Where the shadowy waves
Are as green as the forest's night:—
Outspeeding the shark,
And the sword-fish dark,
Under the ocean-foam,
And up through the rifts
Of the mountain clifts
They passed to their Dorian home.
And now from their fountains
In Enna's mountains,
Down one vale where the morning basks,
Like friends once parted,
Grown single-hearted,
They ply their watery tasks.
At sunrise they leap
From their cradles steep
In the cave of the shelving hill;
At noontide they flow
Through the woods below,
And the meadows of Asphodel:

And at night they sleep
In the rocking deep
Beneath the Ortygian shore ;—
Like spirits that lie
In the azure sky,
When they love, but live no more.

Shelley.

· 158 ·

SONG OF THE GREEKS.

Again to the battle, Achaians !
Our hearts bid the tyrants defiance,
Our land, the first garden of Liberty's tree—
It has been, and shall yet be, the land of the free;
For the cross of our faith is replanted ;
The pale dying crescent is daunted,
And we march that the footprints of Mahomet's slaves
May be washed out in blood from our forefathers' graves.
Their spirits are hovering o'er us,
And the sword shall to glory restore us.

Ah ! what though no succor advances,
Nor Christendom's chivalrous lances
Are stretched in our aid—be the combat our own !
And we'll perish or conquer more proudly alone;
For we've sworn by our country's assaulters,
By the virgins they dragged from our altars,
By our massacred patriots, our children in chains,
By our heroes of old, and their blood in our veins,
That, living, we will be victorious,
Or that, dying, our deaths shall be glorious.

A breath of submission we breathe not;
The sword that we've drawn we will sheathe not!
Its scabbard is left where our martyrs are laid,
And the vengeance of ages has whetted its blade.

Earth may hide—waves ingulf—fire consume us,
But they shall not to slavery doom us;
If they rule, it shall be o'er our ashes and graves;
But we've smote them already with fire on the waves.
And new triumphs on land are before us;
To the charge!—Heaven's banner is o'er us.

This day, shall ye blush for its story,
Or brighten your lives with its glory.
Our women, oh say, shall they shriek in despair,
Or embrace us from conquest with wreaths in their hair?
Accursed may his memory blacken,
If a coward there be that would slacken
Till we've trampled the turban, and shown ourselves worth
Being sprung from and named for, the godlike of earth.
Strike home, and the world shall revere us
As heroes descended from heroes.

Old Greece lightens up with emotion
Her inlands, her isles of the ocean;
Fanes rebuilt and fair towns shall with jubilee ring,
And the nine shall new-hallow their Helicon's spring;
Our hearths shall be kindled in gladness,
That were cold and extinguished in sadness;
Whilst our maidens shall dance with their white waving arms,
Singing joy to the brave who delivered their charms,
When the blood of yon Mussulman cravens,
Shall have crimsoned the beaks of our ravens.
                                    Thomas Campbell.

· 159 ·

CHEVY-CHASE.

God prosper long our noble king,
    Our lives and safeties all;
A woful hunting once there did
    In Chevy-Chase befall.

To drive the deer with hound and horn
  Earl Percy took his way;
The child may rue that is unborn
  The hunting of that day.

The stout Earl of Northumberland
  A vow to God did make,
His pleasure in the Scottish woods
  Three summer days to take—

The chiefest harts in Chevy-Chase
  To kill and bear away;
These tidings to Earl Douglas came
  In Scotland, where he lay;

Who sent Earl Percy present word
  He would prevent his sport;
The English Earl, not fearing that,
  Did to the woods resort,

With fifteen hundred bowmen bold,
  All chosen men of might,
Who knew full well in time of need
  To aim their shafts aright.

The gallant grey-hounds swiftly ran
  To chase the fallow deer;
On Monday they began to hunt
  When daylight did appear;

And long before high noon they had
  A hundred fat bucks slain;
Then having dined, the drovers went
  To rouse the deer again.

The bowmen mustered on the hills,
  Well able to endure;
Their backsides all with special care,
  That day were guarded sure.

The hounds ran swiftly through the woods
   The nimble deer to take,
That with their cries the hills and dales
   An echo shrill did make.

Lord Percy to the quarry went,
   To view the slaughtered deer;
Quoth he, "Earl Douglas promised
   This day to meet me here;

"If that I thought he would not come
   No longer would I stay;"
With that a brave young gentleman
   Thus to the Earl did say:

"Lo, yonder doth Earl Douglas come,
   His men in armor bright;
Full twenty hundred Scottish spears
   All marching in our sight;

"All men of pleasant Teviotdale,
   Fast by the river Tweed;"
"Then cease your sports," Earl Percy said,
   "And take your bows with speed;

"And now with me, my countrymen,
   Your courage forth advance;
For never was there champion yet,
   In Scotland or in France,

That ever did on horse-back come,
   But if my hap it were,
I durst encounter man for man,
   With him to break a spear."

Earl Douglas on his milk-white steed,
   Most like a baron bold,
Rode foremost of his company,
   Whose armor shone like gold.

" Show me," said he, " whose men you be,
    That hunt so boldly here,
That, without my consent, do chase
    And kill my fallow deer."

The first man that did answer make,
    Was noble Percy he—
Who said, " We list not to declare
    Nor show whose men we be ;

" Yet we will spend our dearest blood
    Thy chiefest harts to slay."
Then Douglas swore a solemn oath,
    And thus in rage did say :

" Ere thus I will out-bravèd be,
    One of us two shall die :
I know thee well, an Earl thou art—
    Lord Percy, so am I.

" But trust me, Percy, pity 'twere,
    Any great offence to kill
Any of these our guiltless men,
    For they have done no ill.

" Let you and I the battle try,
    And set our men aside."
" Accursed be he," Earl Percy said,
    " By whom this is denied."

Then stepped a gallant squire forth,
    Witherington was his name,
Who said, " I would not have it told
    To Henry, our king for shame,

" That e'er my captain fought on foot,
    And I stood looking on.
Ye be two Earls," said Witherington,
    " And I a squire alone ;

" I'll do the best that do I may,
  While I have power to stand;
While I have power to wield my sword,
  I'll fight with heart and hand."

Our English archers bent their bows—
  Their hearts were good and true;
At the first flight of arrows sent,
  Full fourscore Scots they slew.

Yet stays Earl Douglas on the bent,
  As chieftain stout and good;
As valiant captain all unmoved,
  The shock he firmly stood.

His host he parted had in three,
  As leader ware and tried:
And soon his spearmen on their foes
  Bore down on every side.

Throughout the English archery
  They dealt full many a wound;
But still our valiant Englishmen
  All firmly kept their ground.

And throwing straight their bows away
  They grasped their swords so bright;
And now sharp blows, a heavy shower,
  On shields and helmets light.

They closed full fast on every side—
  No slackness there was found;
And many a gallant gentleman
  Lay gasping on the ground.

In truth it was a grief to see
  How each one chose his spear,
And how the blood out of their breasts
  Did gush like water clear.

At last these two stout earls did meet ;
  Like captains of great might,
Like lions wode, they laid on lode,
  And made a cruel fight.

They fought until they both did sweat,
  With swords of tempered steel,
Until the blood, like drops of rain,
  They trickling down did feel.

" Yield thee, Lord Percy ! " Douglas said,
  " In faith I will thee bring
Where thou shalt high advanced be
  By James, our Scottish king.

" Thy ransom I will freely give,
  And this report of thee :
Thou art the most courageous knight
  That ever I did see."

" No, Douglas," quoth Earl Percy then,
  " Thy proffer I do scorn ;
I will not yield to any Scot
  That ever yet was born."

With that there came an arrow keen
  Out of an English bow,
Which struck Earl Douglas to the heart ;
  A deep and deadly blow :

Who never spake more words than these ;
  " Fight on, my merry men all ;
For why, my life is at an end ;
  Lord Percy sees my fall."

Then leaving life, Earl Percy took
  The dead man by the hand ;
And said, " Earl Douglas, for thy life
  Would I had lost my land.

" In truth my very heart doth bleed
　With sorrow for thy sake ;
For sure a more redoubted knight
　Mischance did never take."

A knight among the Scots there was,
　Who saw Earl Douglas die,
Who straight in wrath did vow revenge
　Upon the Earl Percy :

Sir Hugh Montgomery was he called,
　Who, with a spear full bright,
Well mounted on a gallant steed
　Ran fiercely through the fight ;

And past the English archers all,
　Without a dread or fear ;
And through Earl Percy's body then
　He thrust his hateful spear ;

With such vehement force and might
　He did his body gore,
The staff ran through the other side
　A large cloth-yard and more.

So thus did both those nobles die,
　Whose courage none could stain,
An English archer then perceived
　The noble Earl was slain :

He had a bow bent in his hand,
　Made of a trusty tree ;
An arrow of a cloth-yard long
　To the hard head drew he :

Against Sir Hugh Montgomery
　So right the shaft he set,
The gray goose wing that was thereon
　In his heart's blood was wet.

This fight did last from break of day
  Till setting of the sun ;
For when they rung the evening-bell,
  The battle scarce was done.

With stout Earl Percy there were slain
  Sir John of Egerton,
Sir Robert Ratcliff and Sir John,
  Sir James that bold baron.

And with Sir George and stout Sir James,
  Both knights of good account,
Good Sir Ralph Raby there was slain,
  Whose prowess did surmount.

For Witherington my heart is woe
  That ever he slain should be,
For when his legs were hewn in two
  He knelt and fought on his knee.

And with Earl Douglas there was slain
  Sir Hugh Montgomery,
Sir Charles Currel that from the field
  One foot would never flee.

Sir Charles Murray of Ratcliff too,
  His sister's son was he ;
Sir David Lamb, so well esteemed.
  But saved he could not be.

And the Lord Maxwell in like case
  Did with Earl Douglas die ;
Of twenty hundred Scottish spears,
  Scarce fifty-five did fly.

Of fifteen hundred Englishmen,
  Went home but fifty-three ;
The rest in Chevy-Chase were slain,
  Under the greenwood tree.

"Next day did many
widows come,
Their husbands to
bewail."—*p. 257.*

Next day did many widows come,
  Their husbands to bewail;
They washed their wounds in brinish tears,
  But all would not prevail.

Their bodies, bathed in purple blood,
  They bore with them away;
They kissed them dead a thousand times,
  Ere they were clad in clay.

The news was brought to Edinburgh,
  Where Scotland's king did reign,
That brave Earl Douglas suddenly
  Was with an arrow slain:

"Oh heavy news," King James did say,
  "Scotland can witness be
I have not any captain more
  Of such account as he."

Like tidings to King Henry came
  Within as short a space,
That Percy of Northumberland
  Was slain in Chevy-Chase:

"Now God be with him," said our king,
  "Since 'twill no better be;
I trust I have within my realm
  Five hundred good as he:

"Yet shall not Scots or Scotland say
  But I will vengeance take:
I'll be revengèd on them all,
  For brave Earl Percy's sake."

This vow full well the king performed
  After at Humbledown;
In one day fifty knights were slain,
  With lords of high renown:

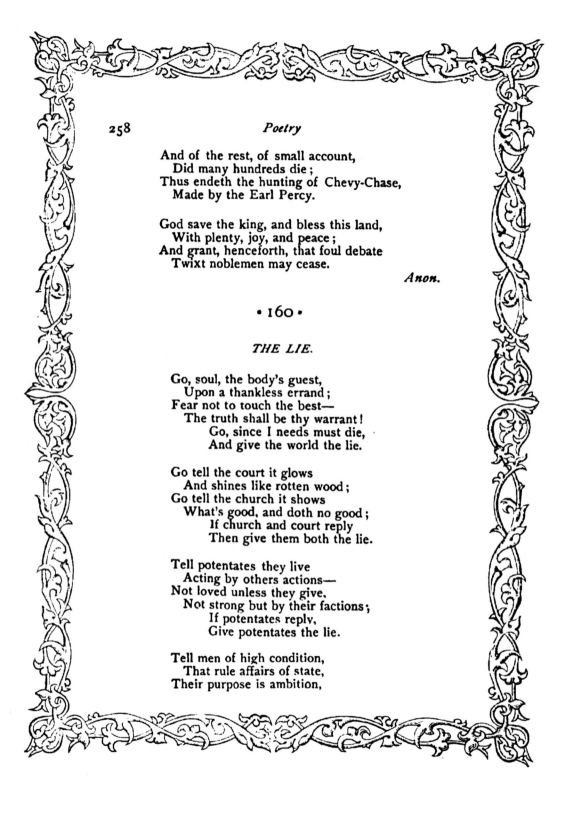

And of the rest, of small account,
 Did many hundreds die;
Thus endeth the hunting of Chevy-Chase,
 Made by the Earl Percy.

God save the king, and bless this land,
 With plenty, joy, and peace;
And grant, henceforth, that foul debate
 Twixt noblemen may cease.

         Anon.

· 160 ·

THE LIE.

Go, soul, the body's guest,
 Upon a thankless errand;
Fear not to touch the best—
 The truth shall be thy warrant!
  Go, since I needs must die,
  And give the world the lie.

Go tell the court it glows
 And shines like rotten wood;
Go tell the church it shows
 What's good, and doth no good;
  If church and court reply
  Then give them both the lie.

Tell potentates they live
 Acting by others actions—
Not loved unless they give,
 Not strong but by their factions;
  If potentates reply,
  Give potentates the lie.

Tell men of high condition,
 That rule affairs of state,
Their purpose is ambition,

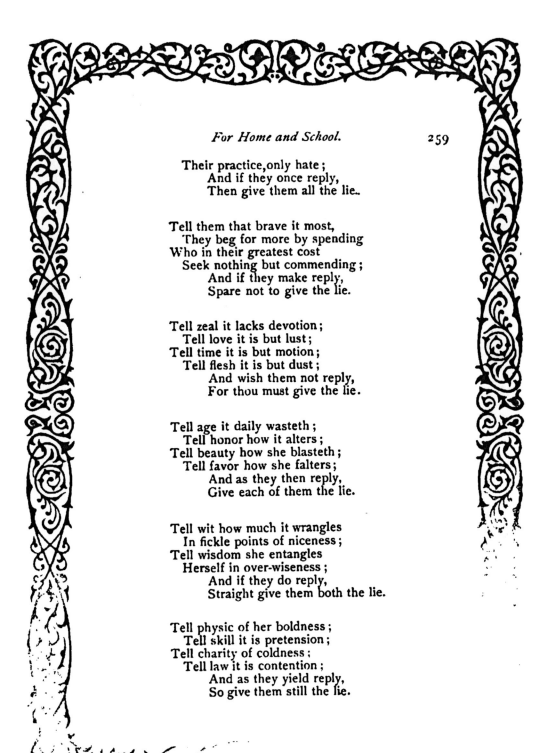

Their practice, only hate;
  And if they once reply,
  Then give them all the lie.

Tell them that brave it most,
  They beg for more by spending
Who in their greatest cost
  Seek nothing but commending;
    And if they make reply,
    Spare not to give the lie.

Tell zeal it lacks devotion;
  Tell love it is but lust;
Tell time it is but motion;
  Tell flesh it is but dust;
    And wish them not reply,
    For thou must give the lie.

Tell age it daily wasteth;
  Tell honor how it alters;
Tell beauty how she blasteth;
  Tell favor how she falters;
    And as they then reply,
    Give each of them the lie.

Tell wit how much it wrangles
  In fickle points of niceness;
Tell wisdom she entangles
  Herself in over-wiseness;
    And if they do reply,
    Straight give them both the lie.

Tell physic of her boldness;
  Tell skill it is pretension;
Tell charity of coldness;
  Tell law it is contention;
    And as they yield reply,
    So give them still the lie.

Tell fortune of her blindness,
Tell nature of decay;
Tell·friendship of unkindness,
Tell justice of delay;
And if they dare reply,
Then give them all the lie.

Tell arts they have no soundness,
But vary by esteeming;
Tell schools they want profoundness,
And stand too much on seeming;
If arts and schools reply,
Give arts and schools the lie.

Tell faith it's fled the city;
Tell how the country erreth;
Tell, manhood shakes off pity;
Tell, virtue least preferreth;
And if they do reply,
Spare not to give the lie.

So, when thou hast, as I
Commanded thee, done blabbing—
Although to give the lie
Deserves no less than stabbing—
Yet stab at thee who will,
No stab the soul can kill.
Walter Raleigh.

•161•

THE IVY GREEN.

Oh! a dainty plant is the Ivy green,
That creepeth o'er ruins old!
Of right choice food are his meals, I ween,
In his cell so lone and cold.

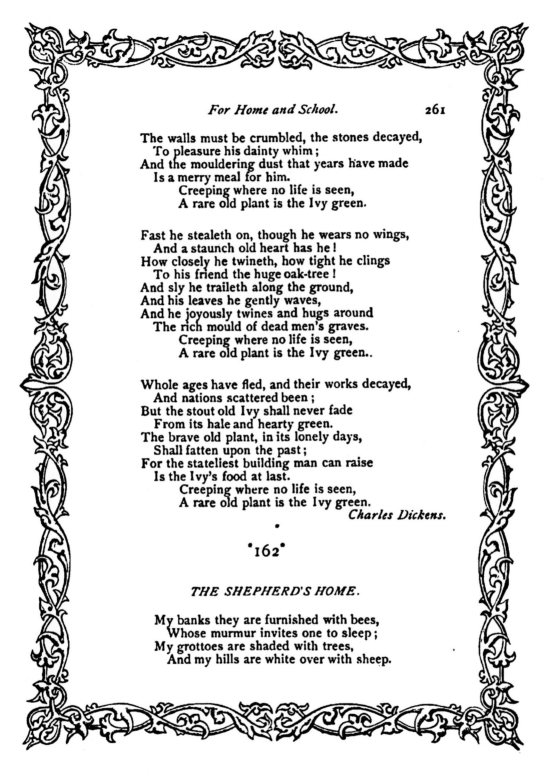

The walls must be crumbled, the stones decayed,
  To pleasure his dainty whim;
And the mouldering dust that years have made
  Is a merry meal for him.
      Creeping where no life is seen,
      A rare old plant is the Ivy green.

Fast he stealeth on, though he wears no wings,
  And a staunch old heart has he!
How closely he twineth, how tight he clings
  To his friend the huge oak-tree!
And sly he traileth along the ground,
And his leaves he gently waves,
And he joyously twines and hugs around
  The rich mould of dead men's graves.
      Creeping where no life is seen,
      A rare old plant is the Ivy green..

Whole ages have fled, and their works decayed,
  And nations scattered been;
But the stout old Ivy shall never fade
  From its hale and hearty green.
The brave old plant, in its lonely days,
  Shall fatten upon the past;
For the stateliest building man can raise
  Is the Ivy's food at last.
      Creeping where no life is seen,
      A rare old plant is the Ivy green.
                              Charles Dickens.

•162•

THE SHEPHERD'S HOME.

My banks they are furnished with bees,
  Whose murmur invites one to sleep;
My grottoes are shaded with trees,
  And my hills are white over with sheep.

I seldom have met with a loss,
   Such health do my fountains bestow;
My fountains all bordered with moss,
   There the harebells and violets blow.

Not a pine in the grove is there seen,
   But with tendrils of woodbine is bound;
Not a beech's more beautiful green,
   But a sweet-briar entwines it around.
Not my fields in the prime of the year,
   More charms than my cattle unfold;
Not a brook that is limpid and clear,
   But it glitters with fishes of gold.

I have found out a gift for my fair,
   I have found where the wood-pigeons breed;
But let me such plunder forbear,
   She will say 'twas a barbarous deed;
For he ne'er could be true, she averred,
   Who would rob a poor bird of its young;
And I loved her the more when I heard
   Such tenderness fall from her tongue.
                              William Shenstone.

· 163 ·

JAFFAR.

Jaffar the Barmecide, the good Vizier,
The poor man's hope, the friend without a peer.
Jaffar was dead, slain by a doom unjust;
And guilty Haroun, sullen with mistrust
Of what the good, and e'en the bad might say,
Ordained that no man living from that day
Should dare to speak his name on pain of death.
All Araby and Persia held their breath.

All but the brave Moudeer.—He, proud to show
How far for love a grateful soul could go,
And facing death for very scorn and grief,
For his great heart wanted a great relief,
Stood forth in Bagdad, daily in the square
Where once had stood a happy home, and there
Harangued the tremblers at the scymitar
On all they owed to the divine Jaffar.

" Bring me this man," the caliph cried : the man
Was brought, was gazed upon. The mutes began
To bind his arms. " Welcome, brave cords," cried he ;
" From bonds far worse Jaffar delivered me ;
From wants, from shames, from loveless household fears ;
Made a man's eyes friends with delicious tears ;
Restored me. loved me, put me on a par
With his great self. How can I pay Jaffar ? "

Haroun, who felt that on a soul like this
The mightiest vengeance could but fall amiss,
Now deigned to smile, as one great lord of fate
Might smile upon another half as great.
He said, " Let worth grow frenzied if it will ;
The caliph's judgment shall be master still.

Go, and since gifts so move thee, take this gem,
The richest in the Tartar's diadem,
And hold the giver as thou deemest fit,"
" Gifts ! " cried the friend. He took ; and holding it
High toward the heavens, as though to meet his star,
Exclaimed, " This too, I owe to thee, Jaffar."

Leigh Hunt.

• 164 •

THE MAY QUEEN.

You must wake and call me early, call me early. mother dear;
To-morrow'll be the happiest time of all the glad New-Year;
Of all the glad New-Year, mother, the maddest merriest
 day;
For I'm to be Queen o' the May, mother, I'm to be Queen o'
 the May.

There's many a bright, black eye, they say, but none so
 bright as mine;
There's Margaret and Mary, there's Kate and Caroline;
But none so fair as little Alice in all the land they say:
So I'm to be Queen o' the May, mother, I'm to be Queen o'
 the May.

I sleep so sound all night, mother, that I shall never wake,
If you do not call me loud when the day begins to break;
But I must gather knots of flowers, and buds and garlands
 gay;
For I'm to be Queen o' the May, mother, I'm to be Queen
 o' the May.

As I came up the valley, whom think ye I should see,
But Robin leaning on the bridge beneath the hazel-tree?
He thought of that sharp look, mother, I gave him yester-
 day,—
But I'm to be Queen o' the May, mother, I'm to be Queen
 o' the May.

He thought I was a ghost, mother, for I was all in white,
And I ran by him without speaking, like a flash of light.
They call me cruel-hearted, but I care not what they say,
For I'm to be Queen o' the May, mother, I'm to be Queen o'
 the May.

" For I 'm to be Queen o' the May, mother,
I 'm to be Queen o' the May."—*p. 264.*

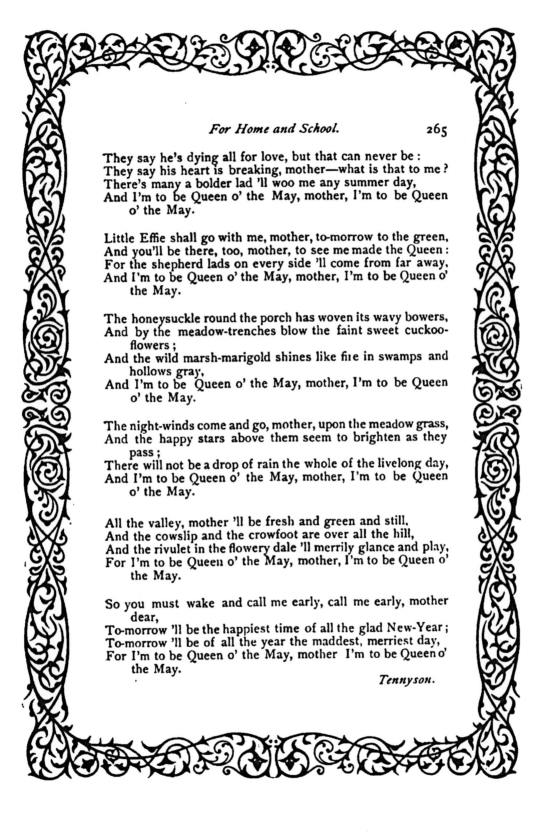

They say he's dying all for love, but that can never be :
They say his heart is breaking, mother—what is that to me ?
There's many a bolder lad 'll woo me any summer day,
And I'm to be Queen o' the May, mother, I'm to be Queen
    o' the May.

Little Effie shall go with me, mother, to-morrow to the green,
And you'll be there, too, mother, to see me made the Queen :
For the shepherd lads on every side 'll come from far away,
And I'm to be Queen o' the May, mother, I'm to be Queen o'
    the May.

The honeysuckle round the porch has woven its wavy bowers,
And by the meadow-trenches blow the faint sweet cuckoo-
    flowers ;
And the wild marsh-marigold shines like fire in swamps and
    hollows gray,
And I'm to be Queen o' the May, mother, I'm to be Queen
    o' the May.

The night-winds come and go, mother, upon the meadow grass,
And the happy stars above them seem to brighten as they
    pass ;
There will not be a drop of rain the whole of the livelong day,
And I'm to be Queen o' the May, mother, I'm to be Queen
    o' the May.

All the valley, mother 'll be fresh and green and still,
And the cowslip and the crowfoot are over all the hill,
And the rivulet in the flowery dale 'll merrily glance and play,
For I'm to be Queen o' the May, mother, I'm to be Queen o'
    the May.

So you must wake and call me early, call me early, mother
    dear,
To-morrow 'll be the happiest time of all the glad New-Year ;
To-morrow 'll be of all the year the maddest, merriest day,
For I'm to be Queen o' the May, mother I'm to be Queen o'
    the May.

Tennyson.

• 165 •

MY LOST YOUTH.

Often I think of the beautiful town
    That is seated by the sea ;
Often in thought go up and down
The pleasant streets of that dear old town,
    And my youth comes back to me.
        And a verse of a Lapland song
        Is haunting my memory still :
        " A boy's will is the wind's will,
And the thoughts of youth are long, long thoughts."

I can see the shadowy lines of its trees,
    And catch, in sudden gleams,
The sheen of the far surrounding seas,
And islands that were the Hesperides
    Of all my boyish dreams.
        And the burden of that old song
        It murmurs and whispers still :
        " A boy's will is the wind's will,
And the thoughts of youth are long, long thoughts."

I remember the black wharves and the slips
    And the sea-tides tossing free ;
And Spanish sailors with bearded lips,
And the beauty and mystery of the ships,
    And the magic of the sea.
        And the voice of that wayward song
        Is singing and saying still :
        " A boy's will is the wind's will,
And the thoughts of youth are long, long thoughts."

I remember the bulwarks by the shore,
    And the fort upon the hill;
The sunrise gun, with its hollow roar
The drum-beat repeated o'er and o'er,
    And the bugle wild and shrill.
        And the music of that old song
        Throbs in my memory still:
        " A boy's will is the wind's will,
And the thoughts of youth are long, long thoughts."

I remember the sea-fight far away,
    How it thundered o'er the tide,
And the dead captains, as they lay
In their graves, o'erlooking the tranquil bay,
    Where they in battle died.
        And the sound of that mournful song
        Goes through me with a thrill:
        " A boy's will is the wind's will,
And the thoughts of youth are long, long thoughts."

I can see the breezy dome of groves,
    The shadows of Deering's woods;
And the friendships old and the early loves
Come back with a sabbath sound, as of doves
    In quiet neighborhoods.
        And the verse of that sweet old song
        It flutters and murmurs still:
        " A boy's will is the wind's will,
And the thoughts of youth are long, long thoughts."

I remember the gleams and glooms that dart
    Across the schoolboy's brain;
The song and the silence in the heart,
That in part are prophecies, and in part
    Are longings wild and vain.
        And the voice of that fitful song
        Sings on and is never still:
        " A boy's will is the wind's will,
And the thoughts of youth are long, long thoughts."

There are things of which I may not speak ;
    There are dreams that cannot die
There are thoughts that make the strong heart weak,
And bring a pallor into the cheek,
    And a mist before the eye.
        And the words of that fatal song
        Come over me like a chill ;
        " A boy's will is the wind's will,
And the thoughts of youth are long, long thoughts."

Strange to me now are the forms I meet
    When I visit the dear old town ;
   But the native air is pure and sweet,
And the trees that o'er shadow each well-known street,
As they balance up and down,
        Are singing the beautiful song
        Are sighing and whispering still ;
        " A boy's will is the wind's will,
And the thoughts of youth are long, long thoughts."

And Deering's Woods are fresh and fain,
    And with joy that is almost pain
My heart goes back to wander there,
And among the dreams of the days that were,
   I find my lost youth again.
        And the strange and beautiful song
        The groves are repeating it still :
        " A boy's will is the wind's will,
And the thoughts of youth are long. long thoughts."
                  Henry W. Longfellow.

• 166 •

MY PLAYMATE.

The pines were dark on Ramoth hill,
  Their song was soft and low;
The blossoms in the sweet May wind
  Were falling like the snow.

The blossoms drifted at our feet,
  The orchard birds sang clear;
The sweetest and the saddest day
  It seemed of all the year.

For, more to me than birds or flowers,
  My playmate left her home,
And took with her the laughing spring,
  The music and the bloom.

She kissed the lips of kith and kin,
  She laid her hand in mine;
What more could ask the bashful boy
  Who fed her father's kine?

She left us in the bloom of May:
  The constant years told o'er
Their seasons with as sweet May morns
  But she came back no more.

I walk with noiseless feet, the round
  Of uneventful years;
Still o'er and o'er I sow the spring
  And reap the autumn ears.

She lives where all the golden year
  Her summer roses blow;
The dusky children of the sun
  Before her come and go.

There haply with her jewelled hands
  She smooths her silken gown,—
No more the homespun lap wherein
  I shook the walnuts down.

The wild grapes wait us by the brook,
  The brown nuts on the hill,
And still the May-day flowers make sweet
  The woods of Follymill.

The lilies blossom in the pond,
  The bird builds in the tree,
The dark pines sing on Ramoth hill
  The slow song of the sea.

I wonder if she thinks of them,
  And how the old time seems,—
If ever the pines of Ramoth wood
  Are sounding in her dreams.

I see her face, I hear her voice;
  Does she remember mine?
And what to her is now the boy
  Who fed her father's kine?

What cares she that the orioles build
  For other eyes than ours,—
That other hands with nuts are filled,
  And other laps with flowers?

O playmate in the golden time;
  Our mossy seat is green,
Its fringing violets blossom yet,
  The old trees o'er it lean.

The winds so sweet with birch and fern
 A sweeter memory blow;
And there in spring the veeries sing
 The song of long ago.

And still the pines of Ramoth wood
 Are moaning like the sea,—
The moaning of the sea of change
 Between myself and thee.

John G. Whittier.

• 167 •

GLENARA.

O heard ye yon pibroch sound sad in the gale.
Where a band cometh slowly with weeping and wail ;
'Tis the chief of Glenara laments for his dear ;
And her sire, and the people are called to her bier.

Glenara came first with the mourners and shroud ;
Her kinsmen they followed, but mourned not aloud :
Their plaids all their bosoms were folded around ;
They march'd all in silence,—they look'd on the ground.

In silence they reached over mountain and moor,
To a heath where the oak-tree grew lonely and hoar :
"Now here let us place the grey stone of her cairn ;
Why speak ye no word ?"—said Glenara the stern.

"And tell me, I charge you ! ye clan of my spouse,
Why fold ye your mantles, why cloud ye your brows ?"
So spake the rude chieftain : no answer is made :
But each mantle unfolding a dagger displayed.

"I dreamt of my lady, I dreamed of her shroud,"
Cried a voice from her kinsmen all wrathful and loud ;
"And empty that shroud and that coffin did seem ;
Glenara ! Glenara ! now read me my dream ! "

O ! pale grew the cheek of that chieftain I ween,
When the shroud was unclosed, and no lady was seen ;
When a voice from the kinsmen spoke louder in scorn,
'Twas the youth who had loved the fair Ellen of Lorn.

"I dreamed of my lady, I dreamt of her grief,
I dreamed that her lord was a barbarous chief :
On a rock in the ocean fair Ellen did seem :
Glenara ! Glenara ! now read me my dream."

In dust low the traitor has knelt to the ground,
And the desert revealed where his lady was found ;
From a rock of the ocean that beauty is borne—
Now joy to the house of fair Ellen of Lorn !
                                        Thomas Campbell.

· 168 ·

SWEET AND LOW.

Sweet and low, sweet and low,
   Wind of the western sea,
Low, low, breathe and blow,
   Wind of the western sea !
Over the rolling waters go ;
   Come from the dying moon, and blow,
Blow him again to me ;
   While my little one, while my pretty one, sleeps.

Sleep and rest, sleep and rest,
   Father will come to thee soon;
Rest, rest, on mother's breast,
   Father will come to thee soon;
Father will come to his babe in the nest;
   Silver sails all out of the west,
Under the silver moon;
   Sleep, my little one, sleep, my pretty one, sleep.
                 Alfred Tennyson.

• 169 •

EACH AND ALL.

Little thinks, in the field, yon red-cloaked clown
Of thee from the hill-top looking down;
The heifer that lows in the upland farm,
Far-heard, lows not thine ear to charm;
The sexton, tolling his bell at noon,
Deems not that great Napoleon
Stops his horse, and lists with delight,
While his files sweep round yon Alpine height;
Nor knowest thou what argument
Thy life to thy neighbor's creed has lent.
All are needed by each one—
Nothing is fair or good alone.

I thought the sparrow's note from heaven,
Singing at dawn on the alder bough;
I brought him home in his nest, at even,
He sings the song, but it pleases not now;
For I did not bring home the river and sky;
He sang to my ear—they sang to my eye.

The delicate shells lay on the shore;
The bubbles of the latest wave
Fresh pearls to their enamel gave,
And the bellowing of the savage sea
Greeted their safe escape to me.

I wiped away the weeds and foam—
I fetched my sea-born treasures home;
But the poor unsightly, noisome things
Had left their beauty on the shore,
With the sun and the sand, and the wild uproar.

The lover watched his graceful maid,
As 'mid the virgin train she strayed;
Nor knew her beauty's best attire
Was woven still by the snow-white choir.
At last she came to his hermitage,
Like the bird from the woodlands to the cage;
The gay enchantment was undone—
A gentle wife, but fairy none.

Then I said, "I covet truth;
Beauty is unripe childhood's cheat—
I leave it behind with the games of youth."
As I spoke, beneath my feet
The ground-pine curled its pretty wreath,
Running over the club-moss burrs;
I inhaled the violet's breath;
Around me stood the oaks and firs;
Pine-cones and acorns lay on the ground;
Over me soared the eternal sky,
Full of light and of deity;
Again I saw, again I heard,
The rolling river, the morning bird;
Beauty through my senses stole—
I yielded myself to the perfect whole.

Ralph Waldo Emerson.

• 170 •

LUCY.

Three years she grew in sun and shower;
Then Nature said, " A lovelier flower
On earth was never sown :
This child I to myself will take ;

She shall be mine, and I will make
A lady of my own.

" Myself will to my darling be
Both law and impulse : and with me
The girl, in rock and plain
In earth and heaven, in glade and bower
Shall feel an overseeing power
To kindle or restrain.

" She shall be sportive as the fawn
That wild with glee across the lawn
Or up the mountain springs ;
And hers shall be the breathing balm,
And hers the silence and the calm
Of mute, insensate things.

" The floating clouds their state shall lend
To her ; for her the willow bend ;
Nor shall she fail to see
E'en in the motions of the storm
Grace that shall mould the maiden's form
By silent sympathy.

" The stars of midnight shall be dear
To her ; and she shall lean her ear
In many a secret place
Where rivulets dance their wayward round,
And beauty born of murmuring sound
Shall pass into her face.

" And vital feelings of delight
Shall rear her form to stately height,
Her virgin bosom swell ;
Such thoughts to Lucy I will give
While she and I together live
Here in this happy dell."

Thus Nature spake—The work was done—
How soon my Lucy's race was run!
She died, and left to me
This heath, this calm and quiet scene;
The memory of what has been,
And never more will be.

                              William Wordsworth.

• 171 •

THE CHAMBERED NAUTILUS.

This is the ship of pearl, which, poets feign,
        Sails the unshadowed main;
        The venturous barque that flings
On the sweet summer wind its purple wings
In gulfs enchanted, where the syren sings
        And coral reefs lie bare;
Where the cold sea-maids rise to sun their streaming hair.

Its webs of living gauze no more unfurl;
        Wrecked is the ship of pearl!
        And every chambered cell
Where its dim-dreaming life was wont to dwell,
As the frail tenant shaped his glowing cell,
        Before thee lies revealed,
Its irised ceiling rent, its sunless crypt unsealed.

Year after year beheld the silent toil
        That spread his lustrous coil;
        Still, as the spiral grew,
He left the past year's dwelling for the new,
Stole with soft step its shining archway through,
        Built up its idle door,
Stretched in his last found home, and knew the old no more.

Thanks for the heavenly message brought by thee,
        Child of the wandering sea,
        Cast from her lap, forlorn!
From thy dead lips a clearer note is borne

Than ever Triton blew from wreathèd horn!
 While on mine ear it rings
Through the deep caves of thought. I hear a voice that
 sings—

Build thee more stately mansions, O my soul,
 As the swift seasons roll!
 Leave thy low-vaulted past!
Let each new temple, nobler than the last,
Shut thee from heaven with a dome more vast,
 Till thou at length art free,
Leaving thine out-grown shell by life's unresting sea!
 Oliver W. Holmes.

•172•

A MADRIGAL.

Crabbèd age and youth
 Cannot live together:
Youth is full of pleasance,
Age is full of care;
Youth like summer morn,
Age like winter weather,
Youth like summer brave,
Age like winter bare:
Youth is full of sport,
Age's breath is short,
Youth is nimble, Age is lame:
Youth is hot and bold,
Age is weak and cold,
Youth is wild, and Age is tame:—
Age, I do abhor thee,
Youth, I do adore thee;
O! my Love, my Love is young!
Age, I do defy thee—
O sweet shepherd, hie thee,
For methinks thou stay'st too long.
 William Shakespeare.

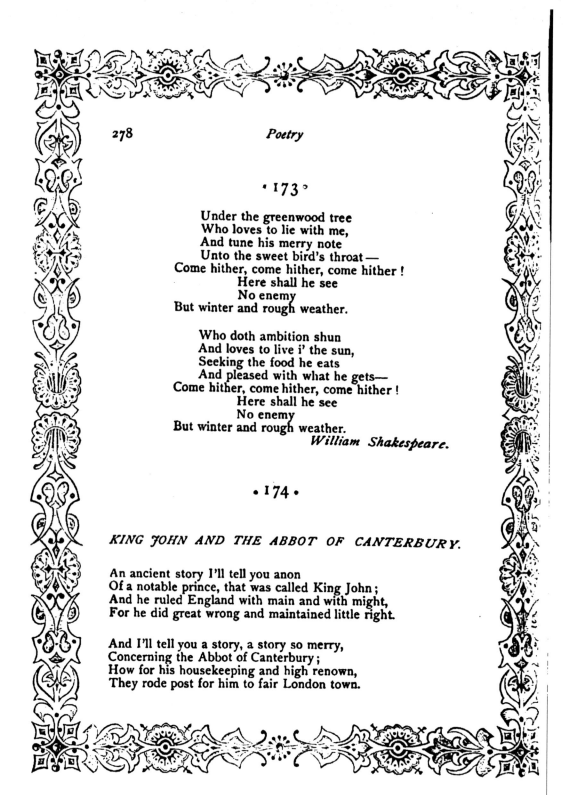

• 173 •

Under the greenwood tree
Who loves to lie with me,
And tune his merry note
Unto the sweet bird's throat —
Come hither, come hither, come hither !
Here shall he see
No enemy
But winter and rough weather.

Who doth ambition shun
And loves to live i' the sun,
Seeking the food he eats
And pleased with what he gets—
Come hither, come hither, come hither !
Here shall he see
No enemy
But winter and rough weather.

William Shakespeare.

• 174 •

KING JOHN AND THE ABBOT OF CANTERBURY.

An ancient story I'll tell you anon
Of a notable prince, that was called King John;
And he ruled England with main and with might,
For he did great wrong and maintained little right.

And I'll tell you a story, a story so merry,
Concerning the Abbot of Canterbury;
How for his housekeeping and high renown,
They rode post for him to fair London town.

" Under the greenwood tree
Who loves to lie with me?"—*p. 278*

" Who doth ambition shun,
  And loves to live i' the sun,
  Seeking the food he eats,
  And pleased with what he gets."—*p. 278.*

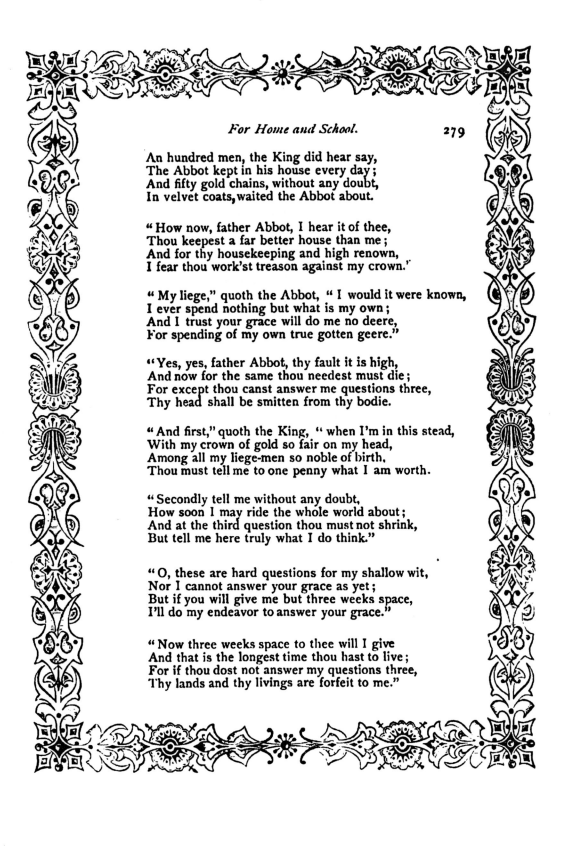

An hundred men, the King did hear say,
The Abbot kept in his house every day;
And fifty gold chains, without any doubt,
In velvet coats, waited the Abbot about.

"How now, father Abbot, I hear it of thee,
Thou keepest a far better house than me;
And for thy housekeeping and high renown,
I fear thou work'st treason against my crown.'

"My liege," quoth the Abbot, "I would it were known,
I ever spend nothing but what is my own;
And I trust your grace will do me no deere,
For spending of my own true gotten geere."

"Yes, yes, father Abbot, thy fault it is high,
And now for the same thou needest must die;
For except thou canst answer me questions three,
Thy head shall be smitten from thy bodie.

"And first," quoth the King, "when I'm in this stead,
With my crown of gold so fair on my head,
Among all my liege-men so noble of birth,
Thou must tell me to one penny what I am worth.

"Secondly tell me without any doubt,
How soon I may ride the whole world about;
And at the third question thou must not shrink,
But tell me here truly what I do think."

"O, these are hard questions for my shallow wit,
Nor I cannot answer your grace as yet;
But if you will give me but three weeks space,
I'll do my endeavor to answer your grace."

"Now three weeks space to thee will I give
And that is the longest time thou hast to live;
For if thou dost not answer my questions three,
Thy lands and thy livings are forfeit to me."

Away rode the Abbot all sad at that word,
And he rode to Cambridge and Oxenford;
But never a doctor there was so wise,
That could with his learning an answer devise.

Then home rode the Abbot of comfort so cold,
And he met his shepherd agoing to fold:
"How now, my lord Abbot, you are welcome home;
What news do you bring us from good King John?"

"Sad news, sad news, shepherd, I must give,
That I have but three days more to live;
For if I do not answer him questions three,
My head will be smitten from my bodie.

"The first is to tell him there in that stead,
With his crown of gold so fair on his head,
Among all his liege-men so noble of birth,
To within one penny of what he is worth.

"The second, to tell him without any doubt,
How soon he may ride this whole world about;
And at the third question I must not shrink,
But tell him there truly what he does think."

"Now cheer up, sir Abbot, did you never hear yet
That a fool he may teach a wise man wit?
Lend me horse, and serving men, and your apparel,
And I'll ride to London to answer your quarrel.

"Nay, frown not if it hath been told unto me,
I am like your lordship as ever may be;
And if you will but lend me your gown
There is none shall know us in fair London town."

"Now horses and serving men thou shalt have,
With sumptuous array most gallant and brave,
With crozier, and mitre, and rochet and cope,
Fit to appear 'fore our father the Pope."

" Now welcome, sir Abbot," the King he did say,
" 'Tis well thou'rt come back to keep the day:
For if thou can'st answer my questions three,
Thy life and thy living both saved shall be.

" And first, when thou seest me here in this stead,
With my crown of gold so fair on my head,
Among all my liege men so noble of birth,
Tell me to one penny what I am worth."

" For thirty pence our Saviour was sold
Among the false Jews as I have been told;
And twenty-nine is the worth of thee,
For I think thou art one penny worser than he."

The King he laughed, and swore by St. Bittel,
" I did not think I had been worth so little !
Now secondly tell me without any doubt
How soon I may ride this whole world about."

" You may rise with the sun, and ride with the same,
Until the next morning he riseth again;
And then your grace need not make any doubt,
But in twenty-four hours you'll ride it about."

The King he laughed, and swore by St. Jone,
" I did not think it could be gone so soon.
Now from the third question thou must not shrink,
But tell me here truly what I do think."

" Yea. that I shall do and make your grace merry;
You think I'm the Abbot of Canterbury;
But I'm his poor shepherd, as plain you may see,
That am come to beg pardon for him and for me."

The King he laughed, and swore by the mass,
" I'll make thee lord Abbot this day in his place !"
" Nay, nay, my liege, be not in such speed,
For alack, I can neither write nor read."

" Four nobles a week, then, I will give thee,
For this merry jest thou hast shewn unto me ;
And tell the old Abbot, when thou comest home,
Thou hast brought him a pardon from good King John."
                                    Old Ballad.

• 175 •

THE RED RIVER VOYAGEUR.

Out and in the river is winding
    The links of its long, red chain
Through belts of dusky pine-land
    And gusty leagues of plain.

Only, at times, a smoke wreath
    With the drifting cloud-rack joins,—
The smoke of the hunting-lodges
    Of the wild Assiniboins.

Drearily blows the north wind
    From the land of ice and snow ;
The eyes that look are weary,
    And heavy the hands that row.

And with one foot on the water,
    And one upon the shore,
The Angel of shadow gives warning
    That day shall be no more.

Is it the clang of wild-geese ?
    Is it the Indian's yell,
That lends to the voice of the north wind
    The tones of a far off bell ?

The *voyageur* smiles as he listens
　To the sound that grows apace;
Well he knows the vesper ringing
　Of the bells of St. Boniface.

The bells of the Roman Mission,
　That call from their turrets twain,
To the boatman on the river,
　To the hunter on the plain!

Even so in our mortal journey
　The bitter north winds blow,
And thus upon life's Red River
　Our hearts, as oarsmen, row.

And when the Angel of Shadow
　Rests his feet on wave and shore,
And our eyes grow dim with watching,
　And our hearts faint at the oar,

Happy is he who heareth
　The signal of his release
In the bells of the Holy City,
　The chimes of eternal peace!
John G. Whittier.

· 176 ·

Home they brought her warrior dead:
　She nor swooned, nor uttered cry;
All her maidens, watching, said,
　"She must weep or she will die."

Then they praised him, soft and low,
　Called him worthy to be loved,
Truest friend and noblest foe;
　Yet she neither spoke nor moved.

Stole a maiden from her place,
  Lightly to the warrior stepped,
Took the face-cloth from the face:
  Yet she neither moved nor wept.

Rose a nurse of ninety years,
  Set his child upon her knee—
Like summer tempest came her tears—
  "Sweet my child, I live for thee."
                              Alfred Tennyson.

· 177 ·

THE BEGGAR.

A beggar through the world am I,—
From place to place I wander by;
Fill up my pilgrim's scrip for me,
For Christ's sweet sake and charity!

A little of thy steadfastness,
Rounded with leafy gracefulness,
Old oak, give me,—
That the world's blasts may round me blow,
And I yield gently to and fro,
While my stout-hearted trunk below
And firm-set roots unmovéd be.

Some of thy stern, unyielding might
Enduring still through day and night
Rude tempest-shock and withering blight, —
That I may keep at bay
The changeful April sky of chance
And the strong tide of circumstance,—
Give me, old granite gray.

"Home they brought her warrior dead."—*p. 283.*

Some of thy mournfulness serene,
Some of thy never-dying green,
Put in this scrip of mine,—
That griefs may fall like snow-flakes light,
And deck me in a robe of white,
Ready to be an angel bright,—
O sweetly-mournful pine.

A little of thy merriment,
Of thy sparkling, light content,
Give me, my cheerful brook,—
That I may still be full of glee
And gladsomeness, where'er I be,
Though fickle fate hath prisoned me
In some neglected nook.

Ye have been very kind and good
To me, since I've been in the wood,
Ye have gone nigh to fill my heart;
But good by, kind friends, every one,
I've far to go ere set of sun;
Of all good things I would have part,
The day was high ere I could start,
And so my journey's scarce begun.

Heaven help me! how could I forget
To beg of thee, dear violet!
Some of thy modesty,
That flowers here as well, unseen,
As if before the world thou'dst been,
O, give, to strengthen me.

James R. Lowell.

· 178 ·

A FAREWELL.

Flow down, cold rivulet, to the sea,
  Thy tribute wave deliver ;
No more by thee my steps shall be,
  Forever and forever.

Flow, softly flow, by lawn and lea,
  A rivulet, then a river ;
No where by thee my steps shall be,
  Forever and forever.

But here will sigh thine alder tree,
  And here thine aspen shiver ;
And here by thee will hum the bee,
  Forever and forever.

A thousand suns will stream on thee,
  A thousand moons will quiver ;
But not by thee my steps shall be,
  Forever and forever.

Alfred Tennyson.

· 179 ·

FIDELE.

Fear no more the heat o' the sun
  Nor the furious winter's rages ;
Thou thy worldly task hast done,
  Home art gone and ta'en thy wages ;
Golden lads and girls all must,
As chimney-sweepers, come to dust.

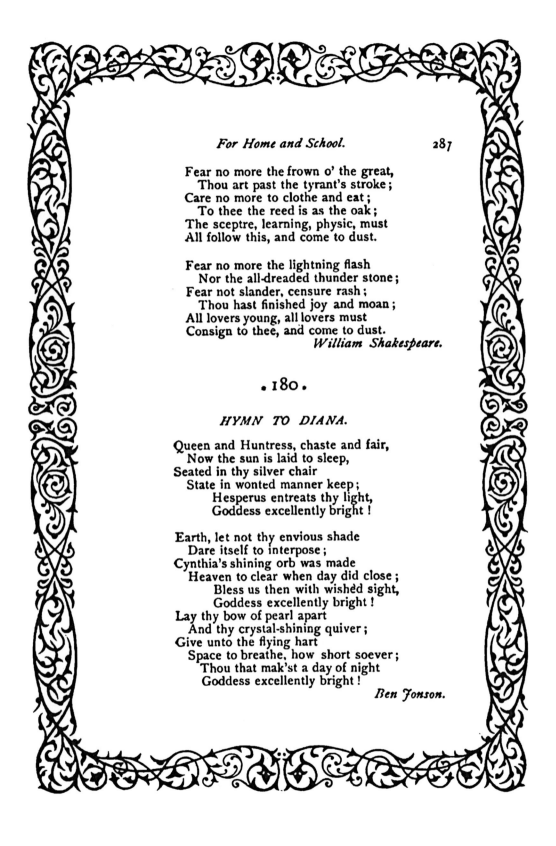

Fear no more the frown o' the great,
  Thou art past the tyrant's stroke;
Care no more to clothe and eat;
  To thee the reed is as the oak;
The sceptre, learning, physic, must
All follow this, and come to dust.

Fear no more the lightning flash
  Nor the all-dreaded thunder stone;
Fear not slander, censure rash;
  Thou hast finished joy and moan;
All lovers young, all lovers must
Consign to thee, and come to dust.
                    William Shakespeare.

. 180 .

HYMN TO DIANA.

Queen and Huntress, chaste and fair,
  Now the sun is laid to sleep,
Seated in thy silver chair
  State in wonted manner keep;
    Hesperus entreats thy light,
    Goddess excellently bright!

Earth, let not thy envious shade
  Dare itself to interpose;
Cynthia's shining orb was made
  Heaven to clear when day did close;
    Bless us then with wishèd sight,
    Goddess excellently bright!
Lay thy bow of pearl apart
  And thy crystal-shining quiver;
Give unto the flying hart
  Space to breathe, how short soever;
    Thou that mak'st a day of night
    Goddess excellently bright!
                    Ben Jonson.

.181.

ODE ON A DISTANT PROSPECT OF ETON COLLEGE.

Ye distant spires, ye antique towers
  That crown the watery glade,
'Where grateful science still adores
  Her Henry's holy shade;
And ye, that from the stately brow
Of Windsor's heights th' expanse below
Of grove, of lawn, of mead survey,
Whose turf, whose shade, whose flowers among
Wanders the hoary Thames along
  His silver-winding way;

Ah happy hills! ah pleasing shade!
  Ah fields beloved in vain!
Where once my careless childhood strayed,
  A stranger yet to pain!
I feel the gales that from you blow
A momentary bliss bestow,
As waving fresh their gladsome wing
My weary soul they seem to soothe,
And, redolent of joy and youth,
  To breathe a second spring.

Say, Father Thames, for thou hast seen
  Full many a sprightly race
Disporting on thy margent green
  The paths of pleasure trace;
Who foremost now delight to cleave
With pliant arm, thy glassy wave?
The captive linnet which enthral?
What idle progeny succeed
To chase the rolling circle's speed
  Or urge the flying ball?

While some on earnest business bent
   Their murmuring labors ply
'Gainst graver hours, that bring constraint
   To sweeten liberty;
Some bold adventurers disdain
The limits of their little reign
And unknown regions dare descry;
Still as they run they look behind,
They hear a voice in every wind
   And snatch a fearful joy.

Gay hope is theirs, by fancy fed,
   Less pleasing when possessed,
The tear forgot as soon as shed,
   The sunshine of the breast;
Theirs buxom health, of rosy hue,
Wild wit, invention ever new,
And lively cheer, of vigor born;
The thoughtless day, the easy night,
The spirits pure, the slumbers light
   That fly th' approach of morn.

Alas! regardless of their doom
   The little victims play!
No sense have they of ills to come
   Nor care beyond to-day;
Yet see how all around them wait
The ministers of human fate
And black misfortune's baleful train!
Ah, show them where in ambush stand
To seize their prey, the murderous band!
   Ah, tell them they are men!

These shall the fury passions tear,
   The vultures of the mind,
Disdainful Anger, pallid Fear,
   And Shame that skulks behind;
Or pining Love shall waste their youth,
Or Jealousy with rankling tooth

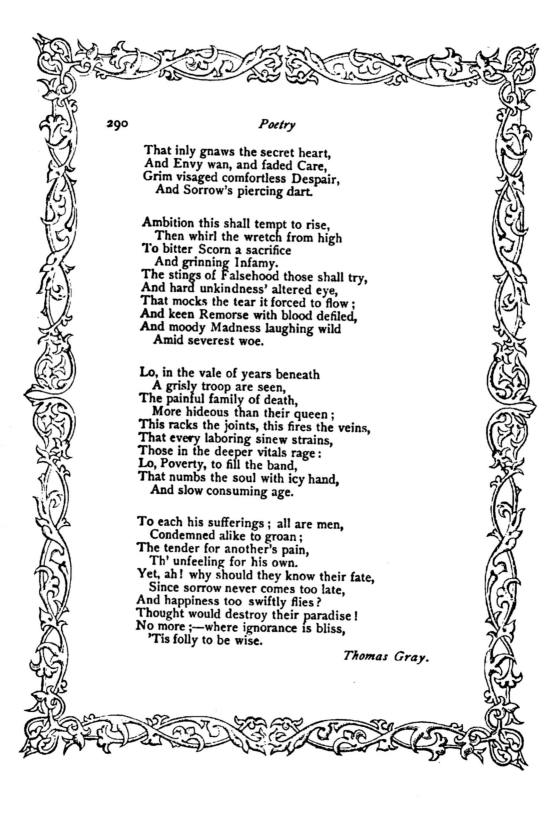

That inly gnaws the secret heart,
And Envy wan, and faded Care,
Grim visaged comfortless Despair,
   And Sorrow's piercing dart.

Ambition this shall tempt to rise,
   Then whirl the wretch from high
To bitter Scorn a sacrifice
   And grinning Infamy.
The stings of Falsehood those shall try,
And hard unkindness' altered eye,
That mocks the tear it forced to flow;
And keen Remorse with blood defiled,
And moody Madness laughing wild
   Amid severest woe.

Lo, in the vale of years beneath
   A grisly troop are seen,
The painful family of death,
   More hideous than their queen;
This racks the joints, this fires the veins,
That every laboring sinew strains,
Those in the deeper vitals rage:
Lo, Poverty, to fill the band,
That numbs the soul with icy hand,
   And slow consuming age.

To each his sufferings; all are men,
   Condemned alike to groan;
The tender for another's pain,
   Th' unfeeling for his own.
Yet, ah! why should they know their fate,
   Since sorrow never comes too late,
And happiness too swiftly flies?
Thought would destroy their paradise!
No more;—where ignorance is bliss,
   'Tis folly to be wise.

                      Thomas Gray.

"Blow, blow, thou winter wind."—*p. 291*.

• 182 •

Blow, blow, thou winter wind,
Thou art not so unkind
As man's ingratitude;
Thy tooth is not so keen
Because thou art not seen,
Although thy breath be rude.
Heigh ho! sing heigh ho! unto the green holly;
Most friendship is feigning, most loving mere folly;
Then, heigh ho! the holly!
This life is most jolly.

Freeze, freeze, thou bitter sky,
Thou dost not bite so nigh
As benefits forgot;
Though thou the waters warp,
Thy sting is not so sharp
As friend remembered not.
Heigh ho! sing heigh ho! unto the green holly;
Most friendship is feigning, most loving mere folly;
Then, heigh ho! the holly!
This life is most jolly.

William Shakespeare.

• 183 •

THE LOST LOVE.

She dwelt among the untrodden ways
  Beside the springs of Dove;
A maid whom there were none to praise,
  And very few to love.

Poetry

A violet by a mossy stone
  Half-hidden from the eye !
—Fair as a star, when only one
  Is shining in the sky.

She lived unknown, and few could know
  When Lucy ceased to be ;
But she is in her grave, and O,
  The difference to me !
                William Wordsworth.

• 184 •

ELEGY.

WRITTEN IN A COUNTRY CHURCHYARD.

The curfew tolls the knell of parting day,
The lowing herd winds slowly o'er the lea,
The ploughman homeward plods his weary way,
And leaves the world to darkness and to me.

Now fades the glimmering landscape on the sight,
And all the air a solemn stillness holds,
Save where the beetle wheels his droning flight,
And drowsy tinklings lull the distant folds ;

Save that from yonder ivy-mantled tower
The moping owl does to the moon complain
Of such as, wandering near her secret bower,
Molest her ancient solitary reign.

Beneath those rugged elms, that yew-trees shade
Where heaves the turf in many a mouldering heap
Each in his narrow cell for ever laid,
The rude forefathers of the hamlet sleep.

The breezy call of incense-breathing morn,
The swallow twittering from the straw-built shed,
The cock's shrill clarion, or the echoing horn,
No more shall rouse them from their lowly bed.

For them no more the blazing hearth shall burn
Or busy housewife ply her evening care ;
No children run to lisp their sire's return,
Or climb his knees, the envied kiss to share

Oft did the harvest to their sickle yield,
Their furrow oft the stubborn glebe has broke ;
How jocund did they drive their team afield !
How bowed the woods beneath their sturdy stroke !

Let not Ambition mock their useful toil,
Their homely joys, and destiny obscure ;
Nor Grandeur hear with a disdainful smile
The short and simple annals of the poor.

The boast of heraldry, the pomp of power,
And all that beauty, all that wealth e'er gave
Await alike th' inevitable hour ;—
The paths of glory lead but to the grave.

Nor you, ye proud, impute to these the fault
If Memory o'er their tomb no trophies raise,
Where through the long-drawn aisle and fretted vault
The pealing anthem swells the note of praise.

Can storied urn or animated bust
Back to its mansion call the fleeting breath ?
Can Honor's voice provoke the silent dust,
Or Flattery soothe the dull cold ear of Death ?

Perhaps in this neglected spot is laid
Some heart once pregnant with celestial fire ;
Hands that the rod of empire might have swayed,
Or waked to ecstasy the living lyre ;

But Knowledge to their eyes her ample page
Rich with the spoils of time, did ne'er unroll;
Chill Penury repressed their noble rage,
And froze the genial current of the soul.

Full many a gem of purest ray serene
The dark unfathomed caves of ocean bear:
Full many a flower is born to blush unseen,
And waste its sweetness on the desert air.

Some village Hampden, that with dauntless breast
The little tyrant of his fields withstood,
Some mute inglorious Milton here may rest,
Some Cromwell, guiltless of his country's blood.

Th' applause of listening senates to command,
The threats of pain and ruin to despise,
To scatter plenty o'er a smiling land,
And read their history in a nation's eyes

Their lot forbade; nor circumscribed alone
Their growing virtues, but their crimes confined;
Forbade to wade through slaughter to a throne,
And shut the gates of mercy on mankind;

The struggling pangs of conscious truth to hide,
To quench the blushes of ingenuous shame,
Or heap the shrine of Luxury and Pride
With incense kindled at the Muse's flame.

Far from the madding crowd's ignoble strife
Their sober wishes never learned to stray;
Along the cool sequestered vale of life
They kept the noiseless tenor of their way.

Yet e'en these bones from insult to protect
Some frail memorial still erected nigh,
With uncouth rhymes and shapeless sculpture decked,
Implores the passing tribute of a sigh.

Their name, their years, spelt by the unlettered Muse,
The place of fame and elegy supply:
And many a holy text around she strews
That teach the rustic moralist to die.

For who, to dumb forgetfulness a prey,
This pleasing, anxious being e'er resigned,
Left the warm precincts of the cheerful day,
Nor cast one longing, lingering look behind?

On some fond breast the parting soul relies,
Some pious drops the closing eye requires;
E'en from the tomb the voice of Nature cries,
E'en in our ashes live their wonted fires.

For thee, who, mindful of th'unhonor'd dead,
Dost in these lines their artless tale relate;
If chance, by lonely Contemplation led,
Some kindred spirit shall inquire thy fate,—

Haply some hoary-headed swain may say,
Oft have we seen him at the peep of dawn
Brushing with hasty steps the dews away,
To meet the sun upon the upland lawn;

There at the foot of yonder nodding beech
That wreathes its old fantastic roots so high,
His listless length at noon-tide would he stretch,
And pore upon the brook that babbles by.

Hard by yon wood, now smiling as in scorn,
Muttering his wayward fancies he would rove;
Now drooping, woeful wan, like one forlorn,
Or crazed with care, or crossed in hopeless love.

One morn I missed him from the accustomed hill,
Along the heath, and near his favorite tree;
Another came; nor yet beside the rill,
Nor up the lawn, nor at the wood was he;

The next, with dirges due in sad array
Slow through the church-way path we saw him borne,—
Approach and read (for thou canst read) the lay
Graved on the stone beneath yon aged thorn.

The Epitaph.

Here rests his head upon the lap of earth
A youth to Fortune and to Fame unknown;
Fair Science frowned not on his humble birth,
And Melancholy marked him for her own.

Large was his bounty, and his soul sincere;
Heaven did a recompense as largely send;
He gave to Misery all he had, a tear,
He gained from Heaven, 'twas all he wished, a friend.

No farther seek his merits to disclose,
Or draw his frailties from their dread abode,
There they alike in trembling hope repose,
The bosom of his Father and his God.

Thomas Gray.

• 185 •

STANZAS FROM " IN MEMORIAM."

Now fades the last long streak of snow,
  Now burgeons every maze of quick,
  About the flowering squares, and thick
By ashen roots the violets blow.

Now rings the woodland loud and long,
  The distance takes a lovelier hue,
  And drowned in yonder living blue
The lark becomes a sightless song.

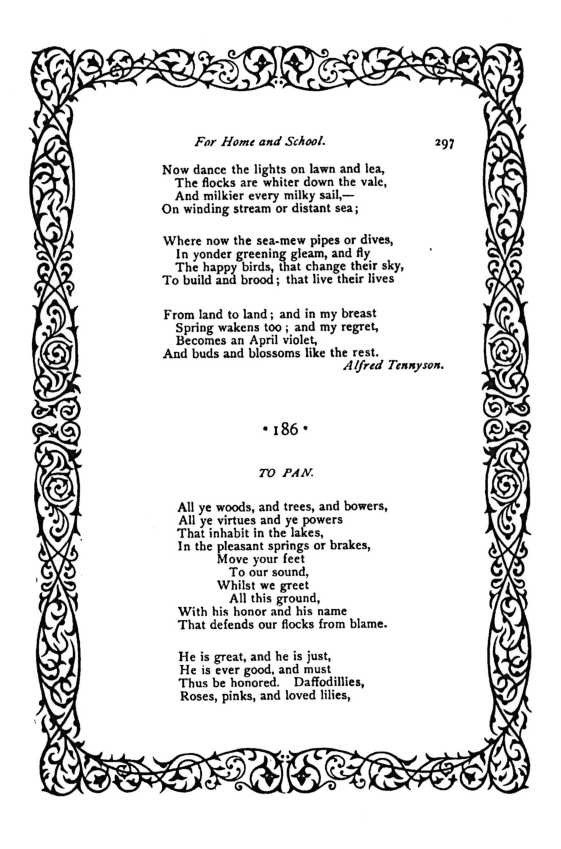

Now dance the lights on lawn and lea,
　The flocks are whiter down the vale,
　And milkier every milky sail,—
On winding stream or distant sea;

Where now the sea-mew pipes or dives,
　In yonder greening gleam, and fly
　The happy birds, that change their sky,
To build and brood; that live their lives

From land to land; and in my breast
　Spring wakens too; and my regret,
　Becomes an April violet,
And buds and blossoms like the rest.
　　　　　　　　Alfred Tennyson.

• 186 •

TO PAN.

All ye woods, and trees, and bowers,
All ye virtues and ye powers
That inhabit in the lakes,
In the pleasant springs or brakes,
　　Move your feet
　　　To our sound,
　　Whilst we greet
　　　All this ground,
With his honor and his name
That defends our flocks from blame.

He is great, and he is just,
He is ever good, and must
Thus be honored.　Daffodillies,
Roses, pinks, and loved lilies,

Let us fling,
　Whilst we sing,
Ever holy,
　Ever holy,
Ever honored, ever young !
Thus great Pan is ever sung.
Beaumont and Fletcher.

. 187 .

THE DRYADS.

These are the tawny Dryads, who love nooks
In the dry depth of oaks ;
Or feel the air in groves, or pull green dresses
For their glad heads in rooty wildernesses ;
Or on the gold turf, o'er the dark lines
Which the sun makes when he declines,
Bend their linked dances in and out the pines.
They tend all forests old, and meeting trees,
Wood, copse, or queach, or slippery dell o'erhung
With firs, and with their dusty apples strewn ;
And let the visiting beams the boughs among,
And bless the trunks from clingings of disease
And wasted hearts that to the night-wind groan.
They screen the cuckoo when he sings ; and teach
The mother blackbird how to lead astray
The unformed spirit of the foolish boy
From thick to thick, from hedge to bay or beach,
When he would steal the huddled nest away
Of yellow bills upgaping for their food,
And spoil the song of the free solitude.
And they, at sound of the brute, insolent horn,
Hurry the deer out of the dewy morn ;
And take into their sudden laps with joy
The startled hare that did but peep abroad ;
And from the trodden road
Help the bruised hedgehog.   And at rest, they love

The back-turned pheasant hanging from the tree
His sunny drapery;
And handy squirrel, nibbling hastily:
And fragrant hiving bee,
So happy that he will not move, not he,
Without a song; and hidden, loving dove,
With his deep breath; and bird of wakeful glen
Whose louder song is like the voice of life,
Triumphant o'er death's image, but whose deep,
Low lovelier note is like a gentle wife,
A poor, a pensive, yet a happy one,
Stealing, when daylight's common tasks are done,
An hour for mother's work, and singing low
While her tired husband and her children sleep.
Leigh Hunt.

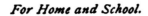

.188.

SIR GALAHAD.

My good blade carves the casques of men,
　My tough lance thrusteth sure;
My strength is as the strength of ten,
　Because my heart is pure.
The shattering trumpet shrilleth high,
　The hard brands shiver on the steel,
The splintered spear-shafts crack and fly,
　The horse and rider reel.
They reel, they roll in clanging lists,
　And when the tide of combat stands,
Perfume and flowers fall in showers,
　That lightly rain from ladies' hands.

How sweet are looks that ladies bend
　On whom their favors fall!
For them I battle till the end,
　To save from shame and thrall;

But all my heart is drawn above,
  My knees are bowed in crypt and shrine:
I never felt the kiss of love,
  Nor maiden's hand in mine.
More bounteous aspects on me beam,
  Me mightier transports move and thrill,
So keep I fair through faith and prayer
  A virgin heart in work and will.

When down the stormy crescent goes,
  A light before me swims,
Between dark stems the forest glows,
  I hear a voice of hymns;
Then by some secret shrine I ride;
  I hear a voice, but none are there;
The stalls are void, the doors are wide,
  The tapers burning fair.
Fair gleams the snowy altar-cloth,
  The silver vessels sparkle clean,
The shrill bell rings, the censer swings,
  And solemn chants resound between.

Sometimes on lonely mountain-meres
  I find a magic bark;
I leap on board; no helmsman steers;
  I float till all is dark.
A gentle sound, an awful light!
  Three angels bear the holy Grail;
With folded feet, in stoles of white,
  On sleeping wings they sail.
Ah, blessed vision! blood of God!
  My spirit beats her mortal bars,
As down dark tides the glory slides,
  And star-like mingles with the stars.

When on my goodly charger borne,
  Through dreaming towns I go,
The cock crows ere the Christmas morn,
  The streets are dumb with snow.

"Fair gleams the snowy altar-cloth,
    The silver vessels sparkle clean,
The shrill bell rings, the censer swings,
    The solemn chants resound between."—*p. 300.*

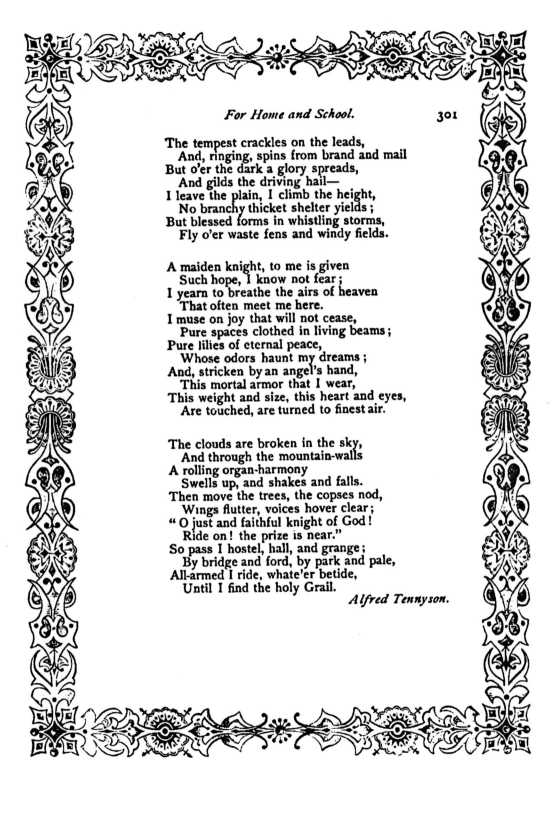

The tempest crackles on the leads,
   And, ringing, spins from brand and mail
But o'er the dark a glory spreads,
   And gilds the driving hail—
I leave the plain, I climb the height,
   No branchy thicket shelter yields;
But blessed forms in whistling storms,
   Fly o'er waste fens and windy fields.

A maiden knight, to me is given
   Such hope, I know not fear;
I yearn to breathe the airs of heaven
   That often meet me here.
I muse on joy that will not cease,
   Pure spaces clothed in living beams;
Pure lilies of eternal peace,
   Whose odors haunt my dreams;
And, stricken by an angel's hand,
   This mortal armor that I wear,
This weight and size, this heart and eyes,
   Are touched, are turned to finest air.

The clouds are broken in the sky,
   And through the mountain-walls
A rolling organ-harmony
   Swells up, and shakes and falls.
Then move the trees, the copses nod,
   Wings flutter, voices hover clear;
"O just and faithful knight of God!
   Ride on! the prize is near."
So pass I hostel, hall, and grange;
   By bridge and ford, by park and pale,
All-armed I ride, whate'er betide,
   Until I find the holy Grail.

                  Alfred Tennyson.

. 189

THE SECRET OF THE SEA.

Ah! what pleasant visions haunt me
  As I gaze upon the sea!
All the old romantic legends,
  All my dreams, come back to me.

Sails of silk and ropes of sendal
  Such as gleam in ancient lore ;
And the singing of the sailors,
  And the answer from the shore !

Most of all, the Spanish ballad
  Haunts me oft, and tarries long,
Of the noble Count Arnaldos
  And the sailor's mystic song.

Like the long waves on a sea-beach,
  When the sand as silver shines,
With a soft, monotonous cadence,
  Flow its unrhymed lyric lines ;—

Telling how the Count Arnaldos
  With his hawk upon his hand,
Saw a fair and stately galley,
  Steering onward to the land :—

How he heard the ancient helmsman
  Chant a song so wild and clear,
That the sailing sea-bird slowly
  Poised upon the mast to hear.

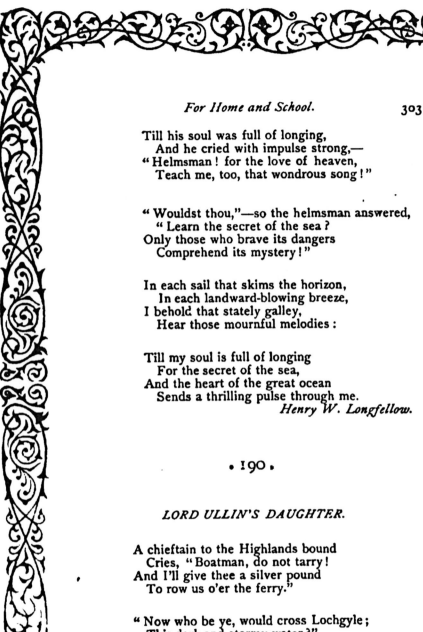

Till his soul was full of longing,
   And he cried with impulse strong,—
"Helmsman ! for the love of heaven,
   Teach me, too, that wondrous song !"

" Wouldst thou,"—so the helmsman answered,
   " Learn the secret of the sea ?
Only those who brave its dangers
   Comprehend its mystery !"

In each sail that skims the horizon,
   In each landward-blowing breeze,
I behold that stately galley,
   Hear those mournful melodies :

Till my soul is full of longing
   For the secret of the sea,
And the heart of the great ocean
   Sends a thrilling pulse through me.
                  Henry W. Longfellow.

• 190 •

LORD ULLIN'S DAUGHTER.

A chieftain to the Highlands bound
   Cries, "Boatman, do not tarry !
And I'll give thee a silver pound
   To row us o'er the ferry."

" Now who be ye, would cross Lochgyle ;
   This dark and stormy water ?"
" O, I'm the chief of Ulva's isle,
   And this, lord Ullin's daughter.

" And fast before her father's men
　　Three days we've fled together,
For should he find us in the glen,
　　My blood would stain the heather.

" His horsemen hard behind us ride ;
　　Should they our steps discover,
Then who will cheer my bonny bride
　　When they have slain her lover ? "

Out spoke the hardy Highland wight,
　　" I'll go, my chief, I'm ready ;
It is not for your silver bright ;
　　But for your winsome lady.

" And by my word, the bonny bird
　　In danger shall not tarry :
So though the waves are raging white,
　　I'll row you o'er the ferry."

By this the storm grew loud apace,
　　The water-wraith was shrieking :
And in the scowl of Heaven, each face
　　Grew dark as they were speaking.

But still as wilder blew the wind,
　　And as the night grew drearer,
Adown the glen rode armed men,
　　Their trampling sounded nearer.

" O haste thee, haste ! " the lady cries,
　　" Though tempests round us gather ;
I'll meet the raging of the skies,
　　But not an angry father."

The boat has left the stormy land,
　　A stormy sea before her,—
When, oh ! too strong for human hand
　　The tempest gathered o'er her.

"His horsemen hard behind us ride."—*p. 304.*

And still they rowed amidst the roar
  Of waters fast prevailing ;
Lord Ullin reached that fatal shore ;
  His wrath was changed to wailing.

For, sore dismayed, through storm and shade
  His child he did discover ;
One lovely hand she stretched for aid,
  And one was round her lover.

" Come back ! come back ! " he cried in grief,
  " Across this stormy water ;
And I 'll forgive your Highland chief,
  My daughter ! oh, my daughter ! "

' Twas vain ; the loud waves lashed the shore,
  Return or aid preventing ;
The waters wild went o'er his child,
  And he was left lamenting.

Thomas Campbell.

• 191 •

TO HIS LOVE.

Shall I compare thee to a summer's day ?
Thou art more lovely and more temperate ;
Rough winds do shake the darling buds of May,
And summer's lease hath all too short a date ;

Sometime too hot the eye of heaven shines,
And often is his gold complexion dimmed
And every fair from fair sometimes declines,
By chance, or nature's changing course, untrimmed.

But thy eternal summer shall not fade
Nor lose possession of that fair thou owest;
Nor shall death brag thou wanderest in his shade,
When in eternal lines to time thou growest.

So long as men can breathe, or eyes can see,
So long lives this, and this gives life to thee.
                              William Shakespeare.

• 192 •

BREAK, BREAK, BREAK.

Break, break, break,
  On thy cold gray stones, O sea!
And I would that my tongue could utter
  The thoughts that arise in me.

O well for the fisherman's boy,
  That he shouts with his sister at play!
O well for the sailor lad,
  That he sings in his boat on the bay!

And the stately ships go on
  To the haven under the hill;
But oh for the touch of a vanished hand,
  And a sound of a voice that is still.

Break, break, break,
  At the foot of thy crags, oh sea!
But the tender grace of a day that is dead
  Will never come back to me.
                              Alfred Tennyson.

" Break, break, break,
   At the foot of thy crags, O Sea ! "—*p. 306.*

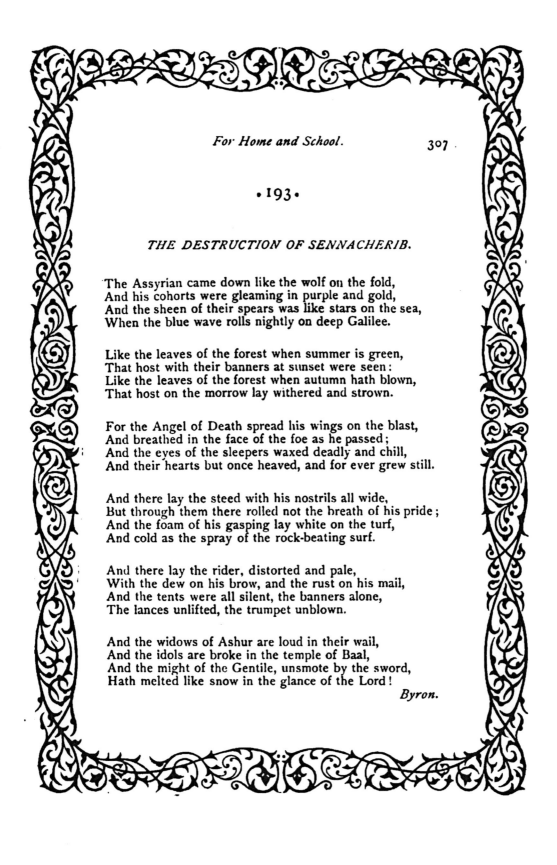

• 193 •

THE DESTRUCTION OF SENNACHERIB.

The Assyrian came down like the wolf on the fold,
And his cohorts were gleaming in purple and gold,
And the sheen of their spears was like stars on the sea,
When the blue wave rolls nightly on deep Galilee.

Like the leaves of the forest when summer is green,
That host with their banners at sunset were seen:
Like the leaves of the forest when autumn hath blown,
That host on the morrow lay withered and strown.

For the Angel of Death spread his wings on the blast,
And breathed in the face of the foe as he passed;
And the eyes of the sleepers waxed deadly and chill,
And their hearts but once heaved, and for ever grew still.

And there lay the steed with his nostrils all wide,
But through them there rolled not the breath of his pride;
And the foam of his gasping lay white on the turf,
And cold as the spray of the rock-beating surf.

And there lay the rider, distorted and pale,
With the dew on his brow, and the rust on his mail,
And the tents were all silent, the banners alone,
The lances unlifted, the trumpet unblown.

And the widows of Ashur are loud in their wail,
And the idols are broke in the temple of Baal,
And the might of the Gentile, unsmote by the sword,
Hath melted like snow in the glance of the Lord!

Byron.

· 194 ·

HYMN.

ON THE MORNING OF CHRIST'S NATIVITY.

It was the winter wild
While the heaven-born child
All meanly wrapped in the rude manger lies ;
Nature in awe to him
Had doffed her gaudy trim,
With her great Master so to sympathize :
It was no season then for her
To wanton with the sun, her lusty paramour.

Only with speeches fair
She woos the gentle air
To hide her guilty front with innocent snow;
And on her naked shame,
Pollute with sinful blame,
The saintly veil of maiden white to throw;
Confounded that her Maker's eyes
Should look so near upon her foul deformities.

But he, her fears to cease,
Sent down the meek-eyed Peace ;
She crown'd with olive green, came softly sliding
Down through the turning sphere
His ready harbinger,
With turtle wing the amorous clouds dividing;
And waving wide her myrtle wand,
She strikes a universal peace through sea and land.

No war, or battle's sound
Was heard the world around ;
The idle spear and shield were high up hung ;

" But peaceful was the night
Wherein the Prince of light
His reign of peace upon the earth began."—*p. 309.*

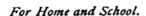

The hooked chariot stood
Unstained with hostile blood;
The trumpet spake not to the armed throng;
And kings sat still with awful eye,
As if they surely knew their sovran Lord was by.

But peaceful was the night
Wherein the Prince of light
His reign of peace upon the earth began;
The winds with wonder whist,
Smoothly the waters kissed
Whispering new joys to the mild ocean—
Who now hath quite forgot to rave,
While birds of calm sit brooding on the charmèd wave.

The stars with deep amaze,
Stand fixed in steadfast gaze,
Bending one way their precious influence;
And will not take their flight
For all the morning light,
Or Lucifer that often warned them thence;
But in their glimmering orbs did glow
Until their Lord himself bespake, and bid them go.

And though the shady gloom
Had given day her room,
The sun himself withheld his wonted speed,
And hid his head for shame,
As his inferior flame
The new-enlightened world no more should need;
He saw a greater sun appear
Than his bright throne, or burning axletree, could bear.

The shepherds on the lawn
Or ere the point of;dawn
Sate simply chatting in a rustic row;
Full little thought they then
That the mighty Pan
Was kindly come to live with them below;

Perhaps their loves, or else their sheep
Was all that did their silly thoughts so busy keep.

When such music sweet
Their hearts and ears did greet
As never was by mortal finger strook—
Divinely-warbled voice
Answering the stringed noise,
As all their souls in blissful rapture took :
The air, such pleasure loth to lose,
With thousand echoes still prolongs each heavenly close.

Nature that heard such sound
Beneath the hollow round
Of Cynthia's seat, the airy region thrilling,
Now was almost won
To think her part was done,
And that her reign had here its last fulfilling ;
She knew such harmony alone
Could hold all heaven and earth in happier union.

At last surrounds their sight
A globe of circular light
That with long beams the shamefaced night array'd,
The helmed Cherubim
And sworded Seraphim
Are seen in glittering ranks with wings displayed,
Harping in loud and solemn choir
With unexpressive notes, to heaven's new-born Heir.

Such music as 'tis said
Before was never made
But when of old the sons of morning sung,
While the Creator great
His constellations set,
And the well-balanced world on hinges hung ;
And cast the dark foundations deep,
And bid the weltering waves their oozy channel keep.

Ring out, ye crystal spheres !
Once bless our human ears,
If ye have power to touch our senses so ;
And let your silver chime
Move in melodious time ;
And let the base of Heaven's deep organ blow ;
And with your ninefold harmony
Make up full consort to the angelic symphony.

For if such holy song
Enwrap our fancy long,
Time will run back, and fetch the age of gold ;
And speckled vanity
Will sicken soon and die,
And leprous sin will melt from earthly mould ;
And Hell itself will pass away,
And leave her dolorous mansions to the peering day.

Yea, Truth and Justice then
Will down return to men,
Orbed in a rainbow ; and, like glories wearing,
Mercy will sit between
Throned in celestial sheen,
With radiant feet the tissued clouds down steering ;
And Heaven, as at some festival
Will open wide the gates of her high palace hall.

But wisest Fate says no ;
This must not yet be so ;
The Babe yet lies in smiling infancy
That on the bitter cross
Must redeem our loss ;
So both himself and us to glorify ;
Yet first, to those ychained in sleep,
The wakeful trump of doom must thunder through the deep ;

With such a horrid clang
As on mount Sinai rang
While the red fire and smouldering clouds out-brake ;

The aged earth aghast
With terror of that blast
Shall from the surface to the centre shake,
When, at the worlds last session,
The dreadful Judge in middle air shall spread his throne.

And then at last our bliss
Full and perfect is,
But now begins ; for from this happy day
The old Dragon, under ground
In straiter limits bound,
Not half so far casts his usurpéd sway ;
And, wroth to see his kingdom fail,
Swindges the scaly horror of his folded tail.

The oracles are dumb ;
No voice or hideous hum
Runs through the archéd roof in words deceiving;
Apollo from his shrine
Can no more divine,
With hollow shriek the steep of Delphos leaving ;
No nightly trance or breathed spell
Inspires the pale-eyed priest from the prophetic cell.

The lonely mountains o'er,
And the resounding shore,
A voice of weeping heard, and loud lament ;
From haunted spring and dale
Edged with poplar pale
The parting Genius is with sighing sent ;
With flower-inwoven tresses torn
The nymphs in twilight shade of tangled thickets mourn

In consecrated earth
And on the holy hearth
The Lars and Lemures moan with midnight plaint ;
In urns, and altars round
A drear and dying sound
Affrights the Flamens at their service quaint ;

"The Babe yet lies in smiling infancy
That on the bitter cross
Must redeem our loss."—*p. 311.*

And the chill marble seems to sweat,
While each peculiar Power foregoes his wonted seat.

Peor and Baalim
Forsake their temples dim,
With that twice battered god of Palestine;
And moonèd Ashtaroth
Heaven's queen and mother both,
Now sits not girt with tapers' holy shine;
The Lybic Hammon shrinks his horn,
In vain the Tyrian maids their wounded Thammuz
    mourn.

And sullen Moloch fled,
Hath left in shadows dread
His burning idol all of blackest hue.
In vain with cymbals ring
They call the grisly king,
In dismal dance about the furnace blue;
The brutish gods of Nile as fast,
Isis, and Orus, and the dog Anubis, haste.

Nor is Osiris seen
In Memphian grove, or green,
Trampling the unshowered grass with lowings loud:
Nor can he be at rest
Within his sacred chest;
Nought but profoundest hell can be his shroud;
In vain with timbrelled anthems dark
The sable stolèd sorcerers bear his worshipped ark.

He feels from Juda's land
The dreaded infant's hand;
The rays of Bethlehem blind his dusky eyn;
Nor all the gods beside
Longer dare abide,
Nor Typhon huge ending in snaky twine:
Our Babe, to show his Godhead true,
Can in his swaddling bands control the damnèd crew.

So, when the sun in bed
Curtained with cloudy red
Pillows his chin upon an orient wave,
The flocking shadows pale
Troop to the infernal jail,
Each fettered ghost slips to his several grave,
And the yellow-skirted fays
Fly after the night steeds, leaving their moon-loved maze.

But see, the Virgin blest
Hath laid her Babe to rest;
Time is, our tedious song should here have ending:
Heaven's youngest-teemèd star
Hath fixed her polish'd car,
Her sleeping Lord with handmaid lamp attending:
And all about the courtly stable
Bright-harnessed angels sit in order serviceable.

John Milton.

• 195 •

SONG

Soldier, rest! thy warfare o'er,
  Sleep the sleep that knows not breaking;
Dream of battled fields no more,
  Days of danger, nights of waking.
In our isle's enchanted hall,
  Hands unseen thy couch are strewing,
Fairy strains of music fall,
  Every sense in slumber dewing,
Soldier, rest! thy warfare o'er,
Dream of fighting fields no more:
Sleep the sleep that knows not breaking,
Morn of toil, nor night of waking.

No rude sound shall reach thine ear,
  Armour's clang, or war-steed champing,
Trump nor pibroch summon here.

Mustering clan, or squadron tramping;
Yet the lark's shrill fife may come
  At the day-break from the fallow,
And the bittern sound his drum,
  Booming from the sedgy shallow.
Ruder sounds shall none be near
Guards nor warders challenge here,
Here's no war steed's neigh and champing,
Shouting clans, or squadron stamping.

Huntsman, rest! thy chase is done,
  While our slumbrous spells assail ye,
Dream not with the rising sun,
  Bugles here shall sound reveillé.
Sleep! the deer is in his den,
  Sleep! thy hounds are by thee lying;
Sleep! nor dream in yonder glen,
  How thy gallant steed lay dying.
Huntsman, rest! thy chase is done,
Think not of the rising sun,
For at dawning to assail ye,
Here no bugles sound reveillé.
                Walter Scott.

• 196 •

A FAREWELL.

My fairest child, I have no song to give you;
  No lark could pipe to skies so dull and grey;
Yet, ere we part, one lesson I can leave you
    For every day.

Be good, sweet maid, and let who will be clever;
  Do noble things, not dream them, all day long:
And so make life, death, and that vast forever
    One grand, sweet song.
           Charles Kingsley.

INDEX TO FIRST LINES.

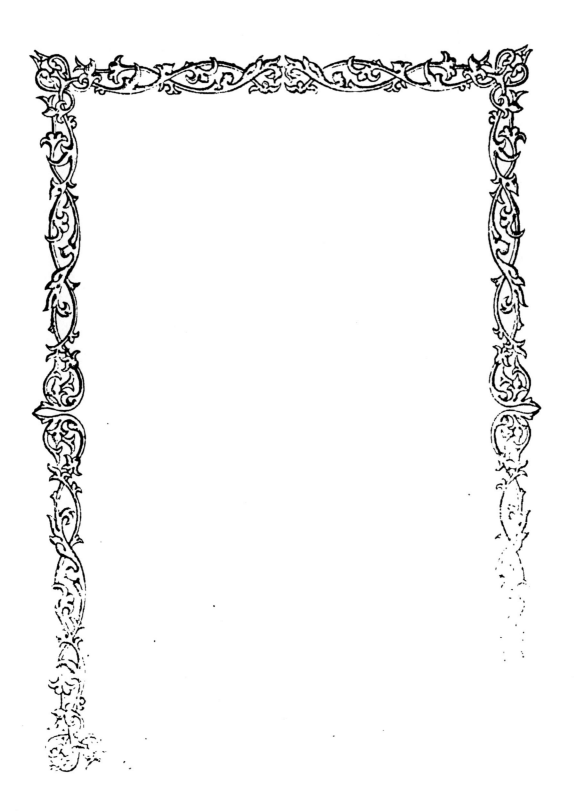

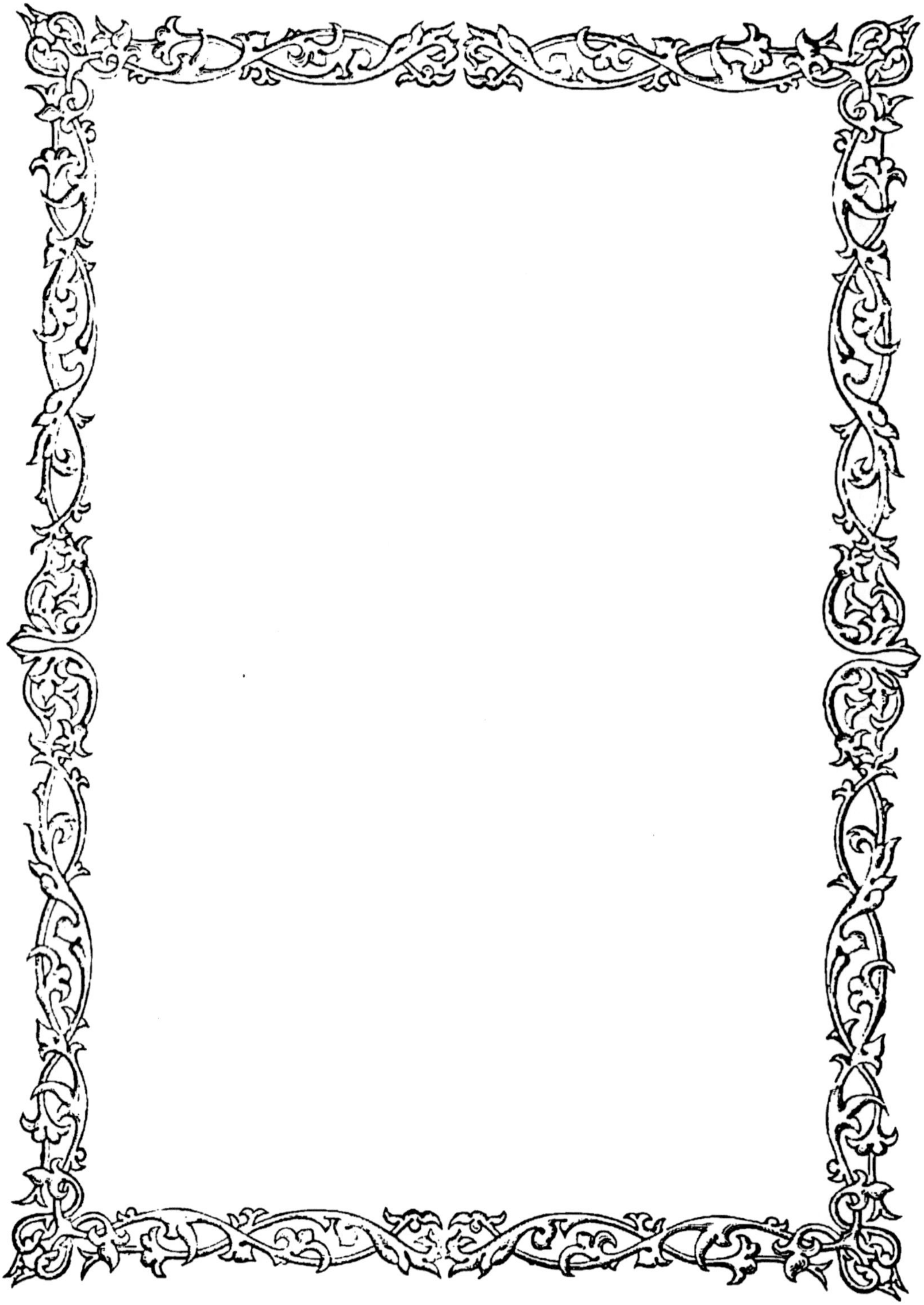

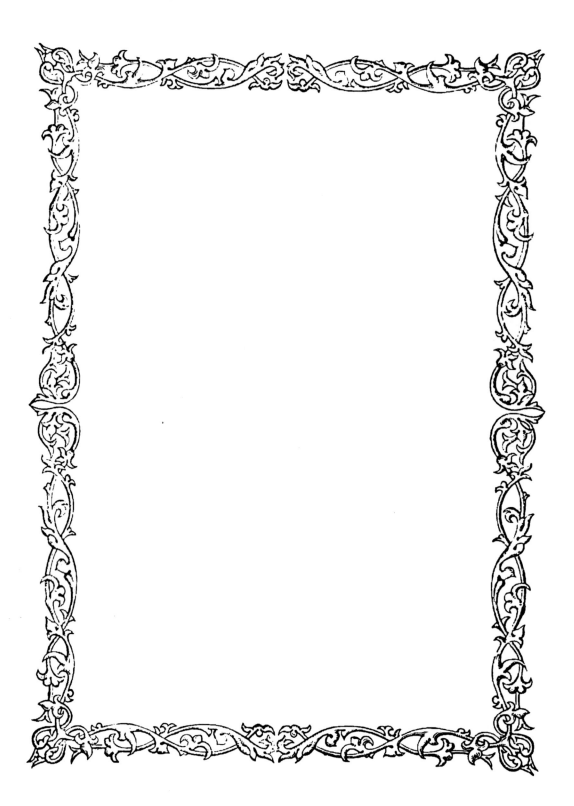

CPSIA information can be obtained at www.ICGtesting.com
Printed in the USA
BVOW04s2150151215

430372BV00009B/58/P